THE ABORIGINAL
TASMANIANS

THE ABORIGINAL TASMANIANS

Lyndall Ryan

University of British Columbia Press

Vancouver and London

THE ABORIGINAL TASMANIANS

This edition for sale in North America only.

© University of Queensland Press, St Lucia, Queensland 1981

Canadian Cataloguing in Publication Data

Ryan, Lyndall, 1943–
   The aboriginal Tasmanians

   Bibliography: p.
   Includes index.
   ISBN 0 7748 0146 8

   1. Tasmanian aborigines – History.
   2. Tasmania – History. I. Title.
   DU473.R92   994.6'0049915   C81 091251 1

International Standard Book Number 0 7748 0146 8

Typeset by University of Queensland Press
Printed and bound by Hedges & Bell Pty Ltd, Melbourne

Contents

Illustrations

Maps

Abbreviations

ABC	Australian Broadcasting Commission
ADB	*Australian Dictionary of Biography*
AIAS	Australian Institute of Aboriginal Studies
ANL	National Library of Australia, Canberra
ANU	Australian National University
AO	Archives Office of New South Wales, Sydney
AP	Arthur Papers, Mitchell Library
BPP	*British Parliamentary Papers*
BT	Bonwick Transcripts, Mitchell Library
CSD	Chief Secretary's Department (Hobart)
CO	Colonial Office (London)
Col.sec.	Colonial secretary (Hobart)
CSO	Colonial Secretary's Office (Hobart)
CN	*Church News*
CT	*Colonial Times*
GO	Governor's Office (Hobart)
HRA	*Historical Records of Australia*
HRNSW	*Historical Records of New South Wales*
HTC	*Hobart Town Courier*
HTG	*Hobart Town Gazette*
J&PP Tas.	*Journal and Papers, Parliament of Tasmania*
J&P LC Tas.	*Journal and Proceedings, Legislative Council of Tasmania*
LA	*Launceston Advertiser*
LSD	Lands and Surveys Department (Hobart)
ML	Mitchell Library (Sydney)
Mil. Ops	*Copies of all Correspondence between Lieutenant-Governor Arthur and His Majesty's Secretary of State for the Colonies, on the Subject of the*

	Military Operations lately Carried on Against the Aboriginal Inhabitants of Van Diemen's Land, BPP, 1831, no. 259, vol. 19.
PD	Premier's Department (Hobart)
PO	Premier's Office (Hobart)
P&P RST	*Papers and Proceedings, Royal Society of Tasmania*
P&P THRA	*Papers and Proceedings, Tasmanian Historical Research Association*
PRO	Public Records Office (London)
PRSV	*Proceedings of the Royal Society of Victoria*
RP	Robinson Papers, Mitchell Library
RQVM	*Records of the Queen Victoria Museum* (Launceston)
RSPS	Research School of Pacific Studies, Australian National University
RST	Royal Society of Tasmania
SG	*Sydney Gazette*
SLSA	State Library of South Australia
SP	Stephens Papers
Tas. Jour. Nat. Sci.	*Tasmanian Journal of Natural Science*
TSA	Tasmanian State Archives
U. Tas.	University of Tasmania, Hobart
VDL	Van Diemen's Land
V&P LC Tas.	Votes and Proceedings, Legislative Council of Tasmania

Acknowledgements

Many people generously assisted me during ten years' researching and writing this book, part of which was originally a doctorate presented to the School of History at Macquarie University in 1975. In Tasmania, Tas Brown and Harry Penrith first opened my eyes to the Aboriginal population and then gave me encouragement to write about them. John Whinray from Flinders Island introduced me to the people on Cape Barren Island, Bill Mollison and Coral Everitt gave me hours of their thoughts and researches on the Cape Barren Islanders and in Launceston, Anne Girard and her children, Duncan and Kirsty, always gave me comfort and support. In Hobart, the staff of the Tasmanian State Archives proved unfailingly helpful through the assistance of Mary McRae who gave permission to reproduce photographs of the Islanders.

I would also like to thank: Sir William Crowther for permission to reproduce *Aborigines at Oyster Cove* by Fanny Benbow; Beatties Studio for permission to reproduce four photographs; the Director of the Tasmanian Museum and Art Gallery; Don Gregg, for permission to reproduce five illustrations; Kim Boyer, Kay Daniels and Mary Murnane who generously provided hospitality and sustenance; the Librarian of the Naval Historical Research Branch Library, Ministry of Defence, for permission to reproduce *Captain Cook's Interview with the natives in Adventure Bay, Van Diemen's Land, January 29, 1777*; the staff of the Mitchell Library for their help and patience; Baiba Irving, the Mitchell Librarian, for permission to reproduce eighteen illustrations; the Australian Institute of Aboriginal Studies and the former principal, Peter Ucko; Barbara Perry from the Pictorial Section of the National Library of Australia for permission to reproduce, *Oyster Cove. An Old Convict Station now inhabited by a few remaining aborigines of Tasmania (c. 1849)*, by Charles Edward Stanley; Sandra Bowdler and Geoff Hope who helped me through three years of rewriting; Win Mumfred who drew the maps; Jennett Moscosco and Irene Saunderson who unscrambled a difficult manuscript; and the School of Humanities at Griffith University which funded the last stages of my work; Warren Osmond to whom I am indebted for ideas, discussion and emotional support; Chris Ronalds, Donalle Wheeler, Bill Thorpe and Claire Williams who never lost faith in me to finish; Manning Clark, who gave me an intellectual framework from which to start looking at the world; and Annie Bickford, who gave so much of her time and energy to this book, I am forever indebted.

Introduction

Ever since the nineteenth century, Australians have accepted without question that the Tasmanian Aborigines perished in 1876 when Truganini died in Hobart. Indeed, the "event" became a source of grim celebration which accorded with another equally pervasive nineteenth century myth, namely, that the Aborigines as a people were inevitably doomed to extinction. The latter myth has been dispelled, although it died hard. No one today would seriously suggest that Aborigines on the Australian mainland have not survived. Aborigines on the Australian mainland are accorded grudging recognition, even if their rights are not.

It may seem odd that one is compelled to make these rather obvious statements about Aborigines. But it is absolutely crucial at the outset to understand that the Tasmanian Aborigines did not die out in 1876 or in any other period in Tasmania's history. Today there are over two thousand Tasmanian Aborigines living in Tasmania and elsewhere. They may not be "fullblooded", but then neither are most mainland Aborigines. However, they are unquestionably descendants of Tasmanian Aborigines, and they retain their identity as Aborigines.

From the very beginnings of European contact and settlement in Tasmania, a viable if tenuous Aboriginal community maintained itself throughout the nineteenth and twentieth centuries despite the ravages of war, dispossession, depopulation, humiliation, and finally the ignominies of twentieth century bureaucratic indifference. This process took place in an environment where the "doomed race" theory was more pervasive than anywhere else in Australia.

Tasmanian Aborigines today are thus living under a greater burden of history than are those on the mainland. Because it is universally believed that they disappeared from history, the surviving Tasmanian Aborigines have had to struggle to be recognized at all. The overriding purpose of this account is to demolish this myth of "the last Tasmanian".

When I began research on the Tasmanian Aborigines ten years ago, I wanted to examine the nature of Aboriginal resistance to pastoral settlers in the 1820s. The seventeen volumes of records in the Tasmanian State Archives documenting the guerilla war between the settlers and Aborigines were my inspiration. But in August 1971, in Launceston, I met the Cape Barren Island people, who confronted me with their Aboriginal community which suffered discrimination in work, health, and housing yet was denied identity as an Aboriginal group. Thus with the myth that the Tasmanian Aborigines had become extinct with the death of Truganini in 1876 in tatters, my work moved in a different direction. I was now confronted with a modern Aboriginal community whose problems were very similar to any Aboriginal group in south-eastern Australia. But the Islanders had a further problem: no one believed they existed. So deeply entrenched was the myth that Truganini was the last of the Tasmanians, and that with her death in 1876 a grisly chapter in Tasmanian history had closed, that to suggest they had survived and some recompense could be made for loss of land was a travesty. The actual documentation of Truganini's death appeared irrefutable proof that the "final solution" which everyone publicly abhorred had been triumphantly attained.

The death of Truganini also coincided with the rise of the science of physical anthropology. In the succeeding eighty years many attempts were made to categorize the "extinct" Tasmanians as the missing link between ape and man. By the beginning of the twentieth century the view was widely held that the Aborigines in Tasmania did not survive European invasion because they were low on the scale of humanity, with such a primitive technology that they had no means to contain or withstand or even adjust to invasion from a technologically superior group. More recently this view has been enlarged to the belief that as a result of ten thousand years of isolation from the Australian mainland, by 1800 the Tasmanians were suffering from "slow strangulation of the mind" and would have died out anyway, regardless of European invasion. So the scientists have helped to expiate the guilt of dispossession.

Only two writers have explored the notion of guilt. James Bonwick in *The Last of the Tasmanians* in 1870 drew the Tasmanian Aborigines as ancient heroes who, when unjustly dispossessed, had died out. In 1948 Clive Turnbull, in *Black War*, drew attention to the dispossession of the Tasmanian Aborigines as a reminder that extermination policies were not exclusive to Nazi Germany. But both writers were in no doubt that the Tasmanian Aborigines had become extinct. Both acknowledged the existence of the Islander community in Bass Strait, but they were quick to point out that it was a "hybrid" or "half-caste" community, and thus not "real" — for in their eyes the community did not retain any of the traditions of the Tasmanian Aborigines before European invasion. Nor could they compare this community to the heroic Aboriginal fighters of the 1820s.

So the myth that the Tasmanian Aborigines became extinct after dispossession because they had lost the will to live was tacked onto the other myth that they had died out because they had no technical, cultural, or even moral means of confronting European invasion. These two myths helped to expiate any guilt about government policies or settlers' dislike of the Aborigines. They became convenient means of easing the consciences of the European Tasmanians and white Australians generally. There was, too, a kind of pride in having achieved the extermination of a whole race — a kind of first for white Australians seeking a place in the world.

The myth of extermination also had other consequences. In carrying the burden of extermination, Tasmania has covered up the dispossession and extermination of Aborigines in other parts of Australia, for the dispossession of the Aborigines in Tasmania was relatively peaceful in comparison with the dispossession and extermination of the Aborigines in western Victoria, western New South Wales, and most of Queensland. Tasmania never experienced the levels of poisoning, trappings, ambushes, and massacres that occurred in other parts of Australia. Yet because most mainland white Australians have been told that Tasmania was the only colony to have exterminated its Aborigines, they failed to question how the Aborigines disappeared from their own environment. So Tasmania has become the scapegoat for the rest of Australia. It was as if, by virtue of being an island, Tasmania was isolated from the rest of Australia when the disease of extermination attacked it. Rather, Tasmania suffered the first and the mildest form of the disease which ravaged mainland Australia unchecked for the next hundred years.

So it was with different perspectives that I began to reconstruct the narrative of relations between Aborigines and Europeans in Tasmania between 1800 and the present. First, not all kinds of European invasion were necessarily destructive of Aboriginal society. Indeed, where invasion did not involve permanent settlement and where there was an overlap of economic pursuits, there existed many opportunities for mutual interaction. The arrival of the sealers as seasonal visitors to the north coast of Tasmania after 1800 provided the Aborigines with the opportunity to incorporate them into their own system of mutual obligation of gift and exchange. For example, the Aboriginal men from one tribe "lent" their wives to the sealers for a short period in return for gifts of flour, seal carcases, and dogs. The sealers then had obligations to assist that tribe in foraging for food or in fighting other tribes. From this interaction the foundations for the present-day community were laid.

Interaction also took place with the agricultural settlers between 1807 and 1820, for they used only small areas of land and did not disrupt the Aborigines' patterns of movement. Where the settlers were prepared to pay rent for their use of Aboriginal land in the form of provisions of potatoes, flour, tobacco, tea, and dogs, some form of mutual co-existence could develop. But interaction and mutual co-existence could not take place with the pastoral settlers who arrived in Tasmania from about 1822 and by 1830 had occupied every available block of grazing land on the island. Their sheep occupied kangaroo hunting grounds, the stock-keepers abducted Aboriginal women, and the settlers refused to provide provisions. In response, the Aborigines in the settled districts tried to drive out the Europeans, partly to assert lost prestige and partly for non-payment of occupation of their land. In the guerilla war that followed, the Aborigines killed nearly two hundred Europeans and severely disrupted the European economy.

The pastoral settlement of Tasmania in the 1820s occurred at the same time as the spread of settlement beyond the Blue Mountains in New South Wales. But in Tasmania it was more controlled, took place in a smaller area, and was always closer to the central administration in Hobart. Between 1822 and 1826, nearly one million sheep occupied the kangaroo hunting grounds of the Midlands Plain, an area of about two hundred square kilometres between Launceston and Hobart. These settlers were attempting to establish a semi-feudal society to provide wool for the factories of Britain.

Governor Phillip had claimed all of eastern Australia for the British Crown when he landed at Sydney in 1788. So the Aborigines were guests on land they had lost without battle and without payment. In return they were classed as British subjects so that they could be brought before the courts for any misdemeanours against the settlers. Phillip could make his proclamation because Captain Cook eighteen years before had written that the Aborigines of New South Wales had no religion, no culture, and no settled way of life — the three essential ingredients for "civilization". And if one had no "civilization", then one could have no land.

At the height of the conflict between the settlers and the Aborigines in Tasmania over ownership of the land, between 1824 and 1834, the British government's representative in the colony, Lieutenant-Governor George Arthur, attempted a series of solutions. First he created a reserve distant from European settlement as a place of

Aboriginal retreat. When the Aborigines failed to go there voluntarily, he ordered a military expedition known as the Black Line to sweep them from the settled districts. Then he commissioned a tradesman, G. A. Robinson, to round up the remaining Aborigines and place them in captivity on Flinders Island in Bass Strait. There the Aborigines were expected to become "civilized by tuition".

By 1832 Arthur realized that in future where other areas of Australia attracted new pastoral settlement a treaty would have to be signed with the Aborigines at the outset. Then, before the spread of settlement, a sympathetic missionary could remove the Aborigines from their land and take them to a place from which they could not escape and where they could learn the rudiments of British civilization. In due course they could enter the unskilled labour force.

In the 1840s, however, neither the British government nor the pastoralists were seriously interested in signing treaties with the Aborigines or in using "humane" means to dispossess them. Rather, the pastoral settlers preferred to rely upon the secret, practical, and cheap activities of the native mounted police forces who dispossessed the Aborigines through search-and-destroy operations beyond the frontier of government control and far from the scrutiny of the urban press.

So the public dispossession of the Aborigines that was so meticulously documented in Tasmania became the private dispossession in the other colonies. The settlers would initiate the original dispersal of the Aborigines and leave the native police forces to do the rest. This form of dispossession was more swift and more complete than in Tasmania. Whole tribes literally disappeared without trace. It was not until the 1880s, with the rise of the philanthropic movement, the desire of the northern pastoralists to have access to cheap, seasonal labour, and the clamour of the townspeople to remove the destitute Aborigines who congregated in their streets, that the reserves were reintroduced.

The new reserves were not established with the same motives as that of Flinders Island — as a place of retreat for the defeated warriors — but as a ration station for the destitute. The conditions were the same, however, and the people who ran the stations were the same. The Aborigines were expected to show gratitude and to die out gracefully. No effort was made to promote Aboriginal survival, and when any group of Aborigines looked like regenerating and becoming an effective political group, their children were removed and the young men banished.

The reserve system was reintroduced to Tasmania in 1881 with the establishment of the Cape Barren Island reserve for the sealing community. Here, in far less rigid conditions than on Flinders Island, the

Islanders were expected to become a self-sufficient farming community despite the fact that the land was largely unsuited to agriculture. Their movements to and from the reserve were controlled; they were threatened with constant eviction and were subject to government regulation but were not entitled to government assistance. There was no opportunity for self-determination. The ultimate irony arrived in 1951 when in accordance with the assimilation policy, the reserve was abolished because the government no longer defined the Islanders as Aborigines.

Tasmania was the cradle of race relations in Australia. It provided the initial interaction between Aborigines and sealers that enabled some Aborigines to survive. It provided the first test of sustained Aboriginal resistance to pastoral settlement, and it provided the first opportunity for the formulation for a sustained and, by comparison with later events, humane policy of dispossession. Tasmania was also the first part of European Australia to deny Aboriginal survival. This book is thus an examination of European attitudes towards Aborigines as well as a narrative of Aboriginal survival.

1

The Aboriginal Landscape

Tasmania is an island of 67,870 square kilometres — almost the same size as Sri Lanka and a little smaller than Ireland. Physically Tasmania is part of Australia but separated from it by the relatively shallow Bass Strait. It lies between 40 and 43½ degrees south of the Equator, which places it within the influence of the roaring forties and produces the island's temperate marine climate of abnormally mild winters and cool summers. Tasmania is also a mountainous island. In the centre, east, and south-east the mountains are plateau-like; in the west they are ridge-like. Very little of the island's surface lies close to sea level, and continuous lowland plains are limited to the extreme north-west and north-east and to the northern Midlands between Launceston and Tunbridge. With these exceptions, the mountains and hills directly adjoin the coast and rise from there to heights of over 1,524 metres, forming a rugged landscape that includes some of the most spectacular mountain scenery in Australia. Tasmania also contains thousands of lakes — the north-east section of the central plateau alone has four thousand. On the west coast the annual rainfall varies between 127 and 381 centimetres, but the high ridge of mountains along the western spine of Tasmania provides a buffer against the roaring forties in the central and eastern part of the island, where the annual rainfall is between 38 and 152 centimetres. With such topography the island abounds in swift-flowing rivers.[1]

The Tasmanian flora is a mixture of Southern Oceanic and Australian components. The high mountains and high rainfall of the western region produce floristic affinities with New Zealand and South America, while the lower and drier eastern region is predominantly Australian in character. A wide range of local environments occurs within these regions; vegetation varies floristically and structurally in response to local conditions. Rainforest occurs in regions where the average yearly rainfall exceeds 139 centimetres, sclerophyll forests

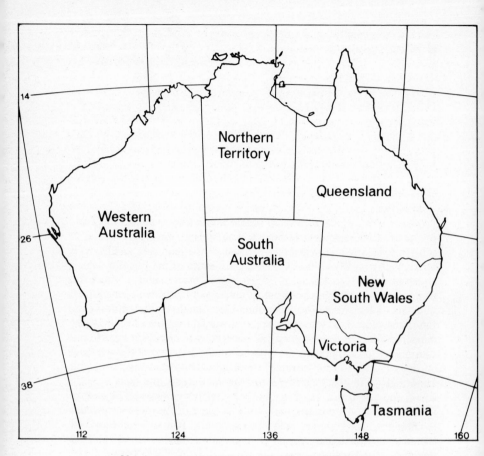

Map 1. Tasmania in relation to the other Australian states

occur in lower rainfall areas, moorland occurs in altitudes above 914 metres in the north and 609 metres in the south, coastal heath is found in the north-east and north-west lowland plains, and the inland plain is open savannah woodland.

Tasmania has a range of fauna closely related to that of the Australian mainland: mammals like the platypus and echidna, a variety of marsupials including several species of kangaroo, as well as the thylacine (Tasmanian tiger) and the Tasmanian devil. It also has several genera of rodents and some bats. All these animals are either contemporary Australian species, related to Australian species, or species that have been in Australia in the past. So Tasmania has some exotic aspects in climate, topography, and flora and fauna, but ultimately its greatest affinities lie with the Australian mainland across Bass Strait. Above all it is an environment well suited to a hunter-gatherer people like the Tasmanian Aborigines.

The sparse information known about the Aboriginal Tasmanians before European invasion at the beginning of the nineteenth century is based on archaeological and ethno-historical sources. Both have limits and are subject to innate limitations. The data can be interpreted to suit different points of view. We do know, however, that Tasmania was first reached by the Aborigines more than twenty thousand years ago when a land bridge linked the island to Australia. As a hunter-gatherer people, they presumably moved across the landscape to take advantage of the food sources available, keeping personal property to a minimum. If our present archaeological record is comprehensive, it seems that they had no metal, dogs, ground-edge axes, or boomerangs. When the sea rose to form Bass Strait ten thousand years ago, the Aborigines in Tasmania became separated from the Australian mainland.[2]

Archaeologists have reached different conclusions about the fortunes of the Tasmanian Aborigines before European contact, based on their interpretations of the material culture. One conclusion is that in the ten thousand years of isolation from the Australian mainland the material culture of the Tasmanian Aborigines, which was originally like that of the Australian Aborigines, became simpler, and that the progressive simplicity and impoverishment of culture and lifestyle led to "a slow strangulation of the mind" (the dropping of scale fish from the diet about four thousand years ago is evidenced to support this view), so at the point of European invasion the Tasmanian Aborigines were at a crucial stage of cultural decline. The other view is that from the moment of isolation from mainland Australia, the Tasmanian Aborigines adapted successfully to their environment, making significant adjustments to their material culture, so that at the point of European contact they were improving their exploitation of the environment. The development of boats in the north-west, south-west, and south-east to exploit seals over the last two thousand years is used as evidence to support this view.[3]

More recent dating of stone implements found on islands in Bass Strait suggest that the Tasmanian Aborigines may not have suffered complete isolation over the last ten thousand years.[4] For the historian who can only examine the material culture, it is hard to take sides and draw conclusions. The archaeology of Tasmania proceeds apace, and fresh interpretations of the era before European contact will soon be offered. But assuming there was a period of isolation and a closed system over the last ten thousand years, it seems that, influenced by environmental changes as well as accelerated genetic change owing to population size, the Aborigines in Tasmania developed a degree of physical and material culture different from that of the Aborigines on the Australian mainland.

The most important changes in physical appearance were the emergence of woolly hair and reddish-brown skin colour. But their size and other physical characteristics varied among themselves as much as in any other Aboriginal group in Australia. A change took place four thousand years ago, when the Tasmanian Aborigines ceased to eat scale fish, ceased to make bone tools, and began to increase their exploitation of land mammals like kangaroos and wallabies, which in turn involved a slight refinement of stone tools. These changes produced by about two thousand years ago a more profitable exploitation of the environment. On the west coast, where the Aborigines found a year-round abundance of food sources like shellfish and important seasonal sources like fur and elephant seals and muttonbirds, as well as kangaroos and wallabies in the spatially limited hinterland, they became more settled in their search for food, living in "semi-permanent" villages where they were less affected by seasonal changes, strong winds, and heavy rains.[5]

Changes in the social, territorial, and religious organization of Aboriginal Tasmanian society over the last ten thousand years are unknown, for the absence of social anthropological research and the poverty of valid ethnographical observations have obscured the cultural base of Aboriginal Tasmanian society. In particular, their religious beliefs were recorded by people who expected the Tasmanians to conform to notions of nationalistic animalism. Thus the men were associated with the sun spirit and the women with the moon. Their religion was thought to be based upon "star gods" and good and bad spirits which could be compared to classical mythology. Their customs appear to have been based upon totems (each tribe taking a designated species as a totem) and taboos, especially concerning whether an individual ate the male or female kangaroo and wallaby. Their spiritual practices were apparently based upon the idea of the good spirit (Noiheener or Parledee), who governed the day, and the bad spirit (Wrageowrapper), who governed the night. These and other spirits were associated with the creation, fire, river, trees, and the dead. The Aborigines carried amulets made from the bones of the dead to ward off harm and illness. Sometimes they lit fires during bad weather, or when rivers were in flood, to appease malignant spirits. As an uncircumcised people they can be compared with the "older" uncircumcised tribes of mainland Australia. Their mythology ascribed the creation of the first Aboriginal, who had a tail like a kangaroo, to a star god who tumbled to earth at Toogee

Low (Port Davey) and who was turned into a large stone. Other traditions hint at epic sea voyages. An overall view could possibly see these traditions as a racial memory of the climatic upheavals which occurred as the sea level rose after the ice age.

The Aborigines believed in a life after death and that a guardian spirit or "soul" who lived within their left breast went to live elsewhere — in the case of the Aborigines from the northern part of the island, the islands in Bass Strait. They also made bark drawings and, in the past, made stone and rock carvings. The significance of their linear, circular, and dot formations is unclear, although they could possibly represent the sun-male and the moon-female deities associated with tribal bands, formations, and numbers or movements in a similar context to their myths and legends.[6]

There is only a hazy picture of the variety of Aboriginal Tasmanian languages and range of thought of the Aborigines. The Tasmanian languages were subject to change, for the Aborigines refrained from naming the dead and elaborate circumlocutions were practised to avoid personal names when referring to the dead. But the most recent reassessment suggests there were two Tasmanian languages, the Northern Tasmanian and Southern Tasmanian. They show some vague typological resemblance to the Australian languages, on a very general level, but there are a number of un-Australian features in them.[7]

In their daily lives, the men carried fire (they were unable to make fire) and hunted kangaroos, wallabies, wombats, potoroos and other animals with implements made of stone, wood, and bone. They loaded their scalp hair with a mixture of grease and ochre, twisting the individual ringlets into tubular masses which hung around the head like the strands of a mop and almost concealed the eyes. They either allowed their beards and moustaches to grow naturally or trimmed or cut them short. If they wore beards, they would also be greased. Sometimes they wore a feather or flower in their hair for ornamentation. They also wore loops of twisted sinews loaded with ochre around their necks and sometimes suspended the jawbone of a dead friend from their necks, bound with string made from a plant fibre.

The women carried the children and their few household effects: water containers and baskets and digging sticks and sometimes stone tools and shells. They searched for roots and small animals and plants and swam and dived to prodigious depths for shellfish. They also climbed trees for possums and made necklaces from tiny shells and wove baskets from grass and reeds. Their major implement was the digging stick. They cropped their heads closely, at most leaving a coronet of short hair, and the arrangement of their scalp hair may have had a significance in the identification of their band or tribe.

Both sexes incised their bodies and rubbed into their wounds powdered charcoal and red ochre mixed with grease, in order to raise high weals on the skin. These cicatrices took the form of lines, dashes, and circles and were to be found principally on the upper arm, chest, shoulder, back, and buttock. Their significance is not definitely known, but in the case of the women they could again have signified band or tribal affiliation.

The Aborigines' stone implements were never mounted in handles; their wooden implements comprised no more than simple spears and waddies, a chisel-like stick, and perhaps a small spatula; and their bone implements were small piercing and spatulate utensils. Apart from these, they had grinding and mortar stones, baskets, water containers, and, in some areas, boats. They made their stone tools by striking flakes of stone off a larger mass. With these they cut up the bodies of animals and the roots and stems of plants in the preparation of food. They also used stone tools in the manufacture of baskets and water containers, in shaping their waddies and spears, and for cutting toeholds in the trunks of trees when climbing. Stone tools – and sometimes abalone shells – were also used for cutting hair.

The spears of the Aborigines were plain wooden lances made from slender stems of the bushy tea-trees. They were from 2.4 to 5.4 metres long and about 1 to 2 centimetres thick, tapering back from a robust point. The Aboriginal men threw their spears in such a way that they spun in flight and were a lethal weapon at sixty to seventy metres.

The men also used a waddy – a wooden rod about 60 centimetres long and 2 to 3 centimetres in diameter, one end bluntly pointed and the other roughened for holding – either to strike a blow or to throw with a rotary motion. The women used a stick sharpened to a chisel-like blade at one end to prise abalones and other molluscs from the rocks, to dig up tubers and roots, to break into the burrows of mutton-birds and penguins, as well as to strip sheets of bark from the trees. They used spatulate and pointed sticks to extract small molluscs from their shells after cooking. They used twisted plant fibres as handles for water containers and as binding for their "relics of the dead". They also used a suitable tough grass for making long ropes with which they climbed trees, and strips of bark for binding the masses of bark or rushes to construct their canoes. [8]

The social organization of the Aboriginal Tasmanian appears to have consisted of three units: (1) the domestic unit, or *hearth group*; (2) the basic social unit or *band*; and (3) the political unit, or *tribe*. The hearth group camped and cooked around a single fire and, on the west coast, occupied a single hut. Its core was a "family" consisting of husband, wife, and children and relatives and sometimes friends and other

relations. The total ranged from two to eleven people. Families were
"invariably monogamous". Men and women married in their late teens,
the husband and wife being about the same age. They remarried quickly
on the death of a spouse, and the new partners assumed responsibility
for the children of previous unions. There were parental prohibitions
and punishments for "wrong" marriages and adultery, and although
"divorce" took place, infidelity, jealousy, and raids for women were the
chief causes of fights, often resulting in the death of some of the principal parties. Thus in several respects, Aboriginal marriage customs
appeared significantly different from some of those practised on the
Australian mainland.[9]

The basic social unit, or band, was "a group of people who called
themselves by a particular name, and were known by that or other
names to other people".[10] Like the hearth group, the band was exoga-
mous; the wife usually moved to her husband's band and claimed it as
her own, although occasionally the reverse happened, particularly if
there had been a quarrel. The band was led by a man, usually older
than the others and who had a reputation as a formidable hunter and
fighter. The leader formed the core of the band, to which were added
his own and other hearth groups. The leader always came from the
territory encompassed by the band. Some European explorers, like
Cook, thought they saw leaders among the Aboriginal Tasmanians
wielding authority and prestige as in European society. But leadership
among the Aboriginal Tasmanians was probably no more developed
than among Aborigines on the Australian mainland before European
invasion.[11]

The band was also the basic unit for feuding with other bands.
Combat usually took the form of ambushes or personal fights. The
band "owned" territory, the core of which was often a rich foraging
zone whose boundaries coincided with well-marked geographical
features like rivers and lagoons. Band ownership of land was probably
formal, but this did not mean that the band foraged only in that area.
Rather, each band foraged widely on the territories of other bands,
sometimes with permission, sometimes without. Thus foraging
depended very much on relations with other bands.[12]

Along the coasts, the bands were regularly spaced, each occupying
some twenty-five to thirty kilometres of coastline, with shorter
distances in the rich western corner of the island and longer ones along
the extreme south-west, where smaller supplies of food were available.
Where coast and inland areas were combined, each band's territory
occupied about 500 to 750 square kilometres. The nature of the food
supply determined the size and number of bands. Several came together
for seasonal visits at places like the north-west coast for sealing and

muttonbirding, at Mount Housetop and Mount Vandyke for mining ochre, which was of great cultural significance as a body adornment, at Moulting Lagoon for gathering swan and duck eggs, at Campbell Town and Ross for kangaroo hunting, and at Recherche Bay for sealing. Each band's year was divided into "private" and "public" periods. No local band maintained exclusive rights to the resources within its boundaries, so that visiting patterns created inter-group relations. Thus hosts in one season became guests in another. Movement was largely seasonal, but it was also determined by personal inclination relating to the settlement of feuds and obligations. No band had a food surplus, for the environment itself was a storehouse. Each band knew where food sources were in abundance at any time of year.[13]

Before European invasion there were at least fifty bands, of which forty-eight have been located. Rhys Jones estimates there were originally seventy to eighty-five. If, as Jones assumes, the average band contained between forty and fifty people, the Aboriginal Tasmanian population would have been between three thousand and four thousand.[14] Each band was associated with a wider political unit, the tribe, which was "that agglomeration of bands which lived in contiguous regions, spoke the same language or dialect, shared the same cultural traits, usually intermarried, had a similar pattern of seasonal movement, habitually met together for economic and other reasons, the pattern of whose peaceful relations were within the agglomeration and of whose enmities and military adventures were directed outside it". Its territory consisted of all the land owned by the constituent bands so that movement outside the territory, and of alien bands inside it, were carefully sanctioned. Such movements usually had reciprocal economic advantages to bands concerned, while trespass was usually a challenge to or punishable by war. Its boundaries ranged from "a sharp well-defined line associated with a prominent geographical feature to a broad transition zone often found between two friendly tribes".[15]

Aboriginal Tasmania consisted of nine tribes, each comprising from five or six to fifteen bands, with an average of nine. Jones estimates the mean population of each tribe to have been between 350 and 470 people, the smallest tribe having about 250 and the largest 700.[16]

Within an area of 67,800 square kilometres the hunter-gatherer population density of Aboriginal Tasmania was one person per thirteen to twenty-three square kilometres. On the rich coastal belt of 1,450 kilometres, an even higher population density of one to two people per square kilometre was achieved. This level was comparable to the high population densities on the rich coastal and riverine regions of mainland Australia and North America.[17]

The tribes fell into three groups. The eastern and northern groups

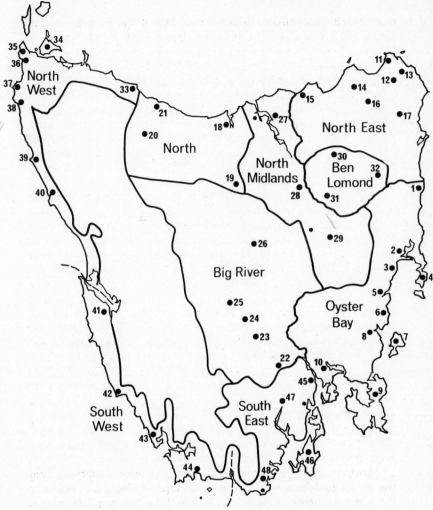

Map 2. Tribal boundaries of the Tasmanian Aborigines; numbers indicate band territories (see table 1 for key)

consisted of the Oyster Bay, North East, and North tribes and had both an extensive coast and hinterland. The midland group, consisting of the Big River, North Midlands, and Ben Lomond tribes, had little or no coastline, while the third, the maritime group, consisting of the North West, South West, and South East tribes, had an extensive coast and

Table 1. Aboriginal Tasmania: tribal groupings and locations

Group	Tribe	Band		Territory of Band
Eastern and northern	Oyster Bay	1	Leetermairremener	St Patricks Head
		2	Linetemairrener	Nth Moulting Lagn
		3	Loontitetermairrelehoinner	Nth Oyster Bay
		4	Toorernomairremener	Schouten Passage
		5	Poredareme	Little Swanport
		6	Laremairremener	Grindstone Bay
		7	Tyreddeme	Maria Island
		8	Portmairremener	Prosser River
		9	Pydairrerme	Tasman Peninsula
		10	Moomairremener	Pittwater, Risdon
	North East	11	Peeberrangner	
		12	Leenerrerter	
		13	Pinterrairer	Uncertain
		14	Trawlwoolway	
		15	Pyemmairrenerpairrener	
		16	Leenethmairrener	
		17	Panpekanner	
	North	18	Punnilerpanner	Port Sorell
		19	Pallittorre	Quamby Bluff
		20	Noeteeler	Hampshire Hills
		21	Plairhekehillerplue	Emu Bay
Midland	Big River	22	Leenowwenne	New Norfolk
		23	Pangerninghe	Clyde-Derwent junct.
		24	Braylwunyer	Ouse and Dee rivers
		25	Larmairremener	West of Dee
		26	Luggermairrernerpairrer	Great Lake
	North Midlands	27	Leterremairrener	Port Dalrymple
		28	Panninher	Norfolk Plains
		29	Tyerrernotepanner	Campbell Town
	Ben Lomond	30	Plangermairreenner	
		31	Plindermairhemener	Uncertain
		32	Tonenerweenerlarmenne	
Maritime	North West	33	Tommeginer	Table Cape
		34	Parperloihener	Robbins Island
		35	Pennemukeer	Cape Grim
		36	Pendowte	Studland Bay
		37	Peerapper	West Point
		38	Manegin	Arthur River mouth
		39	Tarkinener	Sandy Cape
		40	Peternidic	Pieman River mouth
	South West	41	Mimegin	Macquarie Harbour
		42	Lowreenne	Low Rocky Point
		43	Ninene	Port Davey
		44	Needwonnee	Cox Bight
	South East	45	Mouheneenner	Hobart
		46	Nuenonne	Bruny Island
		47	Mellukerdee	Huon River
		48	Lyluequonny	Recherche Bay

Note. Numbers before band names are a key to band locations on map 2.

limited hinterland. All three groups gained coastal and inland access to one another's territory by agreement. In pre-European times no tribes or group of bands lived inland all year round, but there were tribes or groups of bands such as those on the west coast which could live on coastal food sources all year round.[18]

Of the eastern and northern group of tribes, the Oyster Bay tribe was the largest. Their territory, which covered 7,800 square kilometres, including 515 kilometres of coastline, was located along the east coast from St Patricks Head to the Derwent estuary. From there the boundary proceeded along the eastern bank of the Derwent River to the mouth of the Jordan River, which it followed inland to St Peters Pass in the Midlands and then east to the watershed of the South Esk and Macquarie Rivers in the Eastern Tiers and then north-east back to St Patricks Head. The Oyster Bay tribe consisted of ten bands, producing a total population of between seven hundred and eight hundred, making it the largest tribe in Tasmania. The major elements of their diet were shellfish from estuarine beds, kangaroo and possum from the open forests and plains, and a variety of vegetable foods. The bands and their locations were: the Leetermairremener from St Patricks Head, the Linetemairrener from North Moulting Lagoon, the Loontitetermairrelehoinner from North Oyster Bay, the Toorernomairremener from Schouten Passage, the Poredareme from Little Swanport, the Laremairremener from Grindstone Bay, the Tyreddeme from Maria Island, the Portmairremener from Prosser River, the Pydairrerme from Tasman Peninsula, and the Moomairremener from Pittwater and Risdon.[19]

The Oyster Bay people were divided into two groups according to seasonal patterns of movement in their search for food: one from North Oyster Bay to St Patricks Head and the other from Little Swanport to Tasman Peninsula. Each winter would find both groups on the coastal areas of their territories living on shellfish and marine vegetables until the end of July, when swans and ducks arrived in lagoons and riverine areas to lay their eggs and bring up their young. At the end of August the South Oyster Bay people moved inland, the Moomairremener band at Pittwater waiting until September or even October to do so. The Poredareme from Little Swanport, the Laremairremener from Grindstone Bay, the Portmairremener from Prosser River, the Tyreddeme from Maria Island, and the Pydairrerme from Tasman Peninsula moved up the Little Swanport and Prosser rivers to the Eastern Marshes, where there were birds, kangaroos, and wallabies. As summer drew near, they moved further west, hunting and firing the bush for game, moving through St Peters Pass to Blackmans River and to the high country to the west or round the Blue Hill Bluff to Miles Opening and to the Clyde

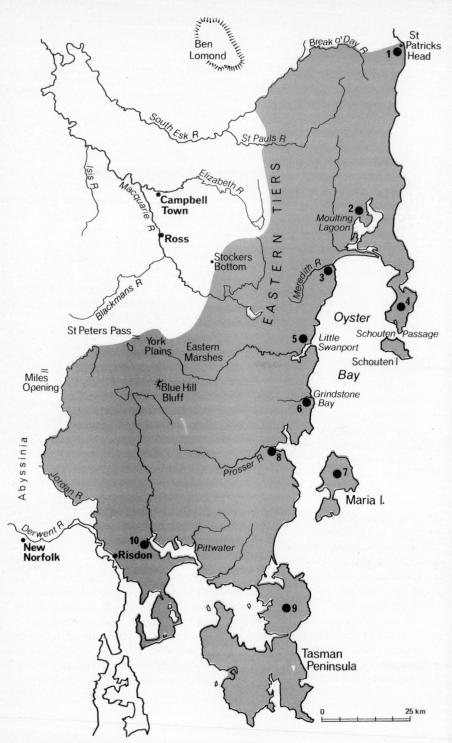

Map 3. Oyster Bay tribe: territory (see table 1 for key for band locations)

Ben Lomond

St Patricks Head

1

Break o' Day R

South Esk R

St Pauls R

Elizabeth R

EASTERN TIERS

Campbell Town

Macquarie R

Isis R

2

Moulting Lagoon

Ross

Stockers Bottom

Meredith R

3

Blackmans R

St Peters Pass

York Plains

Eastern Marshes

5

Oyster

Little Swanport

4

Schouten Passage

Schouten I

Bay

Miles Opening

Blue Hill Bluff

6

Grindstone Bay

Abyssinia

Jordan R

Prosser R

8

7

Maria I.

Derwent R

New Norfolk

10

Risdon

Pittwater

9

Tasman Peninsula

0   25 km

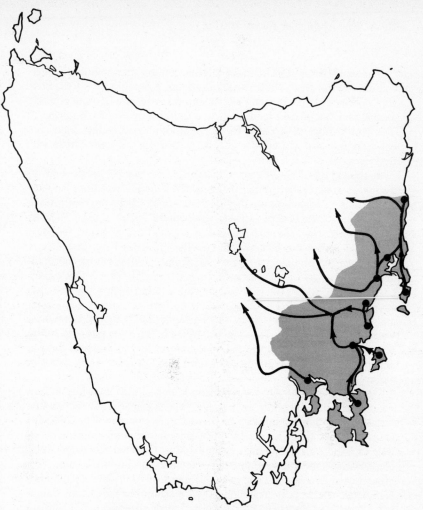

Map 4. Oyster Bay tribe: seasonal movements

and Ouse river valleys in Big River country. The Moomairremener people moved west up the Derwent to New Norfolk, across to Abyssinia, and from there to the Clyde and the Ouse. These were all well-defined routes, usually along the borders of territory, designed for "maximum access and minimum trespass". Not all the people from the Little Swanport area and to the south travelled west every spring and summer, but summer visits to Big River country were common. They returned to the Midlands in late February or early March, arriving back at the coast in June.[20]

The great attractions of the Big River country, particularly the high country to the west, were *Eucalyptus gunii*, a potentially intoxicating gum confined to the central plateau, and the extensive hunting grounds around the Great Lake and along the Clyde and Ouse river valleys.[21] The North West and North people in whose territory lay important ochre mines also visited the Big River country to trade shells and necklaces.

Between August and October the Oyster Bay people north of Little Swanport congregated at rich food-source areas like Moulting Lagoon and Schouten Island, where there were seasonally heavy concentrations of birdlife. At the end of October they moved inland, up the St Pauls and Break o' Day rivers to the Ben Lomond Tier or up the Meredith River and across the Eastern Tiers to the Elizabeth River at Stockers Bottom on the boundary of North Midlands country, across to Campbell Town and to the tiers west of the Isis River. The North Oyster Bay people often spent the summer in these areas. Those in the Ben Lomond Tier returned to the coast at the end of January for sealing and muttonbirding, moving to the Midlands in March for kangaroos, wallabies and possums. Those in the Western Tiers also returned to the Midlands in March, congregating on their boundary at Stockers Bottom and in the marsh country to hunt until they returned to the coast in June.[22]

As with the South Oyster Bay people, not all the North Oyster Bay people left their country in summer, but seasonal visits to the Ben Lomond and North Midlands territories were common. The Midlands areas also provided quarries for the fashioning of stone implements as well as important ceremonial grounds. Most seasonal movement took place in spring and autumn. In the colonial literature there are numerous references to large concentrations of Aborigines in the Midlands area, particularly York Plains, the Eastern Marshes, Ross, Campbell Town, and Stockers Bottom. They were all important kangaroo hunting grounds, all on well-defined routes. The Oyster Bay people had close relations with the Big River tribe, often meeting them at favoured hunting grounds or at important coastal resorts.[23]

To the north of the Oyster Bay people lay the second tribe of the eastern and northern group, the North East people, whose territory included the country east of the Piper River to Cape Portland, then south to St Patricks Head, along the Break o' Day and North Esk Rivers to Launceston and north to the Piper River again. The area was five thousand square kilometres and included 260 kilometres of coastline. There were probably seven bands between fifty and eighty in number, giving a total population of between four hundred and five hundred people. They were the Peeberrangner, the Leenerrerter, the Pinterrairer, the Trawlwoolway, the Pyemmairrenerpairrener, the Leenethmairrener, and the Panpekanner. The exact location of these bands is unknown, since G. A. Robinson, the major source for most information about the Tasmanian tribes, reached this area after the North East tribe had been severely dislocated.[24]

The North East people had heaths and plains behind their coast which they kept open and clear by firing. Game included kangaroos, wallabies, emus, and possums. The coastline and the associated lagoons and estuaries provided abundant seasonal food resources, such as muttonbirds, swans, ducks, and seals. From late July to early September the egging season enticed the bands to congregate around these lagoons and estuaries to collect the eggs of swans and ducks. In summer they hunted fur seals and in autumn muttonbirds. The coast and its immediate hinterland was capable of supporting a high Aboriginal population during most seasons of the year, as well as summer visits from the Ben Lomond and North Midlands tribes. In return, some visited Ben Lomond for ochre and the Tamar Valley to the east.[25]

There were well-marked "roads" consisting of tracks and chains of small plains running east-west near the southern boundary. To the south the rugged mountainous rainforest formed a strong physical barrier with the Ben Lomond and North Midlands peoples. One road led eastwards from the Tamar north to Mount Barrow and on to the upper reaches of Ringarooma River, from which there was a route via the headwaters of the George River to George Bay or the Scamander River on the east coast. Within this wet forested country the Pyemmairrenerpairrener people subsisted on wombats, possums, and echidnas and, for vegetable food, ferns, roots, and fungi of various types. Of all the peoples in Aboriginal Tasmania, the North East people travelled least. A mild climate and abundant resources on both the coast and hinterland gave them an insularity comparable only to the South East people.[26]

The third tribe from the eastern and northern group were the North people, whose territory extended along the north coast from Port Sorell to west of Emu Bay, and then inland west of the Hampshire Hills to the south-west corner of the Surrey Hills and then south of Black Bluff, Middlesex Plains and Mount Roland to the base of the Western Tiers. Then it swung north at Quamby Bluff along the ridge of the Asbestos Range to the coast, west of the Tamar River. The area was 4,700 square kilometres and included 113 kilometres of coastline. The North people had four known bands, the Punnilerpanner from Port Sorell, the Pallittorre from Quamby Bluff, the Noeteeler at the Hampshire Hills, and the Plairhekehillerplue at Emu Bay, with perhaps one or two more

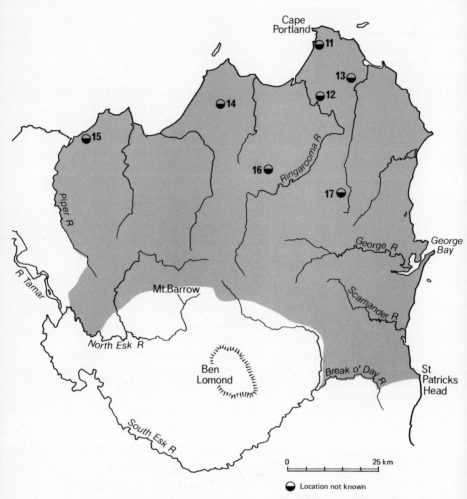

Map 5. North East tribe: territory (see table 1 for key to band locations)

along the coast and associated with the Mersey River, giving an original estimate of two hundred to three hundred people.[27]

The ochre mines of Mount Vandyke, Mount Housetop and St Valentines Peak, which formed the most important sources of ochre on the whole island, were in the country of the North people. Partly related to these mines was a system of well-defined roads or lines of communi-

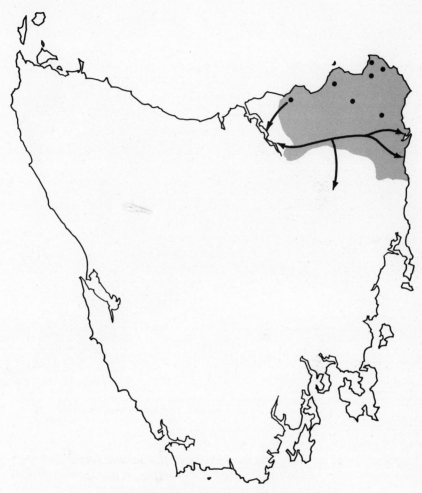

Map 6. North East tribe: seasonal movements

cation which were kept open by firing. A major route ran east-west along the southern boundary of the territory from Norfolk Plains past Quamby Bluff to the Mount Vandyke mine, and then on to the Surrey Hills and eventually across the Norfolk Range to the west coast at Sandy Cape. From this, several routes ran northwards, one from Mount Vandyke to the sea at Port Sorell, another from Mount Housetop to

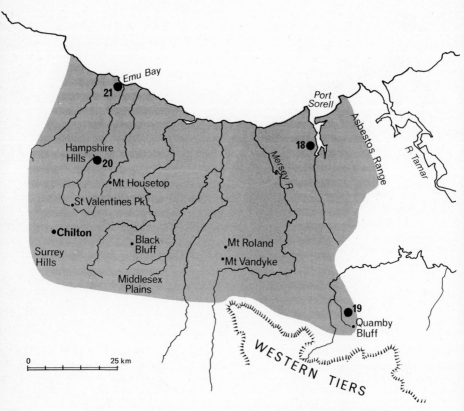

Map 7. North tribe: territory (see table 1 for key to band locations)

Port Sorell, and one from the Surrey Hills to Emu Bay. Running south-wards were the roads to the Big River country, one past Quamby Bluff to the Great Lake, and the other past Cradle Mountain to Lake St Clair. There was also a road running along the coast.[28]

The inland plains were kept open by firing, and on these such game as wallabies, wombats, possums, and emus were hunted and a variety of vegetable foods gathered. Because of the cold conditions and heavy falls of snow in winter, the North people did not occupy this area during that time of year. In early spring, between August and Septem-ber, people congregated at Port Sorell and at the mouths of the north coast rivers to collect the eggs of swans, ducks, and other water birds. Other coastal foods would have included shellfish.

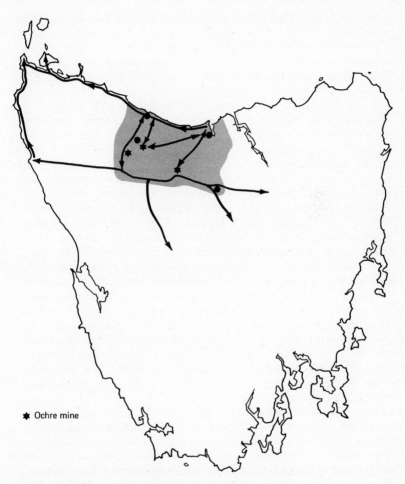

Map 8. North tribe: seasonal movements

To the west, the North people, particularly those from the Surrey Hills and Emu Bay districts, paid regular visits to the coast along the Norfolk Range road. The journey from Chilton in the Surrey Hills to Cape Grim could be travelled in forty-eight hours and was usually made in summer, possibly to take advantage of the sealing season. Excursions were also made to Robbins Island, where, in addition to food, shells were collected for necklaces. In return, the North West people obtained ochre from their visitors as well as rights to visit the inland plains and ochre mines.

To the south-east the North people had access to the high plateau country belonging to the Big River people, travelling there along the Cradle Mountain or Great Lake roads. The lack of a definite pattern of seasonal movement to the eastern boundary suggests that relations between the North people and the North Midlands people were cool or even hostile. In their whole pattern of seasonal movement, the North people had an important localized source – ochre – with which to bargain for reciprocal arrangements with neighbouring tribes.[29]

The Big River people were a midland group, and much of their territory consisted of mountain plateau over six hundred metres above sea level. To the immediate north-west lay the highest mountains in Tasmania, while the country to the south-west was extremely rugged. Although the Big River people had no coastline, they had several lakes whose shorelines totalled more than 240 kilometres, as well as the banks of four rivers with a plentiful supply of birdlife. The Big River was an old name for the River Ouse, which joined the Great Lake, 1,035 metres above sea level, to the Derwent Valley. The territory of the Big River people began near New Norfolk on the Derwent River and moved south along the border of the South East tribe across very high rugged mountains beyond the source of the Derwent River to the south-west corner of the Surrey Hills on the boundary of the North and North West tribes, then east through the extreme western mountains to Quamby Bluff, enclosing all the lake country, and then south along the Western Tiers to St Peters Pass and along the Jordan River back to the Derwent.[30]

Only five bands have been located: the Leenowwenne, from the west bank of the Derwent River above New Norfolk; the Pangerninghe, also on the west bank of the Derwent, opposite its confluence with the Clyde River; the Braylwunyer, who operated between the Ouse and Dee Rivers near where they flowed into the Derwent; the Larmairremener, who came from the high country west of the river Dee; and the Luggermairrernerpairrer, who came from the country near the Great Lake. They probably totalled between four hundred and five hundred people.[31]

Little is known of the Big River people's seasonal movements within tribal territory, but there was some concentration of people on lake shores, particularly those of the Great Lake, the Arthur Lakes, and Lake Echo, and along the rivers that connect the lakes to the Derwent River. Well-marked roads gave access through rough country. Stone implements from the shoreline of Lake Augusta show that the Big River people penetrated into the highest moorland of the central plateau, 1,200 metres above sea level. They may have made periodic excursions into the valleys south-west of the Derwent, but the mountain ranges from this point marked the limit of their occupation.[32]

To the east the Big River people had amicable and co-operative arrangements with some Oyster Bay bands to forage together in each other's territory and used seasonal routes to Pittwater, Oyster Bay, and the Macquarie River. To the north there were two routes leading out of their country. The route most commonly used went past the Great Lake and through a pass in the Western Tiers near Quamby Bluff where it connected with an east-west road running to the ochre mines near Mount Vandyke. The Big River people also went further westwards to the open plains at the Surrey and Hampshire hills and to the ochre mines at Mount Housetop, where they sometimes met coastal bands from the North West tribe. Some Big River bands even went as far as Cape Grim on the west coast, a distance of 240 kilometres from the Great Lake. On these journeys they used either the Norfolk Range road or that to Emu Bay.[33]

The other route to the north led from near Lake St Clair, past Cradle Mountain and Lake Dove, to south of Black Bluff. Much of this route was between nine hundred and twelve hundred metres above sea level but would have given convenient access from the western side of the Big River country to the Surrey Hills plains, Mount Housetop, and the western end of the Norfolk Range road to the west coast.[34]

The ochre mines and the northern roads formed part of the southern boundary of the North tribe, with whom the Big River people usually had amicable relations. The North people were allowed into Big River country as far as the Ouse Valley, while some individuals could have gone as far as Pittwater. To their north-east, relations with the North Midlands people were often hostile, but some North Midlands bands had seasonal access to the high country around the northern part of the Great Lake and the Western Tiers. There was no contact with the South West. The Big River people were the only Aborigines in Tasmania to have regular access to both the east and the west coasts, and its geographically central position enabled them to contact a larger number of Aboriginal families than any other group.[35]

Another midland group, the North Midlands people, occupied both coastal and inland territory. Their boundary ran from the Western Tiers from St Peters Pass to Quamby Bluff in the west, then northwards through the Deloraine district to the western edge of the Tamar Valley and the north coast. The eastern boundary ran from the north coastal Piper River to Launceston then eastwards along the South Esk River valley to St Pauls Dome, then south-westwards along the watershed of the Eastern Tiers back to St Peters Pass. In an area of 6,750 square

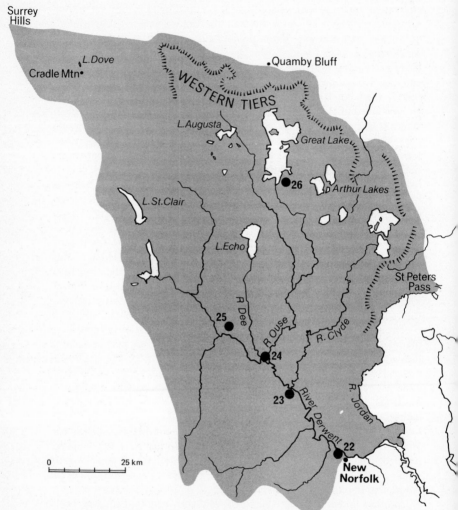

Map 9. Big River tribe: territory (see table 1 for key to band locations)

kilometres they had 160 kilometres of coastline, including both shores of the Tamar estuary. This region forms the driest in Tasmania, particularly in the Campbell Town area of the Midlands Plain. Their diet

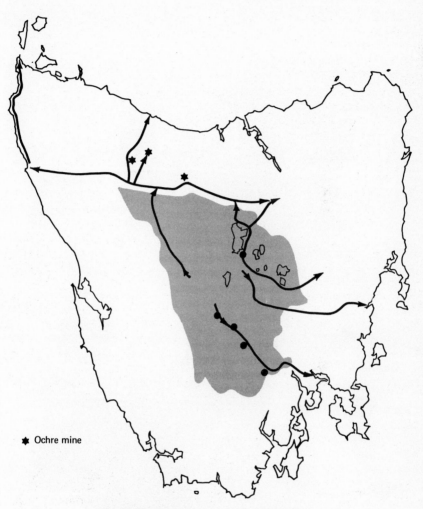

★ Ochre mine

Map 10. Big River tribe: seasonal movements

consisted of shellfish, riverine and estuarine birdlife, kangaroos, wallabies, and possums, and vegetable foods.[36]

There were at least three bands in the North Midlands area, the Leterremairrener (or Port Dalrymple people) at the east Tamar, the Panninher (or Norfolk Plains people) at Norfolk Plains, and the Tyerrernotepanner (or Stoney Creek or Campbell Town people) at

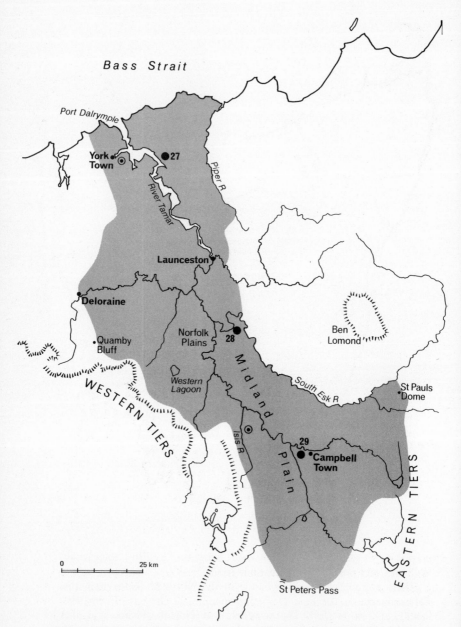

Map. 11. North Midlands tribe: territory (see table 1 for key to band locations)

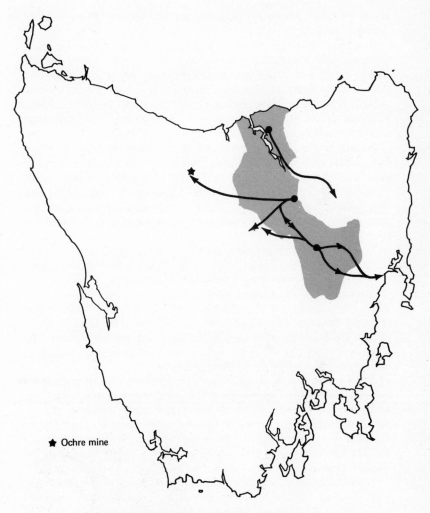

Map 12. North Midlands tribe: seasonal movements

Campbell Town. There was possibly another band at York Town on the western side of the Tamar and another along the Isis. Since the North Midlands people suffered European invasion from the end of 1804, insufficient ethnographic information exists about the boundaries of their bands. With five bands of between sixty and eighty in number, the

North Midlands population probably reached between three hundred and four hundred.[37]

The North Midlands people at the centre of Tasmania had extensive relations, not always harmonious, with surrounding tribes, for the biggest kangaroo hunting grounds in the country lay at Campbell Town and Norfolk Plains. On common territory near Launceston, seasonal tribal concentrations took place. Like the Oyster Bay people, the North Midlands people found it necessary to move to specialist food-source areas according to the season. [38]

In winter the Stoney Creek people had foraging rights in North Oyster Bay; they returned to their own country in spring for extensive kangaroo hunting. They spent the summer in the Western Tiers, sometimes moving along the road to Mount Vandyke for ochre. In autumn they returned again to the Campbell Town area for kangaroos and perhaps for an exchange of ochre with Ben Lomond and Oyster Bay people.[39]

The Norfolk Plains people spent the winter on the lower reaches of the west bank of the Tamar, where they gathered shellfish and swans' eggs. In spring they returned to the kangaroo hunting grounds in their own country. In the summer they moved to the Western Tiers, from where they could use the "ochre road" to Mount Vandyke, and returned to their own country in the autumn. The Norfolk Plains people had extensive relations with the North and Big River people, the former often visiting the Norfolk Plains area to hunt and to catch birds in the marsh area of the Great Western Lagoon.[40]

The Port Dalrymple people spent winter in their own territory along the east bank of the Tamar as far as the coast, moving east in spring and up to the Ben Lomond Tier in summer, returning to their own country at the end of January to await the muttonbird season. They met to exchange shell necklaces for ochre with the Norfolk Plains people and the Ben Lomond people and hunted extensively in the country of the North East people.[41]

Among the three groups of the North Midlands people there was great diversity in their seasonal movements. Their existence depended upon sustained relations with neighbouring tribes and on the full exploitation of seasonal resources.

The third midland group, the Ben Lomond people, had territory that consisted of the Ben Lomond mountain and its neighbourhood. The boundary ran along the South Esk River from the White Hills, south-east of Launceston, to the junction of the Break o' Day River at Fingal, then north to the rainforest of the North Esk River, following the line across the peaks of Mount Saddleback, Ben Nevis, and Mount Barrow and back to the North Esk River outside Launceston. The area was 260 square kilometres and included no coastline except by seasonal access. Ben Lomond dominated the region. Most of the area was open forest with savannah woodlands and open plains, but the northern boundary was dominated by rainforest. The Ben Lomond people probably consisted of three bands of between fifty and eighty in number: the Plangermairreenner, the Plindermairhemener, and the Tonenerweenerlarmenne, reaching a total population somewhere between 150 and 200. They probably had friendly relations with the North Oyster Bay, the North East, and the North Midlands peoples, in the latter case through the Stoney Creek and Port Dalrymple people. One band had foraging rights at North Oyster Bay at Moulting Lagoon between August and October, then moved to the North Midlands territory at Stockers Bottom in November, retiring to the Ben Lomond Tier for the summer. Sometimes they went with some North Midlands people to visit Big River country for hostile purposes. In January they were known to visit the east coast for seals and muttonbirds, returning to the Midlands Plain in autumn and then back to the coast for the winter. Another band spent the winter on the coast with the North East people, retiring to the hinterland for kangaroos in spring and returning to their own country in the summer. The autumn saw a heavy concentration of Ben Lomond people at places like Cape Portland, Waterhouse Point, and Eddystone Point for muttonbirds and seals. A third band wintered with the Port Dalrymple people on the Tamar coast, congregating at the Lower South Esk in spring and autumn and spending the summer in the Ben Lomond Tier. Thus the Ben Lomond people had access to the east and north coasts, the Midland Plain, and the Western Tiers. Their own country was a popular summer resort. It was possible for a band or a member of a band to spend winter on the east coast with the North Oyster Bay people, travel in spring through St Marys Pass to Schouten Passage for eggs, return to the Ben Lomond Tier for the summer, and spend autumn on the Midlands Plain and the following winter at the Tamar coast.[42]

Of the maritime tribes, the North West people occupied the north coast from Table Cape to Cape Grim and down the west coast to Macquarie Harbour. Inland they restricted their occupation to the coastal regions not more than a few miles from the sea, but on the north-west tip the boundary went inland from the Arthur River to Smithton. Since the North West people also regularly visited the Hunter Islands, their tribal area covered 3,400 square kilometres with a coastline of 550 kilometres. As one of the largest tribes in Tasmania — between four hundred and six hundred people — they supported at least eight bands: the Tommeginer from Table Cape, the Parperloihener from Robbins Island, the Pennemukeer from Cape Grim, the Pendowte

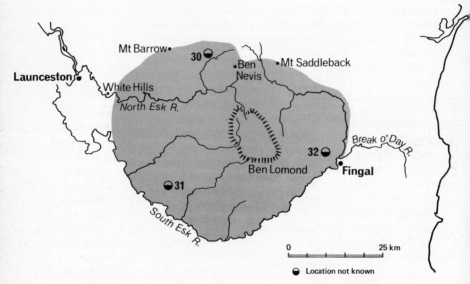

Map 13. Ben Lomond tribe: territory (see table 1 for key to band locations)

from Studland Bay, the Peerapper from West Point, the Manegin from
the mouth of the Arthur River, the Tarkinener from Sandy Cape, and
the Peternidic from the mouth of the Pieman River. [43]

The North West people moved seasonally up and down the coast,
travelling along well-marked footpaths or roads to gain easy access
through swampy country covered with dense scrub. In most cases the
narrow coastal plain marked the limit of inward expansion, since the
dense vegetation, rugged terrain, and huge rainfall formed an effective
barrier to the inland. But the Peerapper from West Point used to forage
inland of Mount Cameron West in the swampy tea-tree and scrub
country round the Welcome River and from there visit Robbins Island
and Circular Head. They also erected beehive-shaped huts in strategic
locations close to foraging areas, so that as the bands travelled along
the coast they could move from one hut to the next, occupying old
huts or building new ones as the occasion demanded. They dug and
kept tidy small wells and placed abalone shells near them as drinking
vessels for travellers.[44]

The individual bands moved in response both to chance events like
"the whims of individuals, fights and deaths" and to more formal
seasonal migration. Every September, for example, the North West

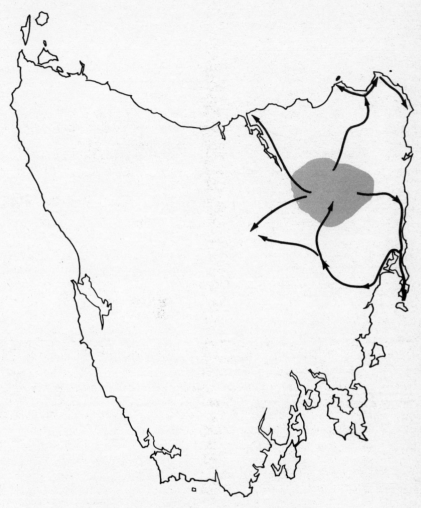

Map 14. Ben Lomond tribe: seasonal movements

people congregated at the mouths of rivers near the coastal lagoons, where swans and ducks laid their eggs. From October to the end of March they exploited the vast muttonbird rookeries on the Hunter Group and on the rocky stacks and were often joined by bands from as far south as Sandy Cape. Since these rookeries were the most extensive

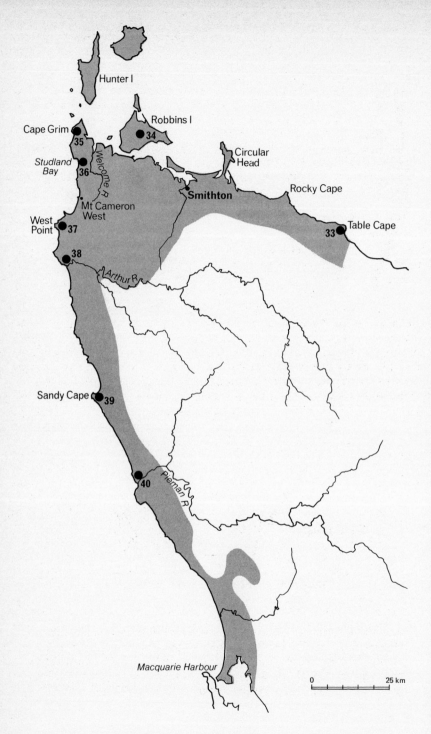

Map 15. North West tribe: territory (see table 1 for key to band locations)

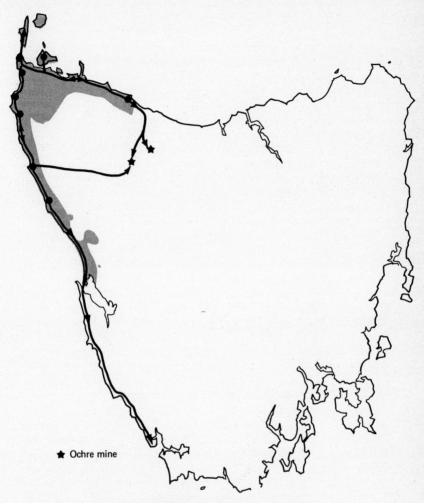

★ Ochre mine

Map 16. North West tribe: seasonal movements

near the Tasmanian mainland, they were able to sustain an Aboriginal
population for much longer than the rookeries near Cape Portland and
at various places on the east coast and at Bruny Island. In early and
mid summer the North West people exploited the elephant sealing
grounds from Sandy Cape north to Mount Cameron West.[45]

From Sandy Cape and the Pieman River the southernmost bands of
the North West people crossed Macquarie Harbour by catamaran to
forage on the south-west coast as far south as Port Davey. In turn the
South West people made visits in summer to Mount Cameron West and
even as far as Cape Grim. The Robbins Island and West Point bands
were also known to have visited the South West people. Although
bands from the North West and South West tribes knew one another
well, relations were not always friendly.

People from Circular Head to Sandy Cape used to travel regularly
into the high inland country belonging to the North people, particularly to the Surrey and Hampshire Hills region to collect ochre. They
travelled through a chain of open plains kept clear by regular firing.
These land excursions were carefully sanctioned and often needed a
band from the North people like the Noeteeler to accompany them.
Unaccompanied visits led to hostility. In return for the use of these
vital inland resources, the coastal bands acted as host for the North
people when they visited Robbins Island for muttonbirds, for sealing,
and for shells to make necklaces. Relations, however, were not always
amicable. The Table Cape people, the Tommeginer, exploited their
position in their relations both with the other North West people and
with the North people. A west coast band, even allowing for its semi-
permanent occupation of areas like West Point, still travelled about
three hundred kilometres a year. The Tarkinener, for example, whose
local residence was at Sandy Cape, in a normal year could travel 130
kilometres north to the Hunter Islands, then 265 kilometres south to
Port Davey and 95 to 130 kilometres inland to the Surrey Hills. Thus
the North West people were another example of an intensely maritime
people exploiting a wide variety of coastal resources.[46]

The second maritime group, the South West people, occupied territory some 450 kilometres from Macquarie Harbour to somewhere
between Cox Bight and South Cape. North of Low Rocky Point, the
boundary cut inland in a straight line to Birch Inlet on the eastern
side of Macquarie Harbour. The area covered 2,860 square kilometres
and supported four bands: the Mimegin from the southern side of
Macquarie Harbour, the Lowreenne from Low Rocky Point, the Ninene
from Port Davey, and the Needwonnee from Cox Bight. With a population of between fifty and seventy for each band, the total population
for the South West people was between two hundred and three
hundred.[47]

The economy of the South West people was focused on the seashore
and the coastal plain immediately behind it. Major foods were shellfish, crayfish, seals, wombats and macropods. Vegetable foods were less
abundant and thus not as important in the diet as they were elsewhere

in Tasmania. Like the North West people, the South West bands lived in local "villages" of beehive-shaped huts situated close to fresh water and food-collecting areas. Movement was mostly parallel to the coast along well-defined footpaths where huts were numerous. Rivers and harbours were crossed by catamarans. During the winter the bands tended to stay in their local residences, shellfish forming the staple diet until the egging season in late winter, when they moved towards Macquarie Harbour or Port Davey. They obtained ochre at Cox Bight. Outside the region, the South West people had access north across Macquarie Harbour or east along the coast past South East Cape to Recherche Bay. No route led to central or eastern Tasmania. They had close relations with the North West people and often visited Mount Cameron West and Cape Grim during the sealing and muttonbirding seasons. To the east they visited the Maatsuyker and De Witt Islands during the summer to hunt seals. Here they would sometimes meet South East people. In winter they sometimes visited the South East people at Bruny Island.[48]

The Ninene, or Port Davey people, in the course of a year would travel from Recherche Bay to Mount Cameron West, a distance of four hundred kilometres. Since ochre was obtained at Cox Bight they had no need to travel to the Surrey Hills. There was no contact between the South West people and those from the North Midlands, Big River, or Oyster Bay. Like the North West and South East people, the South West people were dependent on the coastal regions for basic food sources. Their ability to travel the whole extent of the west coast and to the D'Entrecasteaux Channel in the south-east were indications of their need for food sources. The presence of ochre at Cox Bight allowed them to take it to the South East people in return for foraging in their area.[49]

The third maritime tribe, the South East people, had territory that covered about 3,100 square kilometres with 555 kilometres of coastline from the west bank of the Derwent from New Norfolk to Storm Bay, all the D'Entrecasteaux Channel and Bruny Island as far as South Cape and extended inland north to the Huon Valley and New Norfolk. There were probably seven bands in this territory in pre-contact times, each band consisting of at least seventy or eighty people.[50]

Four bands were recorded by Europeans: the Mouheneenner from Hobart, the Nuenonne from Bruny Island, the Mellukerdee from the Huon, and the Lyluequonny from Recherche Bay. But there were also bands at North West Bay and at South East Cape. These four recorded bands operated in large groups along a coastline rich in shellfish and in a limited hinterland with ready access to birds, kangaroos, and wallabies. Unlike the Big River and Oyster Bay peoples, the South East people did

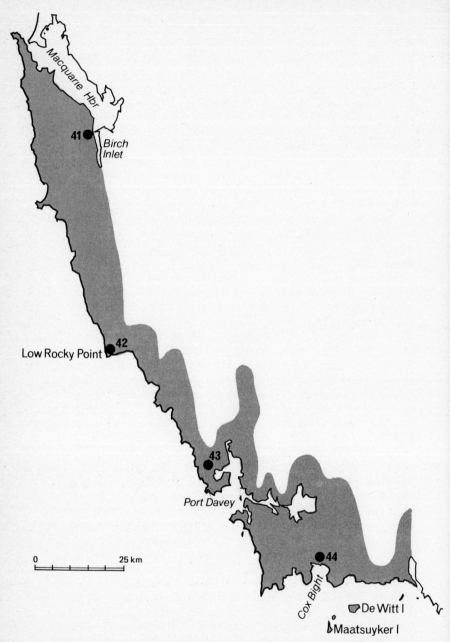

Map 17. South West tribe: territory (see table 1 for key to band locations)

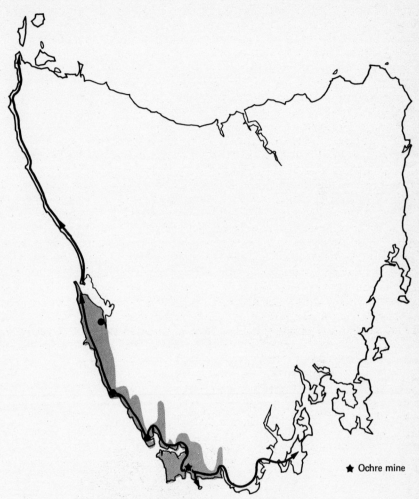

Map 18. South West tribe: seasonal movements

★ Ochre mine

not move inland in spring and summer. Rather, they exploited the coast and immediate hinterland at all seasons of the year. Their different seasonal patterns of movement may have been one reason for the limited contact with the other two tribes despite their proximity.[51]

Seasonal movement for the South East people took place up and down the coast, with occasional excursions into the hinterland. In

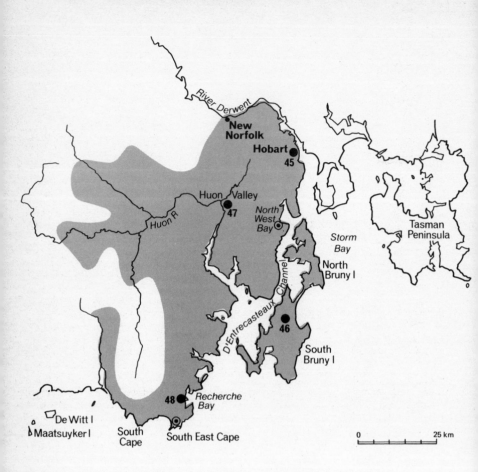

Map 19. South East tribe: territory (see table 1 for key to band locations)

winter they concentrated along the coastline for shellfish; in November they congregated at North Bruny Island for muttonbirds, and in the summer at Recherche Bay for seals. Their diet included shellfish, seals, seabirds, kangaroos, possums, and a variety of marine and terrestrial vegetable food. As the most maritime of the Aboriginal Tasmanians, they were able to use their bark catamarans to shelter in the D'Entre-

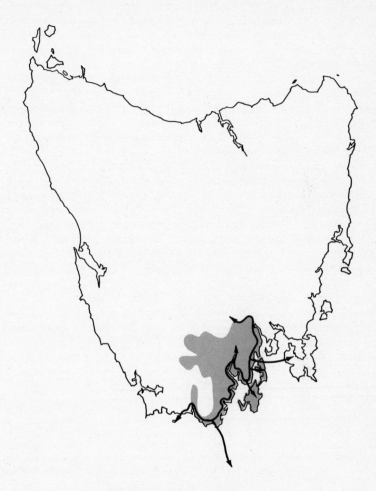

Map 20. South East tribe: seasonal movements

casteaux Channel in all seasons. They made frequent short voyages between Bruny Island and the Tasmanian mainland, including journeys up the Derwent and across the southern straits of the D'Entrecasteaux Channel to Recherche Bay and South East Cape. They also made journeys to Tasman Peninsula, sometimes directly across Storm Bay Passage by catamaran, to the Pydairrerme, the band of Oyster Bay people from that region. These journeys were often for hostile purposes such as the kidnapping of women. Seasonal excursions were made to the Maatsuyker and De Witt Islands to hunt seals, and similar trips may have been made to the Eddystone Rock, twenty-five kilometres off South East Cape. [52]

At the Maatsuyker Group they sometimes met the Needwonnee from Cox Bight and the Ninene from Port Davey. The Ninene people probably visited the South East people every winter to collect swans' eggs. In inclement weather they constructed semicircular bark huts or windbreaks, which differed from the more permanent beehive-shaped huts made by the South West people. [53]

Despite their isolation and "delicate relationship" to the environment, the Aboriginal Tasmanians were not incapable of absorbing or adjusting to the presence of an invader. Rather it was the type of invasion and restraints placed upon their existence that would govern their reaction. Where these invasions threatened their existence, the Aborigines would use the resources of the environment to resist. For in the two thousand to three thousand years before the Europeans came, the Aborigines in Tasmania were physically enlarging their ecological universe — creating productive tracts out of non-productive vegetation, journeying to islands to the north and south. Perhaps, in time, they would have recolonized the mainland, reversed the tide of history, and defied those who would later place them at the bottom of the ladder of humankind. [54]

NOTES

1. J. L. Davies, ed., *Atlas of Tasmania* (Hobart: Department of Lands and Surveys, 1965), pp. 1–5.
2. A. G. Thorne, "The Racial Affinities and Origins of the Australian Aborigines", in *Aboriginal Man and Environment in Australia,* ed. D. J. Mulvaney and J. Golson (Canberra: ANU Press, 1971), pp. 316–23; H. J. Lourandos, "Coast and Hinterland: The Archaeological Sites of Eastern Tasmania" (MA thesis, ANU, 1970), pp. 12–14.
3. Rhys Jones, "The Tasmanian Paradox", in *Stone Tools as Cultural Markers: Change, Evolution and Complexity,* ed. R. V. S. Wright (Canberra: AIAS, 1977), p. 203; Sandra Bowdler, "Hunter Hill, Hunter Island" (PhD thesis, ANU, 1979), p. 451.
4. Rhys Jones, "A Note on the Discovery of Stone Tools and a Stratified Prehistoric Site on King Island, Bass Strait", *Australian Archaeology* 9 (1979): 87–94.
5. Lourandos, "Coast and Hinterland", pp. 12–14.
6. "Report of the Aboriginal Affairs Study Group", *J&PP TAS.,* Vol. 199 (1978), no. 94, pp. 19–20.
7. S. A. Wurm, *Languages of Australia and Tasmania* (The Hague: Mouton, 1972), p. 173.

8. N. J. B. Plomley, *The Tasmanian Aborigines* (Launceston: author in association with Adult Education Division, Tas., 1977), pp. 12–22.
9. Rhys Jones, "Tasmanian Tribes" (seminar paper, Dept. of Prehistory, RSPS, ANU, 1971), p. 18.
10. Ibid., p. 20.
11. Ibid., p. 23–24; J. C. Beaglehole, ed., *The Journals of Captain James Cook*, vol. 3 (London: Hakluyt Society, 1967), p. 52.
12. Jones, "Tasmanian Tribes", pp. 20, 24–25.
13. Irven de Vore, "A Hunter-Gatherer Society", in *Man the Hunter*, ed. Richard B. Lee and Irven de Vore (Chicago: Aldine Press, 1968), pp. 11–12; Plomley, *The Tasmanian Aborigines*, p. 26.
14. Jones, "Tasmanian Tribes", pp. 22–23.
15. Ibid., pp. 27–28.
16. Ibid., p. 28.
17. Rhys Jones, "The Demography of Hunters and Farmers in Tasmania", in Mulvaney and Golson, *Aboriginal Man and Environment*, p. 281.
18. Jones, "Tasmanian Tribes", pp. 29–30.
19. Ibid., p. 63; N. J. B. Plomley, *"Friendly Mission: The Tasmanian Journals and Papers of G. A. Robinson 1829–1834*: A Supplement", *P&P THRA* 18, no. 1 (June 1971): 21.
20. Jones, "Tasmanian Tribes", pp. 66–68.
21. Ibid., p. 67.
22. Ibid., pp. 68–70.
23. Ibid.
24. Ibid., p. 107; Plomley, *"Friendly Mission*: A Supplement", p. 21.
25. Jones, "Tasmanian Tribes", pp. 109–10.
26. Ibid., pp. 109–11.
27. Ibid., p. 81; Plomley, *"Friendly Mission*: A Supplement", p. 21.
28. Jones, "Tasmanian Tribes", pp. 84–85.
29. Ibid., pp. 86–88.
30. Ibid., pp. 71–72.
31. Plomley, *"Friendly Mission*: A Supplement", p. 22.
32. Jones, "Tasmanian Tribes", p. 74.
33. Ibid., pp. 74–75.
34. Ibid., pp. 76–77.
35. Ibid., pp. 78–80.
36. Ibid., p. 96.
37. Plomley, *"Friendly Mission*: A Supplement", pp. 21–22.
38. Jones, "Tasmanian Tribes", p. 98.
39. Ibid., pp. 99–100.
40. Ibid., pp. 100–101.
41. Ibid., p. 101.
42. Ibid., pp. 103–5; Plomley, *"Friendly Mission*: A Supplement", pp. 21–22.
43. Jones, "Tasmanian Tribes", p. 40; Plomley, *"Friendly Mission*: A Supplement", pp. 21–22.
44. Jones, "Tasmanian Tribes", pp. 41–43.
45. Ibid., p. 43.
46. Ibid., pp. 46–49.
47. Ibid., p. 51; Plomley, *"Friendly Mission*: A Supplement", p. 22.
48. Jones, "Tasmanian Tribes", pp. 52–55.
49. Ibid., pp. 54–55.
50. Ibid., p. 56.

51. Plomley, *"Friendly Mission*: A Supplement", p. 22.
52. Jones, "Tasmanian Tribes", p. 58.
53. Lourandos, "Coast and Hinterland", pp. 107–8.
54. Bowdler, "Hunter Hill, Hunter Island", p. 451.

2

European Visitors, 1642–1802

On 24 November 1642 Abel Jansz Tasman, commander of the two Dutch East India ships, *Heemskerck* and *Zeehaen,* sighted high land about seventy-two days' voyage from Batavia. He had been sent by the Council of the Dutch East India Company in Batavia to search for a *terra australis* to add to the existing European knowledge of that area of the South Seas, to explore the south-east coast of New Guinea and the islands near by, and to find new sea routes to Chile and the Spanish American empire. Thus the voyage was typical of the time – to search for new routes, new markets, and new resources.

But this new land, which he called Van Diemen's Land after the governor of Batavia, was too far south for spices and too close to the rim of the earth which Tasman believed was the home of freaks and monsters. For he knew that the Carthaginian voyager Hanno had come upon a country far from anywhere, "very barbarous and full of wilde Beasts . . . and round about the Mountaine inhabit men of divers shapes . . . We heard Phifes and the noise and sound of Cimbals".[1] So he set out to find evidence of their existence.

At North Bay his men heard "certain human sounds, and also sounds nearly resembling music of a trump, or a small gong, not far from them, though they had seen no-one". They saw "two trees about 2 or 2½ fathom in thickness, measuring 60 to 65 feet from the ground to the lowermost branches which trees bore notches made with flint implements, the bark having been removed for the purpose; these notches, forming a kind of steps to enable persons to get up the trees and rob the birds' nests in their tops." They also saw smoke arising from the trees. Tasman concluded that "there must be men here of extraordinary stature".[2]

He planted in Prince of Wales Bay a pole with the company's mark carved into it and the flag of the Prince of Orange so that those who came after them would know they had been there and had taken

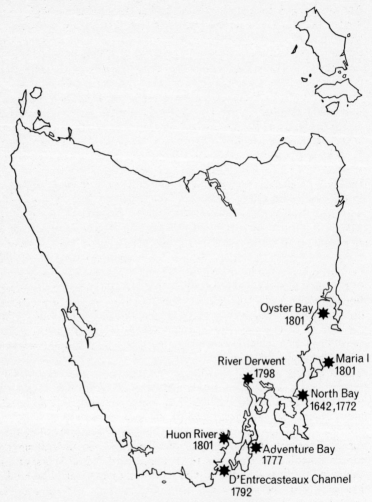

Map 21. Landings of European explorers

possession of the land. It was also to indicate new ownership to the native inhabitants "who did not show themselves, though we suspect some of them were at no great distance and closely watching our proceedings".[3]

Tasman saw no profit in Van Diemen's Land, for the unseen inhabitants, regardless of their size, had nothing to offer the Dutch trader. Nor could his Christian beliefs, which had taught him to look on all human beings as stained by original sin of their common ancestors, allow him to regard these unseen inhabitants as fit owners of the land. For since the discovery of the West Indies by Columbus in 1492, the European had always believed in his right to possess lands beyond the horizon. Such lands were the gifts of Christ, whether the discoverer be of the Catholic or Protestant faith. Tasman departed, and the Dutch East India Company took no further interest in its new possession.

Trade also brought the next visitor to Van Diemen's Land 130 years later. Nicholas Marion du Fresne set off from Mauritius late in 1771 in *Le Mascarin* together with *Le Marquis de Castries* to explore the southern Pacific and to determine whether Tasman's route to Van Diemen's Land was a practical one for French merchantmen *en route* to China, in order to bypass the Dutch East Indies. Marion knew a great deal about the inhabitants of the Pacific since the voyage of Bougainville to Tahiti in 1768. Having been influenced by Rousseau, Bougainville had returned to Europe with positive evidence of the "noble savage" in the inhabitants of Tahiti, who lived on the very rim of paradise in a warm and sensuous climate. They suffered neither from vicious disease nor from religious bigotry. "I never saw men better made," Bougainville wrote, "and whose limbs were more proportionate: in order to paint Hercules or a Mars, one could nowhere find such beautiful models."[4] Tahiti, he concluded, was like an Elysian field, Paradise before the fall of Man, where people lived in a natural state of innocence enjoying its bounty.

By comparing the noble savage of Tahiti to Greek gods, Bougainville reinforced Rousseau's belief that the happiest state of mankind was not the earliest, "when man was primeval, a solitary, moving, stupid but unmoral beast, but in the intermediate state (*la société naissante*), between the primitive and the civilised, a state which was reached after the development of language, the family and the discovery of simpler arts, not yet become noxious to their inventor".[5] For Rousseau, the beginning of the end of this idyllic though not perfect phase of human life came with the invention of metallurgy and agriculture. Thus the inhabitants of the Pacific belonged to *la société naissante*.

Marion had set out on his voyage confident of his ability to communicate with the noble savage. He would send naked Frenchmen on shore whenever naked inhabitants were encountered. He would watch for a sign of peace or friendship and then present gifts to show that the inhabitants of "civilized" France were greeting the noble savages of the South Seas in peace and friendship. Then he would arrange for an exchange of ideas about the "state of nature".[6]

Van Diemen's Land was the first port of call on this tragic voyage, and Marion lost no time in putting his plan into action. On the morning of 7 March 1772, at North Bay, sailors and officers in two cutters set off to explore. As they neared the shore they saw some Aborigines running down the beach. At this moment Duclesmeur, the second in command of the expedition, noted: "The women took refuge in the woods with their children; we did not see them again."[7] One of the men came forward and entered the water, but after a few steps he stopped and made signs to the French that they should go to him. Marion ordered the two sailors who had volunteered to go naked to swim ashore, where one of the older Aboriginal men presented them with a firebrand, which the French took as a sign of peace. Duclesmeur continued:

> Our men accepted it and gave a mirror to the old man. His astonishment and that of the other savages showed incomprehension as one after another saw themselves in it. The colour of the two sailors did not surprise them less and after they had examined them closely they put down their spears and danced before them. This reception was such as to give confidence and M. Marion determined on landing. The spot where we disembarked was dominated by a large rock of which the natives were in possession. However, several of them came down and presented us with fire which we accepted, giving them in our turn some scraps of cloth and some knives . . . Of a truth our small numbers had not up till then caused any uneasiness, but they appeared greatly alarmed at the arrival of a third boat and made all sorts of menacing demonstrations to prevent a landing. M. Marion, not wishing to excite them, ordered the longboat to stop rowing, but its impetus brought it close to the shore. The savages rained on us a shower of spears and stones, one of which wounded M. Marion on the shoulder and another struck me on the leg. We discharged several shots at them and at once they took to flight uttering frightened cries.[8]

Crozet, the second in command of the *Marquis de Castries,* later recorded that several inhabitants were wounded and at least one killed in the ensuing skirmish. Upon his return to France, Crozet explained to Rousseau the terrible events of Van Diemen's Land and those in New Zealand which had led to Marion's death. Rousseau was horrified. "Is it possible", he replied, "that the good Children of Nature can really be so wicked?" Although Duclesmeur saw both incidents as a result of a misunderstanding of the intentions of the French rather than any "natural viciousness" on the part of the Aborigines, the concept of the noble savage had been tarnished. Crozet's statement became "an important landmark in the transition from the European concept of the noble savage to its opposing concept, the ignoble savage".[9]

Nearly four years later Captain James Cook, in the *Resolution* and the *Discovery* during his last voyage to the Pacific, visited Adventure Bay at Bruny Island, off the south-east coast of Van Diemen's Land. He anchored on 26 January 1777 and stayed four days. Cook had read of Marion's clash with the Aborigines, but he had encountered many people in the Pacific from the "soft primitives" of Tahiti to the "hard primitives" of New South Wales. He preferred the hard primitives because they lived "in a Tranquillity which is not disturb'd by the Inequality of Condition".[10] Thus Cook was "responsive to those aspects of primitivistic thought which viewed the life of nature as a renunciation of the luxuries and excesses of civilization in which the virtues of endurance and courage were called into continuous operation by the vicissitudes of daily life".[11]

In the late afternoon of the third day, about ten Aborigines were observed walking along the beach. Cook hastened ashore to greet them. He took only four or five men in a longboat and commanded the others to remain out of sight, for it was important, Cook believed, to establish his leadership and authority to the Aborigines. Upon landing, several men came out of the bush without fear and expressed no interest in his gift of beads. Rather, they preferred his striped coat. One of Cook's sailors sketched the occasion. One Aboriginal man held something like a spear in his hand in a striking position, but when one of the English crew gave a friendly sign of welcome, he dropped it and came down from the edge of the wood with three others. The rest soon followed. Cook noted that these people were naked and wore no ornaments except the large punctures or ridges raised on the skin. He found them

> of the common stature but rather slender; their skin was black and also their hair, which was as woolly as any native of Guinea, but they were not distinguished by remarkable thick lips nor flat noses, on the contrary their features were far from disagreeable; they had pretty good eyes and their teeth were tolerable even but very dirty; most of them had their hair and beards anointed with red ointment and some had their faces painted with the same composition.[12]

Despite his admiration for these "hard primitives", Cook considered they had insufficient civilization to justify their continued enjoyment of their country. He could find no evidence of religion or cultivation of the soil or of settled law, which in British terms rendered the land "practically unoccupied". As a result, he did not believe that the Aborigines would oppose European settlement. He knew that one day the British would stretch their empire to the Pacific, and Van Diemen's Land with its temperate climate seemed well suited to the English temperament.

Like so many of Cook's observations upon inhabitants of the Pacific,

1. *Captain Cook's interview with the natives in Adventure Bay, Van Diemen's Land, January 29, 1977.* (by an unknown artist) From Fannin, P. A Collection of drawings and sketches. Original in library of the Naval Historical Branch, British Ministry of Defence London.

his views of the Aborigines of Van Diemen's Land were the first of any ethnographic significance. They remained the prevailing view in British circles until occupation of the island in 1803.

On 21 April 1792 Bruni d'Entrecasteaux, commander of the French ships *La Recherche* and *L'Espérance*, arrived at an uncharted bay on the south-eastern coast of Van Diemen's Land. His ships carried some of the brightest talents the French scientific world had to offer. The French National Assembly had seen d'Entrecasteaux's expedition as an opportunity to conduct a detailed scientific survey of the southern lands and southern oceans. Among the scientific staff was Jacques-Julien Houton de Labillardière, aged thirty-four, naturalist and surgeon. Labillardiere belonged to that French scientific school of the Enlightenment which espoused republican principles and exemplified the ideals of Rousseau's romantic naturalism — the "hard primitivism" of the noble savage. He believed that the hard primitives were endowed with the virtues that all good eighteenth century republicans aspired to: "simple in [their] needs and desires, self-disciplined, courageous, and with a great capacity for endurance". The noble savage of this type had become "a symbol of revolutionary freedom and ideal perfectibility".[13] For Labillardière believed that man, even when pursuing the gratification of animal instincts, was possessed of nobler faculties, "of liberty to choose among different objects and impediments, and of reason to direct him in that choice". No one tribe of mankind was naturally of an order superior to the rest, "or had any shadow of right to infringe, far less to abrogate, the common claims of humanity".[14] The boasted civilization of Europe was the result of a few happy discoveries, such as the use of iron, rather than any superiority of intellect.

Labillardière's first observations led him to believe that the inhabitants of Van Diemen's Land were very hard primitives indeed, for their shelters were threatened both by fire and wind and could easily be swept away. Nor could they lie at ease in these shelters, for the ground was uneven and hard. After three days' constant searching, the naturalist concluded that the "human species" were either very scarce or very shy. When the expedition departed on 17 May to continue charting the newly discovered D'Entrecasteaux Channel, the naturalist lamented that he had only seen them from a considerable distance.[15]

On 22 January 1793 d'Entrecasteaux's expedition returned to the channel, and on 8 February Labillardière, Lahaie the gardener, Piron the artist, and Riche the naturalist from the *Espérance* set off for a two-day field trip. Having spent the night in the open about three kilometres from the shore, Labillardière and Lahaie woke early and set off for a walk, leaving instructions for the others to prepare breakfast. They had not gone far when they saw to their delight a great number of the Aborigines shellfishing on the banks of a lake. The Frenchmen paused, uncertain of the intention of these people. Having the debacle of Marion du Fresne firmly in their minds, they decided to collect their two companions, who had a musket. Once the two others had been aroused, Labillardière prepared a few cartridges and the four men set out across the woods. The Aborigines had seen them coming and had drawn themselves up ready — the men and young boys at the front almost in a semicircle, the women and children well behind. Holding firmly to his belief that they were not hostile, Labillardière stepped foward and offered the oldest men a piece of biscuit. He was rewarded with a dazzling smile and a hand offered in friendship which he gratefully returned. The rest stepped forward and immediately "the best understanding prevailed".[16]

Labillardière counted forty-two people, of whom seven were full-grown men and eight were women. The rest were children. Then he remembered that he had not yet eaten and so gesticulated to his new companions to join him for breakfast. To his great delight they followed him. As soon as they had reached the camp site, one of the men explained by unequivocal signs that he had reconnoitred their camp site during the night. Labillardière was astounded. "Where else in this part of the world", he wrote in his diary that evening, "could we have escaped attack and possible massacre under similar conditions?"[17]

Then Labillardière decided to demonstrate the superiority of his civilization to the Aborigines by firing his musket, but the noise of the explosion so frightened them that he quickly turned to another mark of his civilization — brandy. But the Aborigines did not like that either. Nor would they eat any cheese or bread.

The next morning Labillardière and a larger party of officers and sailors found nineteen Aborigines around three small fires, eating shellfish. They greeted the French with enthusiasm and invited them to share their meal. Labillardière watched with horror as the women, "condemned to the toil", dived for several hours for shellfish and abalone to feed their families. He believed the men should be made to help gather basic food for the family, but they were uninterested in his demonstration with a fish-hook. He noted that the women ate the body of the lobster and gave the claws to their husbands and children but was uncertain whether the body was considered more succulent than the claws.[18]

Labillardiere was bothered by the major role the women assumed in the constant search for food. He had read in Rousseau's *Discourse on the Origins of Inequality* that, at the beginning of social life in man, the male went in search of food and provided sustenance for the

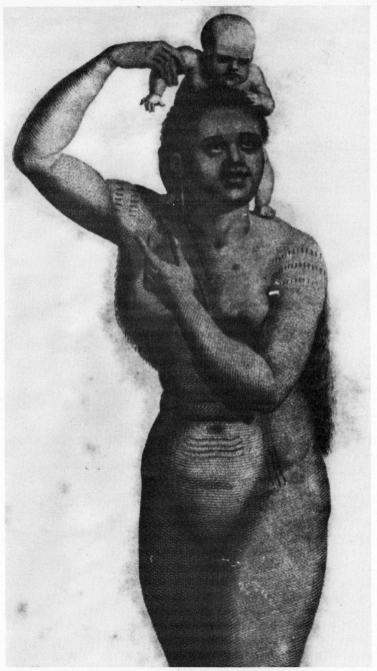

2. Piron, *Woman of Cape Diemen.* From Debrett edition of J. S. Labillardière, *An Account of a Voyage in search of La Perouse . . . 1791, 1792 and 1793,* The Plates, No. VI.

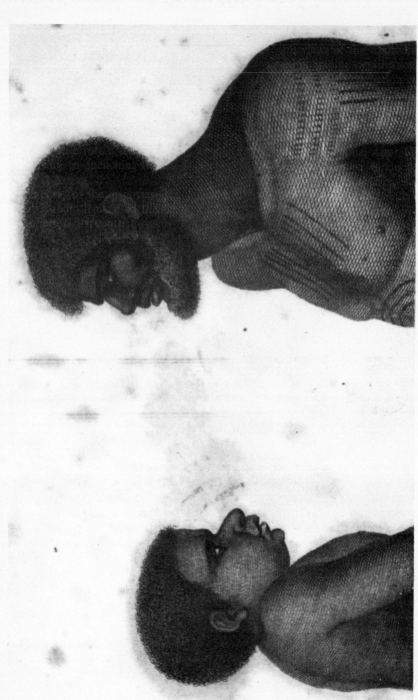

3. Piron, *Boy of Cape Diemen and Man of Cape Diemen.* From Debrett edition of Labillardière, *An Account of a Voyage in search of La Perouse . . . 1791, 1792 and 1793*, The Plates, No. VII.

women, who liked a more sedentary life looking after the shelter as
well as the children. On board the *Recherche* that evening, Labillardière
drew more conclusions. The Aborigines had no beliefs. Each family
appeared to live in perfect independence, although the children were
completely subordinate to their parents and the women subordinate
to their husbands. He believed their language bore no affinity with the
already published vocabulary of east New Holland and that although
covered with vermin they had no trace of disease. He hoped they would
soon take up agriculture and "taste the pleasure of not being obliged
to dive in search of their food, at the risk of being devoured by sharks".
He concluded, "The women who were condemned to this toilsome
occupation will be much more sensible to the value of such a present
than the men." For in agriculture the "proper" role of man the
provider would develop. He regretted that he had been unable to make
the Aborigines recognize the usefulness of other gifts, like fruit-bearing
plants and fish-hooks. But Labillardière believed that the Aborigines of
Van Diemen's Land had come closest to the republican ideal of the
noble savage, for their life was Spartan and their children cheerful.
They were now ready for the next stage of civilization, the introduction
of agriculture and the use of iron. This would probably take place in
contact with the European.[19]

Already a British colony had been formed at Sydney, on the east
coast of New Holland, and it was not long before voyages were made to
determine the geographical limits of the country. In 1795 Bass and
Flinders explored the southern coast of New South Wales, and by 1798
their knowledge of the Aborigines led them to believe that black people
could be readily absorbed into the civilization of the whites without
great bloodshed, although at the Georges River and Lake Illawarra they
had found instances of Aboriginal hostility. In October 1798 they were
commissioned by Governor Hunter to explore the area around the
Furneaux Islands, to determine whether New Holland was separated
from Van Diemen's Land by a strait, and if so to circumnavigate the
island with a view to British settlement. The existence of a strait would
not only shorten the journey from England; it would open up new areas
for whaling and sealing, the industries that had followed the establishment of the settlement at Sydney.[20]

Their only encounter with the Aborigines in Van Diemen's Land
occurred on 28 December at the Derwent River. The two men had
rowed a jolly-boat up the river, and in the late afternoon they saw two
women and a man on the eastern shore. Bass and Flinders landed and,
taking a black swan as a gift, went up to the Aborigines. The two
women ran off, but the man, "short, slight and middle aged", accepted
the swan with rapture. Flinders thought the man resembled the Abori-

gines of New South Wales, but was less Negro-like and more expressive of "benignity and intelligence, than of ferocity or stupidity". But the appearance of their huts led him also to think that they "were more destitute of the comforts and conveniences" than their counterparts in New South Wales.[21]

Bass found the Aborigines inferior in three important areas to those from New South Wales. They had no canoes, no sophisticated hunting weapons, and no satisfactory shelters. But they were neither miserable nor wistful. The real reasons for their apparent differences from the people of New Holland, he concluded, would only be known after prolonged European settlement. Like all the explorers before him, Bass had no belief that these people had any right to their land. They had no interest in agriculture and had no armies to repel an invader. Rather, he believed the Aborigines would benefit from the introduction of European civilization.[22]

Bass and Flinders returned to Sydney, where the news that Van Diemen's Land was separated from New Holland vexed the governor. If the British were to maintain their claim to the island, then it must be settled. This concern was reinforced in 1801 when another French expedition visited Van Diemen's Land. The voyage had been suggested by its commander, Nicholas Baudin, who had already led two scientific expeditions to the Indian Ocean and the West Indies and wanted to take another to the Pacific to pursue the work of d'Entrecasteaux and to visit the Antarctic. His sponsor, the Institut National, was anxious to conduct anthropological observations during the voyage and asked for some guidelines from the Société des Observations de l'Homme, a body devoted to the study of man in his physical, moral, and intellectual existence. One of its members, the philosopher Joseph-Marie Dégerando, submitted a memorandum for use during the voyage called *The Observation of Savage Peoples.* Not only did it reflect the birth of anthropological theory; its philosophical concepts reflected the prevailing spirit of egoism associated with the burgeoning French republic.[23]

Dégerando considered that great mistakes had been made in the past by observers of native peoples because they had been "infected by analogies" drawn from French and European culture. As none had made any attempt to become part of the society under study, the most important aspects — the language and the way of thinking — had been ignored. These mistakes could be overcome by the appointment of a specially trained person to observe the native peoples at close range for long periods. Thus the expedition would have to arrange for "long stays in particular places". Once the groups of people for study had been selected, the language would have to be learnt so that a study of the individual's physical existence — adaptation to climate, sleep patterns, food needs, intellectual capacities, life span, and marriage and family patterns — could be carried out. Then a judgement could be made of the individual's reaction to society at large, and an assessment could be reached of the individual's moral and religious propensities and whether there were any feelings of patriotism. For these were the major facets of any individual's relationship to his society. These long observations would not only give the civilized world the exact specimen cases of the uncivilized world but would also enable the uncivilized world to receive from the civilized the "power to multiply themselves, and to associate themselves with [France] by the ties of a vast confederation". All this could lead to a new world forming itself at the extremities of the earth; "the whole globe covered with happier and wiser inhabitants, more equally provided for, more closely joined".[24]

Twenty-two scientific staff, with an average age of twenty-seven, consisting of botanists, zoologists, mineralogists, painters, draughtsmen, and gardeners, were chosen for Baudin's voyage in the two ships *Le Géographe* and *Le Naturaliste*. The scientists saw themselves as ambassadors of the victorious republic taking a new civilization to the other side of the world. The two zoologists were late appointments, and neither had any anthropological training or experience. Only one, François Péron, aged twenty-five, had received his appointment for any potential interest in anthropology. He was convinced that civilization could be taken to the "noble savage", and his three brief encounters with the Aborigines in Van Diemen's Land confirmed this belief.[25] He ignored Dégerando's instructions to learn the language and spend time with his subjects.

The first encounter took place on 14 January 1801 when Péron and one of the *Géographe*'s officers, Henri de Freycinet, with Lesueur the artist and several seamen, explored the mouth of the Huon River. When two Aboriginal men were seen on top of a hill, the French landed and within a moment were joined by one Aboriginal man twenty-two to twenty-four years of age, "of a strong general appearance, having no other defect than the looseness of joints of his arms and legs, characteristic of his nation". He had a pleasant friendly face, "lively and expressive" eyes, and a manner that "displayed at once both pleasure and surprise". Freycinet and Péron rushed to embrace their host, but were saddened by the "air of indifference" with which the man received this testimony of good will. The man appeared more interested in the colour of the visitors' skins. Further up the hill the French met an older man, who also examined the whiteness of their skins. Having satisfied himself that all was well, he signalled two women and three children a little way off to approach. The sailors joined the party, the

4. N. Petit, *Bana-Ourou, Terre de Diemen.* From Peron, Francois et Freycinet, Louis Claude, *Voyages de Decouvertes aux Terres Australes* Historique, Atlas, no. 4, second edition, Paris, 1824.

young man lit a fire, and all sat down to a shared meal of shellfish, which the French enjoyed enormously. In return the French sang the Marseillaise, which their hosts appeared to find amazing and amusing. Later, one of the young Aboriginal women, who Péron discovered was called Ouré Ouré, rubbed charcoal on her body, which disgusted the

5. N. Petit, *Homme, Terre de Diemen.* From Peron, Francois et Freycinet, Louis Claude, *Voyages de Decouvertes aux Terres Australes* Historique, Atlas, no. 5, second edition, Paris, 1824.

French. Péron could only conclude that fondness for ornament and a sentiment for coquetry prevailed in the hearts of her whole sex.[26]

Like Labillardière, Péron was delighted by the friendliness, kindness, and generosity of the inhabitants. These views were not shared by Leschenault, the other zoologist, who, together with Baudin, Hamelin, captain of the *Naturaliste,* and Petit the artist, discovered some Aborigines further up the D'Entrecasteaux Channel. After a friendly introduction, Petit had been attacked and attempts had been made to take away his sketches. Leschenault angrily confided in his diary that night that, considering the many examples of cruelty and treachery that had been described in all accounts of voyages of discovery, he was astonished to hear sensible people aver that men "in a state of nature" were not wicked and that they were never the aggressors unless provoked. After what he had seen, Leschenault was of the opinion that one could not be too wary of these men whose nature had not been softened by civilization; and that great discretion should be used in landing on shores inhabited by such people. It did not occur to him that the Aborigines were defending their country from attack.[27]

On 31 January Péron encountered about twenty Aborigines on Bruny Island. He turned back, remembering the experiences of his comrades, until he met two officers from the *Naturaliste* who agreed to accompany him. The "miserable horde" were a party of women, the oldest of whom made signs to the Frenchmen to sit down and to lay down their arms. The preliminaries settled, the women squatted on their heels, "and from that moment seemed to show all the natural vivacity of their character without the least reserve". They asked questions, criticized the Frenchmen's appearance, and laughed heartily at their expense. The Frenchmen found the women's physical appearance in the "highest degree disgusting with the exception of two or three young girls whom they found had soft and tender expressions, which was reflected in their manners". Péron later wrote, "Even amongst the most *savage hordes* of the human species the most amiable qualities were found among the young." But he believed there was something unhappy about them all, the result, he felt, of the misery and servitude of having to provide the food. They were, besides, almost all covered with sores, the sad consequence no doubt of the ill-treatment of their "ferocious husbands". Only the eldest woman, who had spoken to them earlier, had preserved any "degree of confidence, liveliness and good temper".[28]

On 18 February the two ships anchored near Maria Island in Oyster Bay, where Péron found an Aboriginal cremation site. He believed these monuments had been erected in piety, affection, and gratitude for the dead, since they were near fresh water in a well-wooded and protected area. Peron found it strange that the Aborigines should burn their dead, when they were "strangers to every principle of social order" and without any apparent rulers, or laws, clothing, or cultivation of any kind, destitute of any material objects, and without any fixed habitation, knowing neither weapons nor implements of any kind apart from a spear and rude club. Since they wandered in families on the seashore, from which they found most of their food, how could they find the resources to build a funeral pyre and to leave gifts? The answer lay, he believed, in the use of fire. Fire had always excited veneration among the ancients — and to the Aborigines of Van Diemen's Land fire must appear superior to all other objects of nature. The cremation sites were the most important discovery Péron made during his visits to Van Diemen's Land, for he believed the key to any civilization lay in the methods of the disposal of the dead.[29]

On 22 February, at Oyster Bay, Peron and some companions had their last encounter with the Aborigines when they discovered fourteen men around a fire. They greeted the French with surprise and pleasure and immediately asked them to sit down. Petit was able to sketch one of them without interference. Péron saw the opportunity to repeat some experiments, first begun in the D'Entrecasteaux Channel, on the natural strength of the people. He had read that of all the attributes of man in a savage state that the apologists had put forward on his behalf, his physical strength was the most constantly praised. Péron had brought with him a machine for testing strength called the Regnier Dynameter. Some of the Aborigines agreed to try it, but the first could not move it and became so enraged that he kicked it. A few others could barely move it. Péron concluded that the strength of the Aborigines was far inferior to that of himself and his other European officers, who delighted in demonstrating their prowess. His observations had shown the Aborigines as being the most savage he had seen, and the Dynameter had shown them as physically the weakest. He concluded that physical strength was not diminished by civilization, nor was it the consequence of a savage state. Rather, the physical degeneration of man could be measured in terms of his remoteness from the state of civilization.[30]

Péron's unscientific conclusion that the Aborigines of Van Diemen's Land were the most removed from European civilization had considerable scientific impact in Europe and formed the basis of the later Social Darwinist belief that they were the missing link between ape and man. More recently this conclusion has formed the basis for the view that the Tasmanian Aborigines were incapable of progressing further along the road of their own civilization because their isolation had caused them to suffer from a slow strangulation of the mind.

But the leader of the expedition, Baudin, had more important concerns. When he discovered that Governor King in Sydney had decided to occupy Van Diemen's Land from fear that the French had designs upon it, Baudin castigated his action. In a letter to King, Baudin questioned the right of Europeans to occupy a country in order to dispossess the native inhabitants. "It would be infinitely more glorious", he wrote, "to mould for society the inhabitants of the various countries over which we have rights, instead of wishing to dispossess those who are so far removed by immediately seizing the soil which they own and which has given them birth."[31] For Baudin had seen the dispossessed Aborigines at Sydney and the great indifference that had developed towards them after thirteen years of European occupation. But King considered that his government had already made an effort to civilize the Aborigines, even if such efforts were secondary to quenching the great British thirst for land.

Thus while Péron had devised a scientific excuse for the dispossession of the Aborigines of Van Diemen's Land, Baudin had raised the political and moral consequences of such action. This conflict has continued to the present.

NOTES

1. Donald E. Frame, ed., *The Complete Works of Montaigne* (London: Hamish Hamilton, 1958), p. 151.
2. J. E. Heeres, ed., *Abel Tasman's Journal of His Discovery of Van Diemen's Land and New Zealand in 1642* (London, 1898), p. 15.
3. Ibid., pp. 15–16.
4. Bernard Smith, *European Vision and the South Pacific 1768–1850* (London: Oxford University Press, 1960), p. 25.
5. Arthur O. Lovejoy and George Boas, *Primitivism and Related Ideas in Antiquity* (Baltimore: John Hopkins Press, 1955), p. 240.
6. Smith, *European Vision*, p. 25.
7. N. J. B. Plomley, ed., *Friendly Mission: The Tasmanian Journals and Papers of George Augustus Robinson 1829–1834* (Hobart: Tasmanian Historical Research Association, 1966), p. 38.
8. Ibid., p. 39.
9. Smith, *European Vision*, p. 87.
10. J. C. Beaglehole, ed., *The Journals of Captain James Cook*, vol. 1 (London: Hakluyt Society, 1955), p. 399.
11. Smith, *European Vision*, p. 126.
12. Beaglehole, *Journals of Captain James Cook*, vol. 3 (1967), p. 52.
13. Smith, *European Vision*, p. 110.
14. H. N. Fairchild, *The Noble Savage: A Study in Romantic Naturalism* (New York: Columbia University Press, 1928), p. 140.
15. J. J. H. de Labillardière, *An Account of a Voyage in Search of La Perouse* (London: Debrett, 1800), vol. 1, p. 136 *et seq.*
16. Ibid., p. 27.
17. Ibid., p. 28.
18. J. J. H. de Labillardière, *An Account of a Voyage in Search of La Perouse* (London: Stockdale, 1800), p. 302.
19. Ibid., pp. 302–13.
20. K. M. Bowden, *The Life of George Bass* (Carlton, Vic.: Melbourne University

Grim in the west to Eddystone Point in the east. Their visits coincided with the Aborigines' summer pilgrimage to the coast for muttonbirds, seals, shellfish, and birds and their eggs. Most Aboriginal groups were at first cautious of these visitors, but it was not long before they were willing to exchange seal and kangaroo skins for tobacco, flour, and tea. This contact intensified when the Aborigines offered women in an attempt to incorporate the visitors into their own society. When the sealers reciprocated by offering dogs, the means were provided for mutually advantageous interaction.

By 1810 the North East people had begun to gather each November at strategic points along the north-east coast, such as Waterhouse Point, Cape Portland, and George Rocks, in anticipation of the sealers' arrival. After their appearance, usually in a whaleboat containing four to six men, a dance would be held, a conference would take place, and an arrangement would be made for a number of women to accompany the sealers for the season. Some women came from the host band, while others were abducted from other bands and sold to the sealers for dogs, muttonbirds, and flour. On other occasions sealers made arrangements to take women for short periods for specific tasks. Sometimes Aboriginal men accompanied sealing parties; one Aboriginal man, Mannalargenna, may have made more than one voyage with the sealers.

By then the seal population had so declined that the large companies had moved to other grounds, but the economic conditions existed for independent sealers to remain and to make their homes on the islands in eastern Bass Strait. Some of these sealers were convicts, some ex-convicts, but most were sailors attracted to the remoteness of the area and the possibility of an existence independent of authority. They took Aboriginal women to live on the islands as their wives, while the Aboriginal men enlisted their support against other Aboriginal bands and accompanied them on short sealing voyages. Such interaction was possible because the sealers made no claim to Aboriginal land.[2]

Once the economic value of Aboriginal women in catching seals was exploited by the sealers, the economy and society of the North East people changed. They now remained on the coast for the whole summer instead of moving inland to hunt kangaroos. In winter they went in search of other bands and tribes along the coast to abduct their women. The power and influence of individual leaders like Mannalargenna, who came from George Bay and spent some years with the band from St Patricks Head, also increased. He led many raids for women on other bands, negotiated with sealers, and quickly saw the value of European dogs to the Aboriginal economy and gift exchange system. Mannalargenna was able to exploit the sealers to the advantage of his own group. The final change was the increasing economic potential of

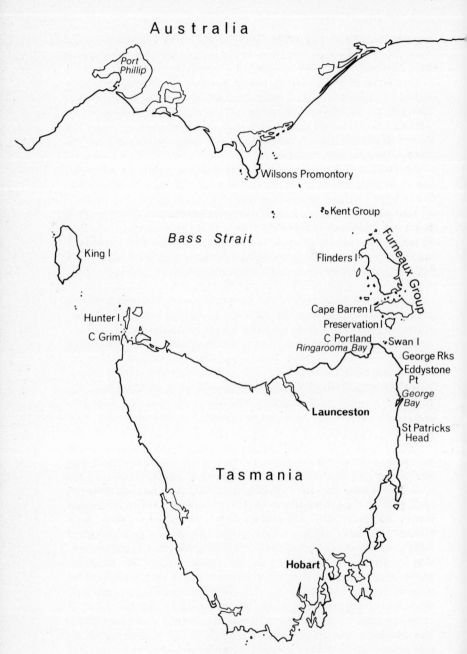

Map 22. Bass Strait

the women. Their skills at first made them chattels in the exchange system devised by the Aboriginal men and the sealers but later proved a useful means with which to bargain for their independence.

The interaction that had developed between the North East people and the sealers was noted by James Kelly during his voyage around Tasmania in 1815 and 1816. With Kelly was the sealer George Briggs, who had at least two Aboriginal women and several children on Cape Barren Island. In January 1816 Kelly and his crew landed in Ringarooma Bay. There they fell in with a band of the North East people numbering two hundred and led by Mannalargenna. Briggs had taken one of Mannalargenna's daughters to Cape Barren Island. Through her, Briggs had obligations to the rest of the band.

Mannalargenna tried to elicit Briggs's assistance to fight a neighbouring band at Eddystone Point, with whom the bushranger Michael Howe and his band had made an alliance. Having no wish to become entangled with Howe, Briggs promised Mannalargenna he would seek help from other sealers at Cape Barren Island. Mannalargenna agreed to this.

Briggs and his companions departed, but they avoided Cape Barren Island and the adjacent north-east coast and sailed instead for George Rocks on the east coast. In breaking his obligations to Mannalargenna, Briggs recognized that he faced future conflict. A few days later Briggs and Kelly fell in with the opposing band led by Tolobunganah near George Rocks. Michael Howe and his party had departed. Tolobunganah, who knew Briggs well, agreed to hire out six women to him for two days to catch seals on George Rocks. In that time they killed 54 seals. Kelly and Briggs subsequently traded 122 carcasses to Tolobunganah for 246 kangaroo skins.[3]

At the sealing camps on Cape Barren, King, Hunter, and Kangaroo islands, the Aboriginal women were the permanent residents, drying and curing seal and kangaroo skins, catching wallabies and possums with dogs, diving for kelp and shellfish, building tentlike huts covered with grass, making baskets and necklaces, and performing ceremonial dances. In the sealing season their skills were used to club seals on remote rocks and islands. In 1820 about fifty sealers and a hundred Aboriginal women and their part-Aboriginal children lived in the strait. The Aboriginal women had become the social guardians and economic exponents of a new society. But by then so few seals remained in the strait that sealing was no longer a profitable pursuit. If the community were to survive, a new economic livelihood had to be found.

In this period of uncertainty the first attempts were made by the Van Diemen's Land government to evict the sealers from the strait, in the belief that most were runaway convicts. Their cohabitation with

Aboriginal women reinforced this belief. Indeed, one historian later wrote: "For thirty years or more . . . the islands . . . [were] an Augean stable which no one took the trouble to clean." Many sealers were driven from the area, and by 1826 only twenty remained at the eastern end of the strait. [4]

Those who stayed were introduced to a new industry — mutton-birding — by the Aboriginal women. Like sealing, muttonbirding is a seasonal industry. The muttonbird, or short-tailed shearwater (*Puffinus tenuirostris*), inhabits the north-east coast of Siberia between June and August, flying south in October to Bass Strait and to the north, east, and west coasts of Tasmania, but particularly to the Furneaux Group. There muttonbirds develop their burrow-like nests in the rookeries at the edge of the sea. During the first week of November they desert the islands, and every burrow is empty. Between 20 and 27 November they return to lay their eggs, which hatch the following February. The parent birds remain for eight to ten weeks, rearing their young, and then depart for Siberia. The young birds follow in the first week in May. Fledglings have always been the mainstay of the annual catch. In the early nineteenth century the muttonbird population reached several hundred million. [5]

Before European contact, the Aboriginal Tasmanians from the northern part of the island gathered along the coastline every November to collect muttonbird eggs. In February they recongregated to eat the young birds. Muttonbirding was more integral to Aboriginal Tasmanian society than sealing, was seasonally more reliable, and was exploited by all ages and both sexes. So when the sealers saw the economic advantages of muttonbirding, they were incorporating a most impor-tant aspect of traditional Aboriginal society into their own.

One of the first sealers to recognize the economic potential of muttonbirding was James Munro, who took up residence on Preserva-tion Island at the eastern end of Bass Strait in 1819 with four Aboriginal women. By 1826 he had several huts, fields of wheat and potatoes, and some livestock and employed fourteen Aboriginal women and thirteen European men in muttonbirding. Munro sold the feathers in Launceston for down, used the oil and fat for fuel, and salted the carcasses for storage against starvation in the winter months. In 1825 he was appointed constable for the area and became the acknowledged spokesman for the "Straitspeople". [6]

The Aboriginal women on Preservation Island adapted their traditional technology to increase the catch. Their digging sticks, origi-nally used to force the birds from their burrows, were converted into spits, so that several birds could be carried at once by stringing them by their beaks along the spit which was then slung across the shoulders.

As the industry became more sophisticated over the next sixty years, both Aboriginal and European skills were used to maximize production. "Birding" gave the community economic security, and thus some independence, and quickly acquired a ritual significance for the people.

By 1830 there were seventy-four Aboriginal women living with sealers in Bass Strait. Twenty-eight came from the North East tribe, twenty-one from the North West, and the remainder from the Ben Lomond, South East, Oyster Bay, and North tribes. In that year the government-appointed conciliator, George Augustus Robinson, arrived in Bass Strait to rescue the Aboriginal women. He regarded all Europeans in the strait as fugitives from the law and all Aboriginal women associated with them as their slaves. When Robinson took most of the women to the temporary Aboriginal establishment on Swan Island, James Munro sought redress from Hobart and returned with a promise from Lieutenant-Governor Arthur that the sealers each had the right to one Aboriginal woman. So at least six were returned. But by then Robinson had decided to set up an Aboriginal establishment on Gun Carriage Island, the centre of the sealing community, and once again they were scattered. However, by 1833 they had returned and re-established themselves.[7]

By 1837 forty Straitspeople remained in small groups over a number of islands at both ends of Bass Strait. From this group — six Aboriginal Tasmanian women, four Aboriginal Australian women, one part-Maori-part-Aboriginal Tasmanian woman, and twelve European men — has emerged the present day Aboriginal community.[8]

The sealers were instrumental in the destruction of a number of Aboriginal tribes on the north coast of Tasmania through exchange and abduction of women, but they also saved Aboriginal Tasmanian society from extinction because their economic activity enabled some of its traditions to continue. Thus the sealers provided a stark contrast to the efforts of the other European invaders, who not only took possession of Aboriginal land and slaughtered the inhabitants but also denied the survivors their identity.

NOTES

1. D. R. Hainsworth, "Iron Men in Wooden Ships: The Sydney Sealers 1800–1820", *Labour History*, no. 13 (Nov. 1967): 19–26; J. S. Cumpston, *Kangaroo Island 1800–1836* (Canberra: Roebuck Books, 1970) and *The Furneaux Group, Bass Strait* (Canberra: Roebuck Books, 1972); Helen Mary Micco, *King Island and the Sealing Trade 1802* (Canberra: Roebuck Society, 1971).

2. Plomley, *Friendly Mission,* p. 179.
3. K. M. Bowden, *Captain James Kelly of Hobart Town* (Carlton, Vic.: Melbourne University Press, 1964), pp. 35–44.
4. *HTG,* 10 June 1826; Welsh to col. sec., 6 June 1827, TSA CSO 1/240/5803; R. W. Giblin, *The Early History of Tasmania,* vol. 2 (Carlton, Vic.: Melbourne University Press, 1939), p. 14; Plomley, *"Friendly Mission:* A Supplement", app. 7.
5. D. L. Serventy, "Mutton-birding", in *Bass Strait: Australia's Last Frontier* (Sydney: ABC, 1969), pp. 53–60.
6. Plomley, *Friendly Mission,* p. 1014; *HTG,* 28 June 1826.
7. Plomley, *Friendly Mission,* pp. 325, 360.
8. N. B. Tindale, "Results of the Harvard–Adelaide Universities Anthropological Expedition", *RQVM,* n.s. 2 (1953): 4.

4

European Invaders: Convicts and Agriculturists, 1803–20

The convict occupation of Van Diemen's Land began in 1803 when the first of three penal settlements under the control of the government of New South Wales was hastily established to forestall French interest in the area. In September, forty-nine convicts and military from Sydney, under the command of Lieutenant John Bowen, arrived at Risdon Cove on the east bank of the River Derwent in the southern part of the island. The following February some two hundred convicts and military under the command of Colonel David Collins arrived from England via Port Phillip and camped at Sullivans Cove, later named Hobart Town, on the opposite bank of the Derwent. In November, 143 convicts and military from Sydney under the command of Lieutenant-Governor William Paterson arrived at Port Dalrymple on the northern side of the island to found York Town at the mouth of the Tamar River.[1]

These footholds had the standing in British law of possessions by discovery and settlement rather than by conquest. Since the British government did not consider the Aborigines a civilized people, they had none of the rights of a conquered nation. They were now British subjects without the rights of British citizenship. Thus the Aborigines had no rights to original land ownership, and any attempts they would make to defend their land could only be defined in British law as criminal in intent. Bowen had no instructions about the Aborigines, not even to the extent of placing them under the "protection" of British law.[2]

Risdon lay in the territory of the Oyster Bay tribe and was the home of the Moomairremener band. It was part of the corridor that gave the Leenowwenne and Pangerninghe bands of the Big River tribe access to the rich shellfish and lagoon areas of the Coal River and Pittwater and to the kangaroo grounds of the east bank of the Derwent. The parkland aspect that attracted Bowen to Risdon had been created by the constant firing of the area by the Moomairremener to flush out game.

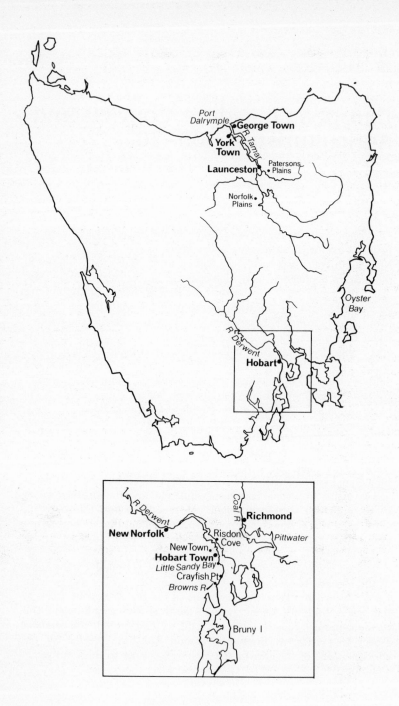

Map 23. Early settlement

When Bowen landed, the Moomairremener in the area vanished. Later "a solitary savage, armed with a spear, . . . entered the camp, and was cordially greeted. He accepted the trinkets which they offered, but he looked on the novelties scattered about without betraying surprise. By his gestures they inferred that he discharged them from their trespass. He then turned towards the woods, and when they attempted to follow, he placed himself in the attitude of menace, and poised his spear."[3] By November the Moomairremener encountered European hunters after their kangaroo. They retaliated by taking the hunters' catch. They also tried to prevent survey parties from pegging out the ground for prospective farms and ships' crews from collecting oysters. Indeed, they made it clear that if the Europeans intended to stay, they must accept some form of mutual obligation.[4]

On 3 May 1804 the uneasy contact became conflict. Some Moomairremener took kangaroos from a gamekeeper just outside the European encampment. Later in the day they surrounded a settler's hut while a larger group visited the settlement. In panic the acting commandant took three soldiers to disperse those at the settler's hut, while the surgeon at the encampment fired a cannon to scatter those at the settlement. In the ensuing skirmish at least three Aborigines were killed. A child orphaned in the massacre was taken by the Europeans and christened Robert Hobart May, the first of many Aboriginal Tasmanian children taken into settlers' homes. The Moomairremener may have drawn some satisfaction from the affray, for at the end of July the Risdon settlement was abandoned and, apart from a government farm, the area remained unoccupied until 1810. The Moomairremener continued to visit the area at least until 1808; their fires were seen every summer and autumn.[5]

At Hobart Town Collins had instructions from London about the Aborigines that were similar to those issued to Governor Phillip sixteen years before:

> to open an intercourse with the natives and to conciliate their good-will, enjoining all persons under your Government to live in amity and kindness with them; and if any person shall exercise any acts of violence against them, or shall wantonly give them any interruption in the exercise of their several occupations, you are to cause such offender to be brought to punishment according to the degree of the offence.[6]

But the last paragraph, which Phillip had so zealously carried out in Sydney, had been deleted. This was: "to procure an account of the numbers inhabiting the neighbourhood of the intended settlement, and report your opinion to one of the Secretaries of State in what manner our intercourse with these people may be turned to advantage to this colony".[7] After sixteen years of European settlement at Sydney, the British government had come to the conclusion that the Aborigines had nothing to offer the colonists. In September Collins wrote to Governor King in Sydney:

> At present we have not had any intercourse with them, which I do not much regret; and not finding any disposition to straggle among my People, I shall wait until my Numbers are increased, when I shall deem it necessary to inform the whole, that.the Aborigines of this Country are as much under the Protection of the Laws of Great Britain, as themselves.[8]

When this occurred, in January 1805, the European population at Hobart Town had reached 481, made up of 327 convicts, 6 emancipists, 49 free settlers, and 99 civil servants and military personnel. The population remained at this level until November 1807.[9]

Hobart Town was in the territory of the Mouheneenner band of the South East people, and the area was known as Nibberloonne or Linghe. The Mouheneenner had a summer camp at Little Sandy Bay called Kreewer. At the time of Collins's arrival the Nuenonne band from Bruny Island were foraging in the area.[10] Woorraddy, a member of that band, later recalled that when his compatriots saw the first ship coming, they were frightened and said it was Wrageowrapper, the devil:

> that when the first people settled they cut down the trees, built houses, dug the ground and planted; that by and by more ships came, then at last plenty of ships; that the natives went to the mountains [Mount Wellington], went and looked at what the white people did, went and told other natives and they came and looked also.[11]

Although the Mouheneenner would not visit the settlement at first, they were friendly to small parties of Europeans they encountered in the bush and were not afraid of a musket. By January 1805 they were venturing to outlying huts at Browns River (now Kingston), Crayfish Point, and New Town, where they offered settlers kelp and crayfish in return for bread and potatoes. But by 1806 these mutual arrangements had begun to break down. The Mouheneenner were attacking Europeans who strayed from settlement, driving off watering parties at Browns River, and setting fire to cornstacks.[12]

Paterson at the Tamar encountered Aboriginal resistance at once. Within two days of landing at York Town in November 1804 his party was confronted by eighty Aborigines. Paterson gave them trinkets, but these proved insufficient payment for trespassing. The next day the Aborigines tried to throw a sentry into the sea. In retaliation an Aboriginal was shot dead. Like Collins, Paterson had also experienced the

Aborigines at Port Jackson and had led a punitive expedition against them at the Hawkesbury River in 1795. Paterson continued this practice at the Tamar, for his people were constantly harassed, particularly between 1804 and 1806, during which time he moved his settlement from York Town to George Town and finally to Launceston.[13]

All three settlements suffered an acute shortage of salt meat provisions within three weeks of their establishment, for no supply ships arrived from Sydney or the Cape of Good Hope. To supplement this loss, small parties of convicts with dogs were sent into the bush to hunt kangaroos. Thus the Aborigines and Europeans were brought into direct competition for the same food resource.

The best kangaroo hunting grounds were at Risdon, Pittwater, and Browns River at the Derwent and the west bank of the River Tamar at Port Dalrymple. A dozen kangaroos a week was considered a good catch. In the fifteen months between the end of August 1804 and October 1805 at the Derwent, over two hundred kangaroos and twenty-five emus were killed by the convict servants of one civil officer alone, and between August and October 1805, the commissariat received 7,740 kilograms of kangaroo meat. Between 1804 and 1808 kangaroo became the major source of fresh meat for the Europeans.[14]

In response to this invasion of their hunting grounds, the Aborigines at first avoided the hunters, then tried to take the kangaroos the hunters had caught. Then the Aborigines killed the hunters' dogs. Finally they took the dogs as payment and found them important and useful assets to their own society. The first European was killed by the Aborigines in 1807. By 1808 conflict between Aborigines and Europeans over kangaroos had so intensified that twenty Europeans and a hundred Aborigines probably lost their lives.[15]

Kangaroo hunting became a lucrative business for the civil and military officers, bringing more profitable returns than agriculture. It also led to a healthy European population, for the only deaths during this period were from misadventure or old age. But by the end of 1808 kangaroos had become a scarce commodity. The kangaroo hunters had to move further from settlements to find kangaroos, which created carriage and storage problems, so that the slowly increasing European population could no longer be guaranteed fresh meat from this source. More importantly, kangaroo hunting encouraged convicts to forsake farming for bushranging.[16]

Most bushrangers were kangaroo hunters and military deserters who preferred the uncertain existence of the bush to the certain use of the lash at the settlements. The first bushrangers were noted in 1805, and by 1808 at least twenty roamed between Hobart Town and Launceston. Some bushrangers cohabited with Aboriginal women.

Others, like Michael Howe, entered into arrangements with particular bands to keep their European pursuers at bay; as late as 1824, Aborigines assisted bushrangers to escape from Europeans. Until 1825, European farmers found bushrangers a more serious threat to their existence than Aborigines.[17]

By 1807, when there were approximately eight hundred Europeans in the colony, kangaroo hunters and bushrangers were the most visible source of annoyance to the Aborigines. Their seasonal pattern of movement had not been disturbed, disease had made no inroads, and they were still the numerical majority. Had settlement remained at this level, Aboriginal and European societies could have adapted to each other's presence. Indeed, the Europeans had brought with them at least one desirable and procurable commodity — the dog — which was quickly absorbed into the Aboriginal economy as a form of gift and exchange.

The agricultural phase of British occupation began in November 1807 when seven hundred settlers arrived from Norfolk Island. They established farms of four to forty hectares at New Norfolk, Browns River, and Pittwater in the south and at Patersons Plains and Norfolk Plains in the north. Between 1811 and 1814 the area under cultivation increased from 3,332 to 12,711 hectares, the number of cattle increased from 421 to 5,060, and the number of sheep from 3,573 to 38,540. The European population increased from 1,198 to 1,898. By 1814 Van Diemen's Land had become a successful agricultural colony.[18]

The agricultural settlers represented the "peasant proprietor" phase of European occupation. Like their counterparts along the Hawkesbury River in New South Wales in the 1790s, most were ex-convicts. Within three months the Aborigines were offering women in return for provisions in another attempt to develop reciprocal arrangements. But the agriculturists who suffered an acute shortage of labour were more attracted to the Aboriginal children as a labour force. For a time some mutual arrangements operated whereby Aboriginal children were "lent" by their parents in exchange for provisions. However, by 1810 Collins was warning the settlers that the kidnapping, rather than borrowing, of Aboriginal chidren would provoke retaliation by their parents. Thomas Davey, who succeeded him as lieutenant-governor in 1813, also condemned the practice. But most settlers believed they were saving the children from starvation and barbarism as well as using them as a cheap labour force. By 1816 kidnapping had become widespread, and in retaliation the Aborigines were raiding huts for provisions, spearing and driving away cattle, burning hayricks, and harassing stockmen. Nevertheless, by 1817 there were at least fifty Aboriginal children in settlers' homes.[19]

Agricultural settlement thus had a profound effect upon the Aborigines, for their labour was in as much demand as their food resources and their land. In their turn the Aborigines considered their seasonal migrations through the agricultural areas as the time for payment, in provisions, for European occupation. The Europeans, however, had no hesitation in defending their farms. By the time William Sorell replaced Davey in April 1817, conflict on the agricultural frontier was over. In April 1818 the *Hobart Town Gazette* reported:

Notwithstanding the hostility which has so long prevailed in the breasts of the Natives of this Island towards Europeans, we now perceive with heartfelt satisfaction the hatred in some measure gradually subsiding. Several of them are to be seen about this town and its environs, who obtain subsistence from the charitable and well-disposed.[20]

These were the "tame mobs", survivors of those bands whose territories were now occupied by the urban areas of Hobart, Richmond, and Launceston. The most prominent tame mob traversed the country between Risdon and Pittwater in the summer and retired to the east coast in winter. It was led by Musquito, a Sydney Aboriginal transported to Van Diemen's Land in 1813 and who had worked both as a stockman and as a guide in search of bushrangers. He had been promised repatriation to Sydney for the capture of bushrangers, but this never happened. He worked as a stock-keeper and in 1816 went to Mauritius with his employer, Edward Lord, to buy cattle. Musquito and his companions openly spurned manual labour, believing that permanent reparations from the European occupiers in the form of provisions were barely sufficient payment for dispossession.[21]

In March 1819, in keeping with Governor Macquarie's policy in New South Wales of "civilizing" those Aborigines who came within the sphere of European settlement, Sorell ordered that all Aboriginal children living with settlers must be sent to the charge of the chaplain, Robert Knopwood, in Hobart and placed in the Orphan School. By 1820 Knopwood had at least twelve children in his care, seven of whom were baptised. Two boys were sent to England for further education in 1821, but both died, one in England, the other upon his return to Hobart in 1827. So unconcerned was Sorell about the "Aboriginal problem" that when he left the colony in 1824 he forgot to mention them in his report on the state of the colony to his successor.[22]

By 1818 the Aboriginal population of Van Diemen's Land had fallen from an estimated four thousand to somewhere below two thousand, while the European population was 3,114. The first fifteen years of European settlement had brought no epidemics, in contrast to Sydney

6. Thomas Scott, *Aborigines in Van Diemen's Land*. From the Papers of Thomas Scott, vol. I. Original in Mitchell Library.

where, in 1789, an outbreak of smallpox severely depleted the local Aboriginal population. Later, in the first few months of 1836, an outbreak of influenza at Port Phillip also decimated the Aboriginal population.

The year 1820 was crucial in European—Aboriginal relations in Tasmania. For the Aborigines, particularly the Oyster Bay and North Midlands tribes, the Europeans were trespassers. The Aborigines were not in despair of the Europeans, but were concerned to control them. There was no question on the part of the Aborigines of their becoming part of European society or culture. Rather, the Aborigines expected the Europeans to adapt to their culture and society. By 1820 the Europeans occupied less than 15 per cent of Van Diemen's Land, but already they had effectively depleted the Oyster Bay and North Midlands tribes. Had European occupation continued piecemeal, the Aborigines and Europeans might have survived in some form of mutual coexistence, and even possibly a multicultural society could have emerged. The rate and type of European occupation in the future would have considerable bearing upon Aboriginal survival.

NOTES

1. *HRA*, III, i, p. 198 and n. 89, pp. 221 and 664.
2. Barry Bridges, "The Aborigines and the Law: New South Wales 1788—1855", *Teaching History* 4, pt 3 (Dec. 1970): 40; *HRA*, III, i, pp. 191—98.
3. John West, *The History of Tasmania*, ed. A. G. L. Shaw (Sydney: Angus and Robertson/Royal Australian Historical Society, 1971), p. 262.
4. Journal of Charles Grimes [James Meehan], 1804, TSA LSD no. 11; Amasa Delano, *A Narrative of Voyages and Travels* (Boston, 1817), p. 440.
5. *Mil. Ops*, pp. 47—55; Mary Nicholls, ed., *The Diary of the Rev. Robert Knopwood 1803—1838* (Launceston: Tas. Hist. Res. Assn., 1977), pp. 51, 52, 55, 57—58; *HRA*, III, i, pp. 242—43; Hugh Anderson, *Out of the Shadow: The Career of John Pascoe Fawkner* (Melbourne: Cheshire, 1962), p. 21.
6. *HRNSW*, vol. 5, p. 18.
7. Ibid., vol. 1, pt. 2, pp. 89—90.
8. *HRA*, III, i, p. 281.
9. Ibid., pp. 281, 371, 529.
10. Plomley, *Friendly Mission*, p. 316.
11. Ibid., p. 376.
12. *Sydney Gazette*, 18 Mar. 1804; James Backhouse, *A Narrative of a Visit to the Australian Colonies* (London, 1843), p. 21; Nicholls, *Diary of the Rev. Robert Knopwood*, pp. 74—75, 104; *Mil. Ops.*, p. 51.
13. Paterson to Banks, 27 Nov. 1804, ML MSS A78—3, pp. 177—79; Barry Bridges, "Aboriginal and White Relations in New South Wales, 1788—1855" (MA thesis, University of Sydney, 1966), pp. 136—39.
14. Rhys Jones, "Tasmanian Aborigines and Dogs", *Mankind*, 7, no. 4 (December 1970): 256—71.

15. Nicholls, *Diary of the Rev. Robert Knopwood,* pp. 128, 140, 146.
16. *HRA,* III, i, pp. 403, 575; "Remarks on the Country and Settlements formed in Van Diemen's Land, 1809", AO 2/8130; West, *History of Tasmania,* p. 560, n. 48.
17. K. M. Bowden, *Captain James Kelly of Hobart Town* (Carlton, Vic.: Melbourne University Press, 1964), p. 39; Launceston Police Office, Depositions, ANL MS 3251; Carl Canteri, "The Origins of Australian Social Banditry: Bushranging in Van Diemen's Land 1805–1818" (typescript, London, 1973).
18. *HRA,* III, i, p. 421; *BPP,* 1816, no. 450, p. 13.
19. Michael Roe, *Quest for Authority in Eastern Australia 1835–1851* (Carlton, Vic.: Melbourne University Press, 1965), p. 35; *Derwent Star,* 29 Jan. 1810; *Mil. Ops,* p. 36; *HTG,* 31 Aug. 1816, 29 Mar., 25 Oct., and 13 Dec. 1817, and 14 Nov. 1818; *HRA,* III, ii, p. 284; *Asiatic Journal,* 1820, pp. 213-20.
20. *HTG,* 25 April 1818.
21. W. Horton to Wesleyan Missionary Soc., 3 June 1823, Bonwick Transcripts, series 1, vol. 4, box 52, pp. 1268–74.
22. Proclamation, 13 Mar. 1819, ML MSS A1352; *HRA,* III, iii, p. 510; Plomley, *Friendly Mission,* p. 475–6 (n. 278).

5

European Invaders:
The Pastoralists, 1820–28

There is no reason to presume that the black natives . . . will oppose
any serious resistance to the extension of future settlements.[1]

From the beginning of 1817, when the European population stood at
2,000, to 1824, when it reached 12,643, over 4,000 free settlers came
to Van Diemen's Land and changed the economic basis of the colony.
These settlers were the new gentry class that commissioner Bigge had
recommended should occupy the "empty" territory of Van Diemen's
Land. By 1830 the European population had reached 23,500, of whom
6,000 were free settlers. They consisted of retired army and naval
officers from the Napoleonic wars, sons of the English, Irish, and
Scottish landed gentry, as well as the sons of colonial officials, all of
whom had capital to invest in the pastoral industry. As evidence of
their wealth and status, they brought letters of recommendation from
the Colonial Office in London to the lieutenant-governor in Van
Diemen's Land suggesting that they receive land grants of between four
hundred and eight hundred hectares each and that they be assigned at
least one convict servant. With their capital, a land grant, a large flock
of sheep, and a cheap convict labour force they were to produce fine
wool for the textile mills of northern England. Pastoralism ushered in
the most severe dislocation to Aboriginal Tasmanian society and the
greatest level of conflict.[2]

In 1823 alone, 175,704 hectares were granted to the new settlers,
the largest alienation of land in a single year in the entire history of
Tasmania. By 1830 nearly half a million hectares had been granted.
Between 1816 and 1823 the sheep population increased from 54,600
to 200,000 and by 1826 had reached 553,698. In 1828 there were
791,120 sheep and by 1830 one million, surpassing for a short time the
number in New South Wales. The eastern Midlands Plain, which had an
annual rainfall of 500 millimetres and which was admirably suited to

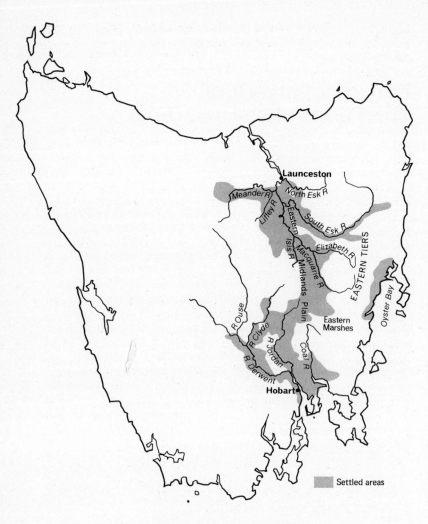

Map 24. Spread of settlement

the production of fine wool, became the centre of this new wave of
expansion. The settlers pushed up the Clyde, Ouse, and Jordan rivers
on the western side of the plain, up the Oyster Bay coast on the eastern
side, along the Liffey, Isis, Macquarie, and Elizabeth rivers in the
centre, and along the North and South Esk rivers at the northern end.

In 1826, in a second wave of pastoral expansion, the settlers pushed along the Meander River west of Launceston. This whole area became known as the "settled districts" and comprised less than 30 per cent of the total area of the island. Even today only about 40 per cent of the total land area has been occupied by Europeans.[3]

Settlement and occupation proceeded "corridor fashion", expropriating Aboriginal hunting grounds but leaving the forested areas unoccupied. In the Clyde River area, settlers occupied the river flats, left the ranges unoccupied, and grazed their sheep in the summer in the high plateau country to the west. In the east, settlers dotted the Oyster Bay coastline, left the Eastern Tiers unoccupied, and grazed their sheep in the Eastern Marshes in summer. This enabled the Aborigines to use the forested areas as bases for raids on settlers' huts. A similar situation occurred in the Moreton Bay pastoral district in south-eastern Queensland between 1842 and 1845. There, large tracts of land unsuitable for grazing were not taken up by the settlers, which allowed the Aborigines to exist on fish and bird and animal life that abounded there for most of the year. These areas also became bases for Aboriginal attacks on stock.[4]

The area of the "settled districts" in Van Diemen's Land coincided with the territory of the Oyster Bay tribe in the east, the Big River tribe west of the Jordan River, the North Midlands tribe from Campbell Town to Launceston in the north, the Ben Lomond tribe on the upper reaches of the South Esk River in the north-east, and the North tribe along the Meander River in the north-west. The sudden appropriation of land in these areas and the arrival of vast numbers of sheep in their kangaroo hunting grounds was the greatest upheaval to their economy these Aborigines had experienced since European invasion. When they began to spear stock and raid stock-keepers' huts, the Aborigines were partly seeking provisions in payment for unauthorized occupation and partly seeking lost prestige. While the Aborigines were prepared to accept "outsiders" into their system of mutual reciprocity, the stock-keepers and settlers had no system for accepting the Aborigines as previous or rightful occupants of the land.

At this stage the Aborigines had not entered the consciousness of the settlers. The few books published about Van Diemen's Land by 1824 had either failed to mention their existence or referred to them briefly as timid, gentle people who would prove no barrier to the expansion of pastoral settlement. The settlers were preoccupied with their desire to establish their new society, which had no immediate place for the Aborigines. The bushrangers were a more salient threat to their existence. But when Aboriginal resistance began, the settlers quickly developed a racist set of attitudes to justify their extermination.

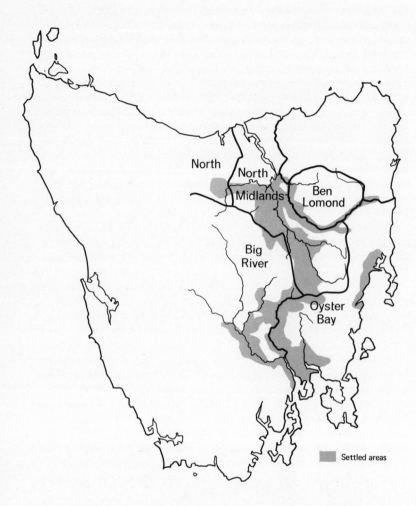

Map 25. Tribal boundaries in relation to settled districts, 1820s

Whereas in 1824 some settlers believed that "God had made of the flesh all nations" and "took in" Aboriginal children to train as labourers, by 1830 most had come to the conclusion that the Aborigines of Van Diemen's Land represented something akin to the orang-outang.[5]

Resistance to pastroal expansion began when the Laremairremener

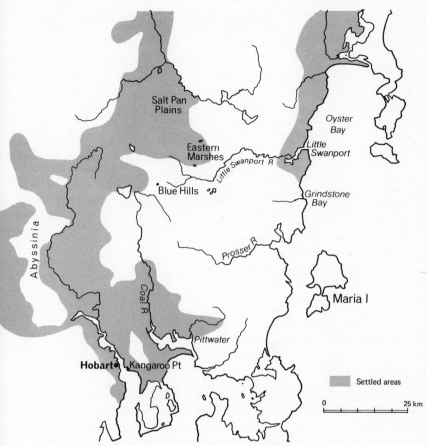

Map 26. Areas of Aboriginal resistance, 1823–24

band of the Oyster Bay tribe, led by the two well-known Aborigines Musquito and Black Jack, killed two stock-keepers at Grindstone Bay on the east coast in November 1823. Four months later, in March 1824, this same band killed two stock-keepers at the Blue Hills and Salt Pan Plains on the edge of the Eastern Marshes. In July they killed another at Little Swanport on the east coast.[6] A month later Musquito and Black Jack were captured near the Little Swanport River and charged with murder. But in October their compatriots attacked a stock-keeper's hut in the Eastern Marshes. The *Hobart Town Gazette* recorded the incident:

As soon as the natives appeared in sight, they were instantly driven back; on which another party directly advanced in an opposite direction and cooed — a signal which was no sooner heard than it was answered by at least 150 more of the same tribe, who armed with spears and waddies, and attended by nearly 50 fine kangaroo dogs, surrounded the house. [The] two servants, each having a musket, defended themselves for five hours, in the best manner they could, from the spears and stones that were thrown at them, until at length the blacks pressed furiously on, and surrounded them with fires — through which, after much struggling, with considerable hazard, the poor fellows . . . escaped. . . . On the following day, they ventured to return, when they found all their provisions, clothes, bedding and utensils had been taken away.[7]

At their trial in December, Musquito and Black Jack pleaded not guilty to the charges of murder, but they could not give evidence because they were not Christians. They were sentenced to hang. No European was ever charged, let alone committed for trial, for assaulting or killing an Aboriginal.

Seven months before, in May 1824, George Arthur arrived in Hobart to become lieutenant-governor of Van Diemen's Land. He had a reputation from his previous post in British Honduras as a man of administrative vigour and moral concern for slaves. He had attacked the cruelty of some slave-owners and had drawn criticism from land-owners for his protection of the illegally enslaved Mosquito Coast Indians. But in Van Diemen's Land Arthur now had the more rigorous task of forging a new society by organizing the increasing numbers of convicts as an unpaid labour force for the new settlers engaged in the production of fine wool. To provide a smooth path for this new society, Arthur expected the Aborigines to abandon their land voluntarily and to accept joyfully the compensation of Christianity. For neither Arthur nor the settlers believed that the Aborigines had any right to their land. But while the settlers saw Aboriginal dispossession as a practical problem, to be solved if necessary by the use of force, Arthur saw Aboriginal dispossession as a moral problem, which had to be solved by peaceful and compassionate means.[8]

In accordance with his instructions from the Colonial Office, Arthur issued a proclamation which placed the Aborigines under the protection of British law and warned the stock-keepers on the frontier that if they continued to "wantonly destroy" the Aborigines, they would be prosecuted. He considered the deaths of some thirteen Europeans in the previous nine months not as the beginning of an offensive by the Aborigines against the spread of pastoral settlement but rather the work of individual "civilized" Aborigines who had left the homes of their European masters to rejoin their own people in the bush.[9]

7. *Colonel George Arthur, Lieutenant-Governor of Van Diemen's Land 1824–1836.* Beattie's Photographs, Hobart.

This view was reinforced in November 1824 when sixty Aborigines visited Hobart Town in search of blankets and provisions. Arthur hastily called a public meeting to discuss the establishment of a "native institution" for them, but after rules and regulations had been drawn up, nothing further was done. Instead they were taken to Kangaroo Point on the river bank opposite the town, where they had an encampment, and were provided with food and clothing. These Aborigines, from the Oyster Bay tribe, came and went "as often as their convenience dictated" for about two years. Another attempt to promote a native institution in 1825 also failed, for the colony was in economic recession, the local clergy were not interested, and bushrangers were considered more dangerous than Aborigines. Indeed, the campaign against the bushrangers from 1824 to 1826 obscured from the settlers and the administration the seriousness of Aboriginal resistance.[10]

When three more Europeans were speared to death in the autumn of 1826, Arthur was still convinced that civilized Aborigines from Kangaroo Point were responsible. The capture of two of these people, Jack and Black Dick, appeared to reinforce this view. So convinced was the chief justice, John Lewes Pedder, that these men were the last of the "depredators" that he appointed counsel and an interpreter on their behalf at their trial. But again the Aborigines were unable to give evidence because they could not take an oath on the Bible. A military jury found them guilty, and the chief justice solemnly announced that they would hang on 16 September. On the day of execution, Arthur issued a government notice which explained that hanging the two Aborigines would "not only prevent further atrocities . . . but lead to a conciliatory line of conduct". While some people thought the executions were a strange method of conciliation, others believed that they would teach the Aborigines a lesson. The Aborigines at Kangaroo Point decamped and never returned.[11]

By November the settlers began to wonder whether the Aborigines were teaching the lessons. Between September and November six Europeans were killed, bringing the total for the year 1826 to twelve. While most were stock-keepers and shepherds, some were also respectable settlers. This spring offensive forced Arthur to the melancholy conclusion that the Aborigines had acquired an implacable hatred of white people. Since he had just added to the settled districts five new Plains, and Waterloo Point — each with a detachment of military, Arthur began to piece together the pattern of Aboriginal resistance from the detailed reports of the settlers, magistrates and military officers. On 29 November he issued a government notice which gave the settlers the right to drive off with force any Aborigines about to attack, rob, or murder them or about to commit a felony. If the settlers could

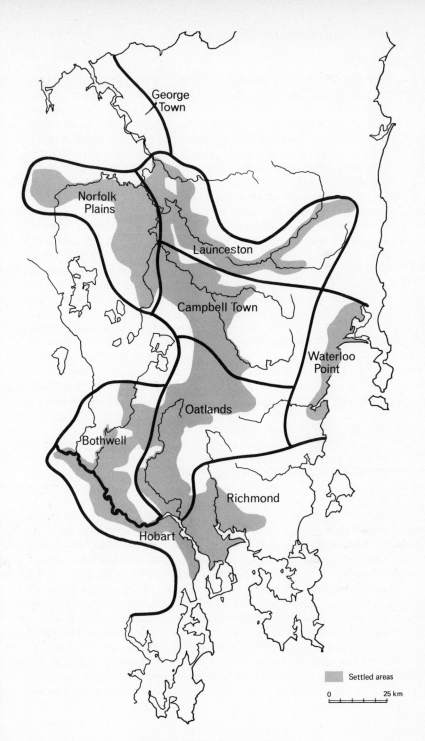

George
Town

Norfolk
Plains

Launceston

Campbell Town

Waterloo
Point

Oatlands

Bothwell

Richmond

Hobart

Settled areas

0   25 km

Map 27. Magisterial areas, 1826

not contend with the Aborigines alone, then they could call upon the nearest detachment of troops for assistance. [12]

The entry of the military and field police led to an immediate affray with forty Oyster Bay Aborigines at Pittwater in which fourteen Aborigines were killed and ten captured. Another group of Big River people were dispersed from the Abyssinia area and two were shot. The situation was similar to that in New South Wales at the beginning of pastoral expansion in 1815. There Governor Macquarie had sent a detachment of soldiers to clear the Appin area of Aborigines in 1816, and in 1824 Governor Brisbane had declared martial law in the Bathurst district while troops cleared that area of Aborigines. The *Colonial Times* also recognized that the government notice was an official declaration of war against the Aborigines. Since it was inevitable, the editor warned, that the settlers would win this war by virtue of superior arms and numbers, it was surely more humane at this time for the government to remove the Aborigines to an island in Bass Strait, rather than sanction their extermination. [13]

But neither the *Colonial Times* nor Arthur was aware that the Aborigines in the settled districts were in a good position to continue guerilla warfare. Because the Aborigines crossed the area every spring and autumn, they were well prepared to raid huts for provisions and to spear those Europeans they despised. About two hundred members of the Oyster Bay tribe, about one hundred from the Big River tribe, and nearly a hundred from the Ben Lomond and North Midlands tribes began to resist pastoral settlement.

West from Launceston, along the Meander River, some of the bloodiest skirmishes of the war were already taking place. In May 1827 the Port Dalrymple band of the North Midlands tribe visited Norfolk Plains (now Longford). First they killed a kangaroo hunter at Western Lagoon in reprisal for shooting Aboriginal men. Then in July they burnt down the house of a prominent settler because his stockmen had seized Aboriginal women. Finally in November they speared three more of this settler's stockmen and clubbed another three to death at Western Lagoon. In retaliation, stock-keepers at Norfolk Plains formed a vigilante group and in December massacred a number of Port Dalrymple Aborigines at the junction of Brumby Creek and the Lake River. At the same time the Big River and Oyster Bay Aborigines attacked stock-keepers with such skill and ferocity that some settlers feared that they had devised a uniform plan of attack. The deaths of thirty Europeans in 1827 appeared to support this view. [14]

If the Aborigines were to be driven from the settled districts, where would they go? Arthur discussed his dilemma with his superiors in

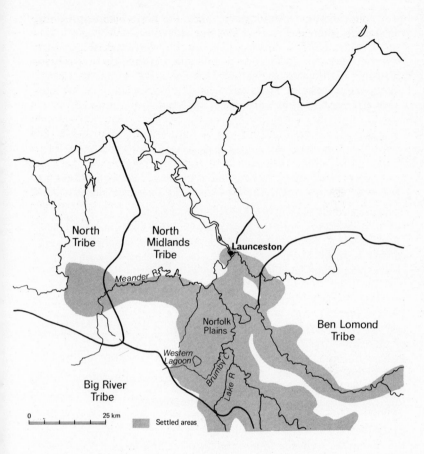

Map 28. Aboriginal resistance, Meander River, 1827

London. To hunt the Aborigines from the island altogether would only aggravate their injuries:

> They already complain that the white people have taken possession of their country, encroached upon their hunting grounds, and destroyed their natural food, the kangaroo; and they doubtless would be exasperated to the last degree to be banished altogether from their favourite haunts; and as they would be ill-disposed to receive instruction from their oppressors, any attempt to civilize them, under such circumstances, must consequently fail.[15]

Arthur suggested instead setting aside the north-east coast of the island as an Aboriginal reserve. This was based on colonial policy in the Cape Colony in South Africa and in Canada, where special areas had been set aside for indigenous populations. Arthur knew from the arguments of Archdeacon Scott in New South Wales that "civilizing" Aborigines in selected areas was against their migratory habits and "their attachment to a savage mode of life". But Arthur believed:

> It is but justice to make the attempt, for, not withstanding the clamour and urgent appeals which are now made to me for the adoption of harsh measures, I cannot divest myself of the consideration that all aggression originated with the white inhabitants, and that therefore much ought to be endured in return before the blacks are treated as an open and accredited enemy by the government.[16]

Arthur was convinced that if someone could be found at this stage to act as an emissary from his government to the Aborigines to explain his views, then the Aborigines would go to this area. Despite his appeals to the magistrates to find a suitable person, none came forward.

The plan, while feasible on paper — and, to Arthur's credit, a manifestation of some understanding of Aboriginal rights — was abhorrent to the press and settlers alike. Had an emissary been found, the Oyster Bay and Big River Aborigines may have been persuaded to go the northeast, for it was not only rich in Aboriginal food resources, the number of Aborigines there had declined from extended conflict with the sealers. European settlement did not spread there until the 1860s. Had Arthur's plan been carried out at this time, the future of the Aboriginal Tasmanians may not necessarily have been brighter, but they could possibly have survived in greater numbers.

Within the colony there was no support for his idea. Most newspapers had come to the conclusion that a military expedition to drive the Aborigines from the whole island was the only answer. The *Hobart Town Courier,* the paper most supportive of Arthur, compared the situation to that in the United States in the 1780s, when the Indians were removed to the other side of the Mississippi River, an area geographically remote from European settlement. The only equivalent place for the Aborigines of Van Diemen's Land was an island in Bass Strait. The *Colonial Times* also considered Van Diemen's Land too small to accommodate two cultures, so that the dispatch of the Aborigines to an island in Bass Strait was the only solution.[17]

By April 1828 Arthur still could not accept the idea of a military expedition either to remove the Aborigines to a reserve in the northeast or to an island in Bass Strait. He wanted the Aborigines to volunteer to go to a reserve. Nor was the Colonial Office of much assistance to him. They agreed that the Aborigines had absurd ideas about their rights over the country in comparison with those of the colonists, but offered Arthur no advice on how to wrest the land from the Aborigines. So Arthur had to confront the problem alone. He recognized that unless some Aboriginal rights were accepted, and that the Aboriginal problem in Van Diemen's Land was resolved equitably, it would be repeated all over Australia where new pastoral settlements were established.[18]

As the autumn of 1828 approached, the Big River and Oyster Bay Aborigines reappeared in the settled districts from the high country behind the River Ouse. The "depredations" began again. At the end of January a band of the Oyster Bay tribe killed a member of a road gang and wounded two others outside Green Ponds. They were still in the area a month later, burning off grassland, harassing sheep, and hunting kangaroos. By March they were in the Eastern Marshes, burning huts and haystacks until they departed down the Little Swanport River for the east coast.[19]

In January 1828 a band of the North Midlands tribe moved from the Ben Lomond Tier to Stockers Bottom in the Eastern Tiers. There they attempted to spear Daniel Cubitt, a stockman who had shot many of them in the past. Again he escaped, but not before they warned him: "We will have you yet." Then as they moved past Campbell Town to the Lake River, plundering huts for provisions, they pursued a settler for some miles. The incident so distressed the man that he abandoned his property, "giving the charge of the place to one poor old man who had been wounded by his master's side." At the Lake River the North Midlands people continued their "hit and run" campaign by plundering several huts in the one day.[20]

In February a band of the North tribe threw a firestick at the hut of a settler named Ritchie on the Meander River and forced the inmates out. Then they took the contents of the hut. This settler had become so vulnerable to attack that he chose another grant. A few days later on the Gog Range this same band told a stock-keeper whom they had tried to kill several times before that they would have him yet, too.[21]

In April a band from the Ben Lomond Aborigines chased one of the stock-keepers of the settler John Batman from a favoured hunting ground at the Ben Lomond Rivulet. With four of his men, Batman set out in pursuit and was joined next day by two soldiers and three field police. The following day Batman came across the Aborigines in camp. With his own men he crept on his hands and knees to within twenty

COPY OF GOVERNOR ARTHUR'S PROCLAMATION TO THE ABORIGINES, 1830

These were placed on trees and in other places frequented by the Tasmanian Aborigines.

8. *Copy of Arthur's Proclamation to the Aborigines, 1828*. Original in Tasmanian Museum and Art Gallery, Hobart. L. G. Shea, Government Printer, Tasmania.

metres before they noticed his presence. After an exchange of spears and gunfire, the Ben Lomond people escaped, leaving one man wounded and Batman in possession of a sixteen-year-old boy, who escaped the following day. A few days later the Ben Lomond people killed a stockman at the River Nile.[22]

One settler wrote in frustration after having been detained in a remote stock hut for several days:

> It is rather alarming living in a Tent surrounded by a set of wretches who value our lives as little as they do the Kangaroos or Opossums. We have been obliged to leave our Firearms at home for the protection of our Properties, now our lives are endangered, and an ingenious death awaits us, our Brains to be beaten out with Waddies by such Ourang Outangs, disgrace it would be to the human race to call them Men.[23]

Other settlers were beginning to expound the view that since the Aborigines had not complied with God's word, "be fruitful, and multiply, and replenish the earth, and subdue it", they should be exterminated. For despite the great pains, others pointed out, taken to "civilize" the Aboriginal children captured years before, they still ran back to the bush at the first opportunity. This was surely an indication of their barbarity.[24]

On 15 April 1828 Arthur issued a proclamation which officially divided the island, so far as the Europeans' relations with the Aborigines were concerned, into the settled and unsettled districts. He placed troops along the frontier of the settled districts at Launceston, at Waterloo Point at Oyster Bay, at Bothwell on the Clyde River, at New Norfolk, at the Isis River, and at Norfolk Plains to prevent the Aborigines from passing through. To indicate to the Aborigines his concern that they should understand government policy, he arranged for a series of boards depicting a cartoon of Aborigines and Europeans living in harmony to be nailed on trees along the frontier. The Aborigines could pass through the settled districts if their leaders applied directly to Arthur for a pass, probably in the form of a brass plate.[25]

During the winter Arthur was confident his plan would succeed. No Aborigines passed through the settled districts and none were seen on the frontier. But by October he had to concede defeat. That spring the Oyster Bay and Big River people launched an unprecedented series of attacks on stock huts in the Eastern Marshes, the Midlands, and the Clyde River, while the Ben Lomond and North Midlands Aborigines razed for the first time huts along the Nile River in the east and the Meander River in the west. For the rest of that spring the settled

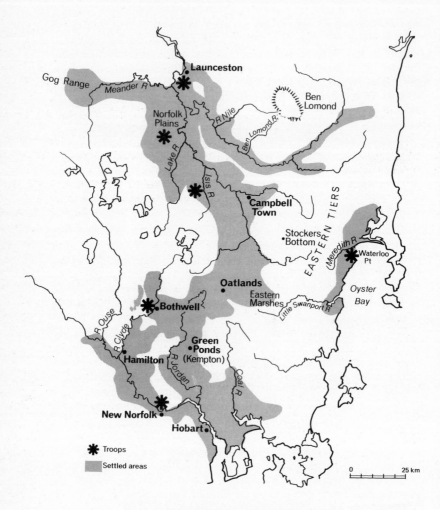

Map 29. Troop depots, 1828

districts were in a state of seige. Not even the capture by John Batman of two young men, four women, and five children of the Oyster Bay tribe at the Meredith River in September calmed the panic.[26] The Colonial Secretary's Office in Hobart Town was flooded with reports from settlers and magistrates pointing out that "not only the whole of

the distant and detached stockkeepers were in imminent daily danger
. . . [but] unoffending and defenceless women and children [had
fallen] victims to the cruelties of those wretched people".[27] In mid-
October the police magistrate at Oatlands, Thomas Anstey, whose area
was the centre of the depredations, wrote: "The natives have uttered
their war whoop and that it is to be a war of extermination even of
defenceless women and children. Their disposition is nearer to the cold
malignity of a wicked spirit than to the frailty and passion of a man."[28]
  On 1 November 1828, after a meeting with the Executive Council,
Arthur declared martial law against the Aborigines in the settled
districts. This meant that the military now had the right to apprehend
without warrant or to shoot on sight any Aboriginal found in the
settled districts. Martial law was that final power colonial governors
could impose upon dissidents under their jurisdiction and was tantamount to a declaration of war. In justification of this most serious
measure, Arthur wrote to his superiors in London:

> All the Aboriginal Tribes of this island with which we are acquain-
> ted, except the tribe who visit Brune Island, are actuated with one
> common purpose of murdering the white inhabitants whenever met
> with, and without distinction of age, sex or condition; that their
> attacks had been unhappily attended with a degree of success which,
> while it appeared to stimulate them to further hostilities, was well
> calculated to produce the great state of alarm which appeared to be
> felt generally by the interior settlers and servants in husbandry.[29]

Martial law had last been declared in Van Diemen's Land in 1816
against the bushrangers. Then it had remained in force for six months.
This time it would continue for more than three years.

NOTES

1. Bigge Report, vol. 3 (1823), quoted in *Black War,* by Clive Turnbull (Melbourne: Cheshire–Lansdowne, 1965), p. 61.
2. R. M. Hartwell, *The Economic Development of Van Diemen's Land 1820–
   1850* (Carlton, Vic.: Melbourne University Press, 1954), pp. 118–25;
   Michael Roe, *Quest for Authority in Eastern Australia 1835–1851* (Carlton,
   Vic.: Melbourne University Press, 1965), p. 99.
3. Peter Scott, "Land Settlement", in *Atlas of Tasmania,* ed. J. L. Davies
   (Hobart: Dept. of Lands and Surveys, 1965), p. 43; Hartwell, *Economic
   Development,* pp. 108–30.
4. R. W. Giblin, *The Early History of Tasmania,* vol. 2, 1804–28 (Carlton,
   Vic.: Melbourne University Press, 1939), p. 297; John C. Taylor, "Race
   Relations in South East Queensland, 1840–1860" (BA thesis, University
   of Queensland, 1967), p. 41.

5. T. Betts, *An Account of the Colony of Van Diemen's Land* (Calcutta, 1830), p. 95.
6. *HTG*, 26 Mar., 2 Apr., and 23 July 1824.
7. Ibid., 29 Oct. 1824.
8. *ADB*, vol. 1, pp. 32–38; C. D. Rowley, *The Destruction of Aboriginal Society* (Canberra: ANU Press, 1970), p. 87.
9. Henry Melville, *The History of Van Diemen's Land From the Year 1824* (Sydney: Horwitz-Grahame 1965), pp. 32–38.
10. *HTG*, 5 Nov., 15 Apr., and 4 Nov. 1824; Mansfield to Arthur, 3 Nov. 1824, and resolutions carried at public meeting, 15 Nov. 1824, Richardson to Arthur, 25 Apr. 1825, TSA GO52/2; Plomley, *Friendly Mission*, p. 49; *Mil. Ops*, p. 39.
11. *Mil. Ops*, pp. 20–21; Melville, *History of Van Diemen's Land*, pp. 56–59; *HTG*, 20 Sept. 1826.
12. Settler to Arthur, 5 Nov. 1826, AP, vol. 28; *Mil. Ops*, pp. 20–21; Arthur to Bathurst, 16 May 1827, *HRA*, III, v, pp. 608–12.
13. Gordon to col. sec., 9 Dec. 1826, TSA CSO 1/331; *HTC*, 15 Nov. 1826; *CT*, 1 Dec. 1826.
14. Smith to col. sec. May 1827, Mulgrave to col. sec. 23 June 1827, Dalrymple to col. sec. 1 July 1827, TSA CSO 1/316; *HTC*, 28 July 1827; Anne McKay, ed., *Journals of the Land Commissioners of Van Diemen's Land 1826–1828* (Hobart: U. Tas./Tas. Hist. Res. Assn., 1962), p. 74; Anstey to Arthur, 4 Dec. 1827, TSA CSO 1/320; *Mil. Ops*, p. 21.
15. *Mil. Ops*, p. 4.
16. Ibid.
17. *HTC*, 5 Apr. 1828; *CT*, 8 Apr. 1828.
18. *Mil. Ops*, p. 8.
19. *HTC*, 25 Jan. and 23 Feb. 1828; Lord to col. sec. 22 Mar. 1828, TSA CSO 1/316.
20. *Mil. Ops*, p. 55.
21. McKay, *Journals of the Land Commissioners*, pp. 78–80.
22. *HTC*, 12 Apr. 1828.
23. McKay, *Journals of the Land Commissioners*, p. 68.
24. Rev. T. Atkins, *Reminiscences of Twelve Years' Residence (1836–1847) in Tasmania and Australia* (Malvern, 1869), pp. 13–14; Mrs A. Prinsep, *The Journal of a Voyage from Calcutta to Van Diemen's Land* (London, 1833), p. 78.
25. *Mil. Ops*, pp. 4–7, 24–25.
26. Ibid., pp. 8, 10–11; Batman to col. sec., 18 Sept. 1828, TSA CSO 1/320.
27. *Mil. Ops*, p. 10.
28. Anstey to Arthur, 13 Oct. 1828, TSA CSO 1/316.
29. *Mil. Ops*, p. 10.

6

War in the Settled Districts, 1829-31: The European Response

> The State of this colony, with reference to the Aborigines, I have now felt for nearly three years to be the most anxious and important concern upon my hands.[1]

The proclamation of martial law on 1 November 1828 took the war between the colonists and the Aborigines into a new phase. Arthur's first response was to establish six roving parties to hunt the two hundred Aborigines from the settled districts or to capture them. This in turn presented a further problem: what to do with those captured. Some were placed in Richmond Gaol, while others became Aboriginal guides for the roving parties. Each roving party was led by a constable of the field police and consisted of an Aboriginal guide and four or five assigned servants with a knowledge of the bush. They were placed under the control of Thomas Anstey at Oatlands, the centre of the settled districts. Three roving parties operated on the eastern Midlands Plain to Oyster Bay, and the others operated in the west in the country of the Big River people. These roving parties, by their composition and tactics, were the precursors of the Native Police established at Port Phillip and the Darling Downs in the 1840s.

The most prominent roving party was led by Gilbert Robertson, chief district constable at Richmond, whose Aboriginal guide was Kickerterpoller, known as Black Tom, who had grown up in a settler's home and returned to the bush when an adolescent. He had joined Musquito's "tame mob" and had earned the anger of many stock-keepers, but had been saved from an extended gaol sentence through the intercession of his white "parents". Robertson's first sortie led to the capture near Great Swanport on 7 November 1828 of five North Midlands Aborigines and their leader Umarrah. Umarrah explained "that white people had been murdered" because they drove the Aborigines off their kangaroo hunting grounds.[2]

The settlers also formed their own parties. Some, like John Batman, hired Aborigines from the Australian mainland to assist them. Using Aborigines from other areas became a common practice of the Native Police in Queensland in the 1850s. The introduction of a bounty in February 1830 of five pounds for every adult Aboriginal captured and two pounds for every child made "black catching" big business. Between November 1828 and November 1830 the roving parties captured about twenty Aborigines and killed about sixty.[3]

The settlers also began to exploit their knowledge of the Aborigines' seasonal patterns of movement. When a band of the Oyster Bay tribe visited Moulting Lagoon in January 1829, they found the settlers waiting for them. Ten were shot dead and three taken prisoner. When a band of Big River people reached the Eastern Marshes in March *en route* to the east coast, Gilbert Robertson's party was waiting and killed five and captured another. But this did not prevent another group of Oyster Bay Aborigines from killing eight assigned servants in the Pittwater area between January and June.[4] Gilbert Robertson had no doubt they were fighting for their country: "They consider every injury they can inflict upon white men as an act of duty and patriotic, and however they may dread the punishment which our laws inflict upon them, they consider the sufferers under these punishments as martyrs of their country . . . having ideas of their natural rights which would astonish most of our European statesmen."[5]

Robertson suggested to Arthur that the Aborigines could be rounded up by a conciliator and moved to an island in Bass Strait, where an establishment could be formed to educate the children. The adults could hunt, visit the children, and receive clothes and rations. Arthur was already forming a similar idea but with the hope that banishment to Bass Strait would not be necessary. In April 1828 five Aborigines from Bruny Island had come to him to complain about a sealer who had abducted three Aboriginal women. He had taken this opportunity to establish a ration station on Bruny in the hope that it would attract other Aborigines from the settled districts. The Bruny people accepted the rations, so in March 1829 Arthur decided to turn the ration station into a mission and to employ a suitable person to run it.[6]

The man appointed, at a salary of a hundred pounds a year, was George Augustus Robinson. He was a free man, forty-one years of age and married with five children. He had arrived in Hobart Town in 1824 to practise as a builder and had made a name for himself as secretary of the Van Diemen's Land Seaman's Friend and Bethel Union Society. His journal suggests that he had been concerned with the welfare of the Aborigines for some years, for his evangelical beliefs had taught him that "this unfortunate race" were his brothers in Christ. Although he believed the Aborigines had no right to their country because they had no civilization, Robinson did believe that they were entitled to know the message of God and to share in the beliefs of British civilization. Armed with the conviction that he could save them from destruction, he set off for Bruny Island at the end of March.[7]

Arthur's decision to appoint a missionary to civilize the Aborigines was not a new departure in the Australian colonies. In New South Wales, convict schoolteachers had been appointed at Black Town and Parramatta to educate the children of the survivors of the massacres of Aborigines along the Hawkesbury River in the 1790s. Then in 1825 the Wesleyan missionary John Harper had been given permission to establish a mission station in the Wellington Valley, to civilize by tuition the survivors of the military expedition which had "cleared" the Bathurst district of Aborigines in 1824. And in 1826 Lancelot Edward Threlkeld, on behalf of the London Missionary Society, had established a mission station at Lake Macquarie for the Aborigines from the remnant tribes. But unlike his missionary predecessors, Robinson was to actively seek out the Aborigines and bring them into captivity.

Having made some move towards the conciliation of the Aborigines, Arthur returned his attention to the frontier. In the winter of 1829 nine roving parties, both government and private, and a hundred troops scoured the settled districts for Aborigines. They found that for the first time the Aboriginal offensive was continuing through the winter. They would have been even more amazed to learn that the number of Aborigines they sought in the settled districts now barely reached a hundred, scarcely one-twentieth envisaged by Arthur and the settlers. But this number did not prevent the Aborigines from continuing the war.

In September they killed four Europeans: a shepherd at the Macquarie River who had his skull fractured by a well-aimed stone, a settler at Great Swanport, an assigned servant who was speared at the River Ouse, and a convict woman near Richmond. In October another assigned servant was killed at Waterloo Point, a settler's hut was plundered near Hamilton and the occupant mortally wounded, a shepherd was killed near Jerusalem, and two others killed at the River Ouse. In November a convict woman was also killed at the Ouse, a stockman was ambushed and killed at Oatlands, a man and a woman murdered at the Clyde River, while another stockman was speared and killed near by. An assigned servant was burnt to death in the house of his master at Bothwell, also on the Clyde, and another killed with a spear at the near by river Ouse. In December, near New Norfolk, another settler was speared and later died from his wounds. Between August and December of 1829 nineteen Europeans lost their lives to the Aborigines.[8]

In the midst of the panic Arthur wrote to the Colonial Office in London: "The species of warfare which we are carrying on with them is of the most distressing nature: — they suddenly appear, commit some acts of outrage, and, then, as suddenly vanish — if pursued, it seems impossible to surround and capture them, and, if the Parties fire, the possibility is that Women and children are the victims."[9]

The summer of 1829/30 was desperate. In January a ticket-of-leave man was killed at the river Ouse, in February a settler and his assigned servant were killed at Jericho, another at the river Clyde, two at Oatlands, and an overseer and another assigned servant at the Ouse. On 19 February a boy aged seven was speared and killed while tending his father's herd of sheep at Constitution Hill near Bagdad. Arthur tried to prevent the last detachment of the 40th Regiment from departing for India and sought the services of another from the 63rd Regiment stationed in Western Australia, but without success. At Bothwell the police magistrate estimated that he needed three times the thirty military already at his disposal to protect the settlers. But the military presence seemed to spur rather than intimidate the Aborigines.[10]

At the Clyde River a regular rendezvous for the Big River people was at Montacute, a farmhouse between Hamilton and Bothwell. Situated at the junction of three ridges which plunged down to the river, it was ideal for Aboriginal ambush. Captain Torlesse, the occupant at this time, built a high brick and stone wall to enclose the homestead and outhouses and at intervals along this wall established positions for firing at the Aborigines. In mid-February 1830, after they had attacked the farmhouse at least six times, Torlesse wrote to Arthur:

> As to the natives, I can assure you we all feel so fearful of their being near us, that we never move without a gun, if the cart has to go to the mill or elsewhere, we lose the service of one man at home, being obliged to send two, one as driver, the other as convoy — Mrs Torlesse is uneasy if I even go so far as the Barn, and even to that short distance I always carry a gun. The trouble and loss they cause and still will cause us is quite paralyzing.[11]

He had to admit that never more than six Aborigines participated in the attacks, but their use of firesticks, the surprise nature of their raids, and their ability to bamboozle the stock-keepers rendered even this small number a formidable danger. Like other settlers in the neighbourhood, Torlesse imagined there were a few hundred Big River people, combining into small groups for raids. He possibly would not have believed that there were only thirty.

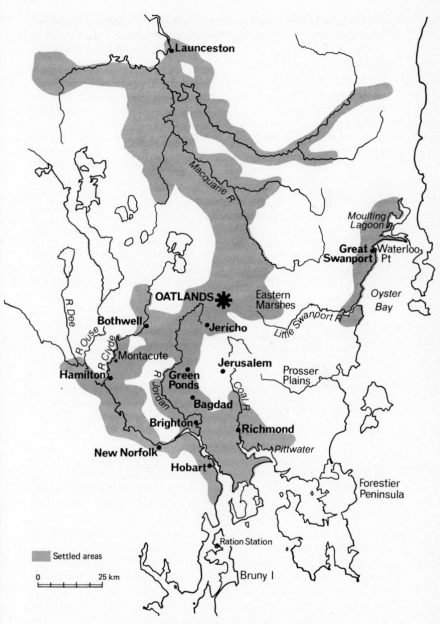

Map 30. Sites of killings by Aborigines, 1829–30

On Sunday 21 February at three o'clock in the afternoon, further up the Clyde, a settler named Sherwin was sitting in the front room of his house when a servant called out, "Fire! Fire! The natives!" Sherwin described the event in a letter to Arthur:

I immediately ran for water, and to alarm the men who were in front of the Hut at the Time — soon after which a fire broke out from the back of the men's hut — we then endeavoured to save the house, but seeing this was impossible, we began to get what things we could from the house: — during this time I never saw a native with the exception of the one who set fire to the house after which he immediately ran away — soon after this I saw smoke arise about 600 or 700 yards from the house, then saw two natives on the hillside. The smoke continued to increase and come nearer. Soon after two natives walked alongside the fences and set fire to them at every 20 or 30 yards distance — then two other Natives appeared on the Rock on the opposite side of the River, seeming to give directions whilst the other 2 still continued to communicate fire to the cross fences and another bringing fire even to the riverside. These 2 joined the others on the Rock and began to leap and use much of their language. "Parrawa Parrawa. Go away you white buggers — what business have you here." One of my men crossing the river with a musket I called to him to come back, when the Natives immediately cried out, "Ah — you coward". For some time they still continued on the Rock making use of such language as above, and constantly raising their hands and leaping.
About 2 hours after the house had been fired, I perceived one skulking round the stacks evidently with the intention of taking some of the articles we had rescued from the flames — my son seeing him first, cried out, "Father — black fellow", he immediately ran round the stacks again and scrambled up some rocks, and on my bringing my piece to a level he immediately fell flat on the Rock — he soon got out of my sight and began shouting. I saw nothing of them afterwards. . . . The Natives were in number about 4 or 5 — one of them always had a firestick in his hand.[12]

The following Saturday, thirty-three settlers along the Clyde assembled at Bothwell to discuss their position. They drew up an address to Arthur warning that unless they were granted increased military protection and unless he abandoned his policy of conciliation they would be driven from their homes. The *Colonial Times* agreed. The dramatic increase in Aboriginal aggression, the editor argued, had eroded any possibility of conciliation. The sooner the Aborigines were rounded up and taken to Bass Strait the better.[13]

In response, Arthur introduced a bounty for captured Aborigines and persuaded the new Anglican archdeacon of Australia, William Grant Broughton, to become temporary chairman of the Aborigines Committee established the previous November to formulate a policy for the future of the captured Aborigines, while it conducted a special inquiry into the origin of the hostility displayed by the "Black Natives of this Island against the Settlers, and to consider the measures expedient to be adopted with a view of checking the devastation of property and the destruction of human lives occasioned by the state of warfare which has so extensively prevailed".[14] Arthur hoped that Broughton's presence would not only lend integrity and independence to the committee but enable a more charitable attitude towards the Aborigines to emerge.

The committee began its investigation on 20 February by writing to the settlers seeking their views on possible means to solve the Aboriginal problem. Some settlers considered the matter so serious that they made the journey to Hobart Town to appear before the committee. They all demanded ruthless measures to expel the Aborigines. One urged that a Maori chieftain and 150 of his followers be employed to capture the Aborigines and remove them to New Zealand to become slaves. Another proposed that decoy huts, containing flour and sugar strongly impregnated with poison, be constructed to drive the Aborigines away. Another pressed for a full-scale military campaign with high bounties for the captured, while others put their faith in the erection of huts with secret rooms, trapdoors, and spring-locks, which would capture Aborigines in search of plunder. Another settler wanted Umarrah to escape with a couple of "lifers" who would then betray the "lurking places of the tribes". Others wanted "dogs to hunt the Aborigines as was done in Cuba and Jamaica with the negroes". This started a lively debate whether the dogs should be "Spanish bloodhounds from Manila" or "pointers which would set upon the natives as if they were quail".[15]

Only one settler, Edward Curr, manager of the Van Diemen's Land Company, acknowledged some form of Aboriginal rights. While never doubting the right of Britain to occupy the island by virtue of its supposed superior civilization, Curr argued that a treaty should have been signed with the Aborigines before land was granted to the settlers and the Aborigines removed "to some other place". Since this had not taken place, it was still the government's duty to remove the Aborigines as quickly as possible.

The committee reported on 19 March. They managed to vindicate Arthur's policies, support the settlers' pleas for more protection, and blame the convict stock-keepers and sealers as the original begetters of poor relations with the Aborigines. The committee saw the Aborigines' attacks upon the settlers not as a resistance tactic to force the settlers off their land, but the result of their inherent "wanton and savage spirit".

The committee believed that since European occupation of Aboriginal land was justified, then the settlers should show every "degree of forebearance and moderation" toward the Aborigines and "use every opportunity to lead them into the paths of civilisation". The committee also pointed out that "in all future attempts at colonization . . . an obligation exists to exercise mercy and justice towards the unprotected savage . . . [for] a neglect of those duties, even by individuals, may ultimately entail upon an entire, an unoffending, community."[16]

The committee recommended that all operations against the Aborigines should be entrusted to the local police magistrate and every police station should have a detachment of mounted police for easy mobility. The field police should be increased, the military should assist the local police magistrate, and the bounty system should be used as an incentive either to keep the Aborigines out of the settled districts or to capture them. Finally, all settlers should be well armed and alert on all occasions with a "watchful regard to the security of their dwellings and possessions"[17] and make sure that the stock-keepers and assigned servants understood the fatal consequences that came about from ill treatment of the Aborigines. Nor should they wantonly shoot kangaroos.

The settlers considered these measures inadequate. The press in Hobart Town and Launceston agreed. In their view the Aborigines were the enemy and nothing short of a full-scale military operation would "teach them a lesson".[18] But Arthur knew that the report would meet with the approval of his superiors in London.

The secretary of state for the colonies, having read the report, supported those of the committee's recommendations that cost no money to implement and then expressed concern lest the Aborigines should be wiped out. He warned Arthur that the British occupation of Van Diemen's Land was not sufficient reason in itself to allow the extermination of a whole people. If the Aborigines were to be exterminated, then evidence would have to be shown of their unusual aggressiveness.[19]

So far as the settlers and the Aborigines Committee were concerned, this unusual aggressiveness came in the winter of 1830. That winter the Big River people, realizing the danger that awaited them from the military and roving parties, as well as the settlers and stock-keepers if they travelled through the settled districts to the east coast, remained in the high country west of the river Ouse. From there they plundered outlying stock huts. By mid-August they had killed twenty Europeans since the beginning of the year. To the settlers near the frontier the report of the Aborigines Committee now appeared a monstrous fraud.

How much longer, one settler wrote to Arthur, could they tolerate the daily fear and anxiety for their safety?

But in Hobart Town, Arthur was reading reports from G. A. Robinson on the west coast and Captain Welsh in the north-west, both of whom had made friendly contacts with Aborigines. For a moment he thought that the war could be stopped, and on 19 August he issued a government notice:

> It is with much satisfaction that the Lieutenant-Governor is at length enabled to announce, that a less hostile disposition towards the European inhabitants has been manifested by some of the aboriginal Natives of this Island, with whom, Captain Welsh and Mr G. A. Robinson have succeeded in opening a friendly intercourse.
>
> As it is the most anxious desire of the government, that the good understanding which has thus happily commenced should be fostered and encouraged by every possible means, his Excellency earnestly requests, that all settlers and others will strictly enjoin their servants cautiously to abstain from acts of aggression against these benighted beings, and that they will themselves personally endeavour to conciliate them wherever it may be practicable: and whenever the Aborigines appear without evincing a hostile feeling, that no attempt shall be made either to capture or restrain them, but, on the contrary, after being fed and kindly treated, that they shall be suffered to depart whenever they desire it.[20]

The next day he warned that the bounty would not be paid for Aborigines captured while holding a friendly intercourse with Europeans in the settled districts. If any Aborigines were shot while attempting to communicate with Europeans, then those responsible would be prosecuted.

The settlers of Jericho viewed "with inexpressible alarm" the consequences of Arthur's statements:

> We are convinced that Your Excellency must be deceived respecting the real state of the Colony and must labour under a mistake as respects our situation. The bringing in of a few inimical blacks — a distinct people from those in the interior and who have not had any intercourse with the European is no criterion to judge of the character of the Aborigines generally as a people, and the events of the last week in this District must convince Your Excellency of the necessity of the most energetic measures as well as for the protection of the Colonists as for the subjection of the Aborigines.[21]

Thomas Anstey wrote that unless sufficient military protection was afforded, the spring of 1830 would be too bloody to remember. The Aborigines Committee agreed. The Aborigines in the settled districts had now become "too much enjoined in the most rancorous animosity to be spared the most vigorous measures against them".[22]

On 27 August Arthur summoned the Executive Council to consider the situation. They deliberated over the address from the settlers of Jericho, they perused Anstey's letter, and they read the report from the Aborigines Committee. They could only concur with their sentiments. The war by the Big River and Oyster Bay Aborigines against the settlers had so intensified that unless some vigorous effort upon an extended scale brought about its end, there would be a great decline in the prosperity of the Colony and the eventual extirpation of the Aboriginal race itself. On the grounds of humanity, the Executive Council taunted Arthur, a full-scale military expedition must take place. Arthur bowed to the inevitable.[23]

He authorized Major Douglas of the 63rd Regiment to draw up a spring offensive against the Big River and Oyster Bay Aborigines. Douglas devised a plan of action whereby the military forces, the field police, and every able-bodied male colonist, whether bond or free, would form a human chain across the settled districts from St Patricks Head on the east coast, through Campbell Town in the midlands to Quamby Bluff in the Western Tiers. With an extra flank at each end of the chain — one stretching from the mouth of the river Ouse past Lake Echo to the Lagoon of Islands, to cover any possible Aboriginal escape to the west; the other in the east concentrated north of Moulting Lagoon between the Swan River and Cape Lodi, to drive any Aborigines in that area in to Freycinet Peninsula — the Black Line, as it was called, would move for three weeks in a pincer movement south and east across the settled districts until it rendezvoused in an area bounded by Sorell at Pittwater, Richmond on the Coal River, and Spring Bay on the east coast. Then the colonists would be sent home, leaving the military forces and the field police to tighten the cordon until they reached East Bay Neck at Forestier Peninsula a month later. There they expected to locate the remaining Aborigines in the settled districts and drive them to Tasman Peninsula, where Arthur had created an Aboriginal reserve. He was still hopeful that the Aborigines could be confined to a portion of their own country rather than be removed to Bass Strait.[24]

The plan was boldly conceived. Had the main target, the Big River and Oyster Bay Aborigines, existed in the numbers envisaged by Major Douglas — between two hundred and five hundred — many would have been captured. However, twenty Big River people had already fled west of the river Ouse, leaving only eleven Oyster Bay people and an equally small number of North Midlands and Ben Lomond people in the settled districts. The plan was similar in strategy to the bounty parties

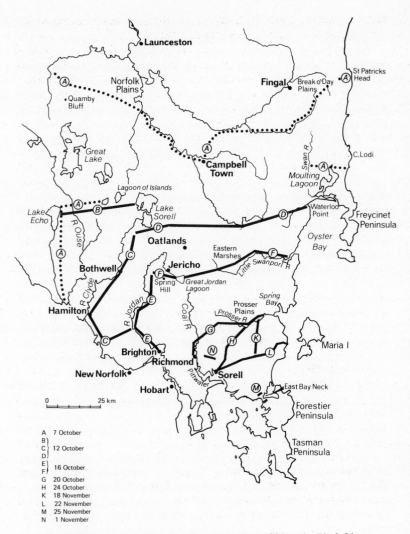

Map 31. Military operations, October–November 1830 – the Black Line

organized by Lieutenant-Governor Davey in 1815 against the bushrangers and similar also to the military expeditions against the Aborigines in New South Wales in 1816 and 1824. But in this operation not
only the colonists played a major part; the Aborigines were expected to

move to a particular place instead of dispersing. The operation also brought about a much needed increase in morale among the settlers.

On 7 October some two thousand men assembled for the Line, five hundred of whom were troops of the 17th, 59th, and 63rd regiments and seven hundred of whom were convicts. The rest were free colonists. They carried a thousand stand of arms, thirty thousand rounds of ammunition, and three hundred pairs of handcuffs. For three weeks they beat bushes, built defensive huts from which to assail their hidden foe, scoured the countryside, got lost in pouring rain, and consumed vast quantities of government stores. Despite the apparent disorganization, the Line dislodged the Oyster Bay people on the east coast so that on 24 October two were captured and two others shot at Prosser Plains. The remaining six or seven moved through the Line to the north-east, realizing they were lucky to escape with their lives. The colonists returned home on 31 October leaving the soldiers and field police to scout the isthmus to Forestier Peninsula until the end of November, when the operation was officially abandoned.[25]

Despite ridicule from the local press, the Line achieved its objective in clearing the settled districts of the Aborigines. It drove the Oyster Bay, North Midlands, and Ben Lomond people to the north-east, where Robinson captured thirteen the following fortnight. It contained the Big River people in their mountain retreat behind the river Ouse and confined the twenty or so Aborigines from North, North East, and North Midlands tribes to the north and west of Launceston, where Robinson captured them the following year.

The settlers of Bothwell and Brighton, at last released from the physical and psychological buffeting of the previous three years, sent addresses of congratulations to Arthur. He in turn reduced the military, disbanded the roving parties, and placed the official pursuit of the Aborigines in the hands of George Augustus Robinson.

The last crisis in the settled districts took place in September 1831 when Aborigines from the North and Big River tribes killed Captain Bartholomew Boyle Thomas and his overseer, William Parker, at Northdown, near Port Sorell.[26] Robinson chose this moment to search for the Big River and Oyster Bay people, and after three months' pursuit he came upon the remaining few near the river Dee. With their capture, martial law was revoked and the settlers were in unfettered possession of the settled districts. In January 1832 the *Hobart Town Courier* wrote: "The large tracts of pasture that have for so long been deserted owing to their murderous attacks on the shepherds and stockhuts, will now be available, and a very sensible relief will be afforded to the flocks of sheep that have been withdrawn from them and pent up on inadequate range of pasture."[27]

From the proclamation of martial law in November 1828 to its revocation in January 1832, eighty-nine Europeans were killed by the Aborigines in the settled districts and twice that number were injured. Of the two hundred Aborigines in the settled districts in 1828, fewer than fifty survived the settlers' guns to surrender to Robinson. While the settlers could now breathe more freely, Arthur had to devise some means of capturing the Aborigines beyond the frontier.

NOTES

1. Arthur to Goderich, 25 Oct. 1831, *BPP* 1834, vol. 44, no. 617, p. 154.
2. Report on proceedings of G. Robertson, 17 Nov. 1828, TSA CSO 1/331.
3. Arthur to col. sec., 27 May 1829, TSA CSO 1/317; Plomley, *Friendly Mission*, pp. 30, 472–74 (n. 277).
4. *LA*, 9 Feb. 1829; *HTC*, 17 Jan. and 7 Mar. 1829; Simpson to Arthur, 17 Feb. 1829, TSA CSO 1/316.
5. Report on proceedings of G. Robertson, 17 Nov. 1828.
6. Welsh to Arthur, 11 Apr. 1828, TSA CSO 1/327; Arthur to col. sec., 23 Apr. 1828, TSA CSO 1/316, and 5 May 1828, TSA CSO 1/740; Govt Notice no. 49, 4 Mar. 1829, *Mil. Ops*, pp. 31–32; *HTG*, 7 Mar. 1829.
7. Plomley, *Friendly Mission*, p. 14.
8. TSA CSO 1/316/7578/1.
9. Arthur to Murray, 12 Sept. 1829, PRO CO 280/21, pp. 334–35.
10. Arthur to Darling, 18 Nov. 1829, ML A1205; Williams to Arthur, 2 Nov. 1829, TSA CSO 1/317.
11. Torlesse to Arthur, 16 Feb. 1830, TSA CSO 1/316.
12. Sherwin to Arthur 23 Feb. 1830, TSA CSO 1/316.
13. Address of the Inhabitants of the Clyde Police District, 27 Feb. 1830, TSA CSO 1/316; *CT*, 19 Feb. 1830.
14. *Mil. Ops*, p. 35.
15. Evidence to the Aborigines Committee, TSA CSO 1/323.
16. *Mil. Ops*, p. 46.
17. Ibid., p. 43.
18. *CT*, 30 July 1830.
19. *Mil. Ops*, pp. 55–57.
20. Ibid., p. 61.
21. Address to His Excellency the Governor by the Settlers of Jericho, 24 Aug. 1830, TSA CSO 1/316.
22. Anstey to Arthur, 22 Aug. 1830, TSA CSO 1/316; Report of the Aborigines Committee, 26 Aug. 1830, TSA CSO 1/319.
23. *Mil. Ops*, pp. 62–64.
24. Ibid., pp. 65–66.
25. James Fenton, *A History of Tasmania* (Hobart, 1884), p. 107; H. J. Emmett, "The Black War in Tasmania", ANL MS 3311; Walpole to col. sec., 27 Oct. 1830, TSA CSO 1/332; Plomley, *Friendly Mission*, p. 489.
26. *Independent* (Launceston) 17 Sept. 1831; Plomley, *Friendly Mission*, pp. 17–18.
27. *HTC*, 14 Jan. 1832.

7

War in the Settled Districts:
The Aboriginal Response

> There is scarcely one among them but what has some monstrous cruelty to relate which had been committed upon some of their kindred or nation or people.[1]

From 1820, the pastoral expansion of Van Diemen's Land ensured the destruction of the Big River, Oyster Bay, Ben Lomond, North Midlands, and North tribes. This chapter will explore the fortunes of one Aboriginal tribe in the settled districts, the Big River people, in their reaction to the pastoral invasion of their territory. The ferocity of their response to European invasion was noted at the time, and their heroic fight deserves some attention.

At the time of European invasion of Van Diemen's Land in 1803, there were probably five bands of the Big River tribe, each consisting of between sixty and eighty people. The first awareness of European invasion for the Big River people came through the Leenowwenne and Braylwunyer bands, whose country lay along the upper Derwent River. Each autumn they usually travelled down the Derwent to Risdon Cove and across to Pittwater, returning in the spring to the high country to the west. They were possibly at Risdon Cove with one of the bands of the Oyster Bay people, the Moomairremener, when John Bowen and his party of convicts and soldiers stepped ashore in September 1803. From the end of 1804 until 1808 the two Big River bands were affected by the acquisition of European dogs and the invasion of hunting grounds in Oyster Bay country. As a result of the increased inter-tribal contention over women and dogs, the Big River population declined. By 1818 the two bands had either joined together or had been absorbed by other Big River groups.

The first direct invasion of their territory came in 1822 when pastoral settlers arrived at the Clyde River, appropriating about forty thousand hectares.[2] Where in one season there had been half a dozen settlers and a few thousand sheep, in the next there were at least sixty settlers and their families and sixty thousand sheep. In the summer of 1822/23 the Big River people saw the pastoralists build huts and depasture sheep along the Clyde, the Ouse, the Shannon, and the Dee rivers as far north as Lake Sorell, and watched the stock-keepers slaughter their kangaroos. In the autumn the Big River people departed for the east coast and upon their return the following spring paid visits to the stock-keepers and exchanged women for bread and potatoes. For a moment it appeared that an acceptable arrangement might be achieved.

But in January 1824, when a stock-keeper at Abyssinia, between the Jordan and Clyde rivers, attempted to take an Aboriginal woman from the Big River people without any remuneration, they promptly speared him and burnt his hut. That winter, when settlers and stock-keepers refused provisions, the Big River people killed three stockmen and a settler, wounded two others, and burnt two stockhuts. The resistance of the Big River people had begun. They believed they were defending their land against invasion, and their methods of attack were acts of patriotism. At this stage they numbered about three hundred.[3]

Big River country was well suited for Aboriginal guerilla activity. It consisted of two major river valleys, the Clyde and the Ouse, with the rivers Shannon and Dee forming significant tributaries, and rugged mountain country surrounded it in the west. It was possible to lie in the hills for days watching stockhuts and houses and to choose the right moment to lay siege. In these conditions the Big River people developed the tactic of burning down huts in retaliation for the failure of settlers and stock-keepers to conform to Aboriginal arrangements. They would ensure that the stock-keeper was inside, throw firesticks at the roof and sometimes down the chimney, and, having smoked the occupant out, they would then take provisions out of the hut. The Oyster Bay people preferred to raid the hut while the occupant was inside and intimidate him into handing over provisions. The North people preferred to kill the occupant of the hut first, then take the provisions. By 1830, all the variations of attack had become common to all groups.

Like the settlers in Oyster Bay country, those moving into the area of Clyde and Ouse rivers occupied the land "corridor fashion". They expropriated the land along the river flats and frontages but left the rugged Western Tiers unoccupied, preferring to use the kangaroo grounds for sheep grazing in the high country to the west. As a result the Big River people were able to remain in the thickly forested mountains and observe settlement along the rivers and the grazing lands behind the ranges. The Western Tiers were perfect cover for attack.

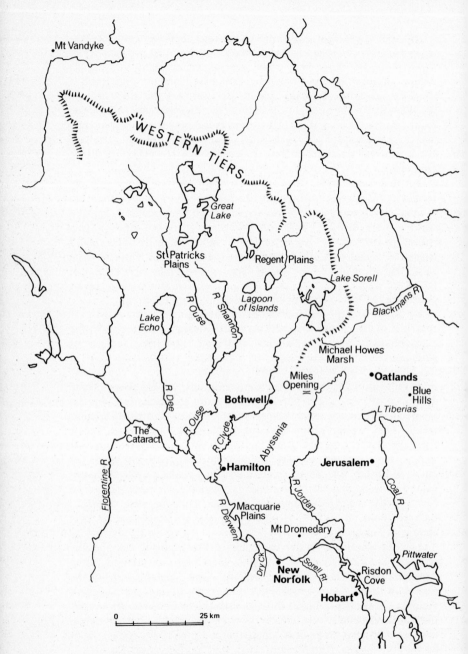

Map 32. Settlement in the territory of the Big River tribe

In 1824 only two bands of the Big River people remained. The Larmairremener, whose territory covered the high country west of the river Dee, bore the brunt of the struggle with the Europeans until 1827. Then the Luggermairrernerpairrer, from the Great Lake, played a more active role. Unlike the Aborigines in some areas of southern Queensland in the 1840s, who stole and hunted cattle for their own use, the Tasmanian Aborigines generally did not eat the Europeans' livestock — in this case sheep — nor did they attempt to destroy them on a large scale. Yet sheep inflicted the greatest damage upon the Aboriginal environment, particularly in dry seasons, in competing with kangaroos for grasslands. The shepherds and stock-keepers also killed vast numbers of kangaroos.

The Aborigines dealt with stock-keepers rather than settlers in their reciprocal arrangements. But they saw the settlers as agents of the stock-keepers and thus part of the reciprocity system into which the stock-keepers had entered. When the stock-keepers failed to fulfil their obligations, the settlers could expect revenge.

In the spring and early summer of 1825/26 the Larmairremener made no attacks on settlers' huts or on stock-keepers, although they moved through the lower Clyde area in November on their way from the east coast to the high plateau country to the west. This "quiet period" reinforced the views of some settlers that the attacks of the previous year had been the work of Europeanized Aborigines who had since been captured.[4]

But in April of 1826 these opinions were revised. As the Larmairremener moved down the north side of the Derwent from New Norfolk to Risdon on their way to Pittwater, they encountered in the Bluff, at Dromedary Mountain, a stock-keeper in possession of one of their women. After accepting provisions from the stock-keeper's master, who refused to return the woman, thirty Larmairremener attacked the settler's hut and killed him. In the pursuit that followed, several Aborigines were wounded.[5]

Then the Larmairremener disappeared into Oyster Bay country, returning to the Abyssinia district the following November. They demanded provisions from stock-keepers as payment for trespass on their kangaroo hunting grounds. When provisions were refused, the Larmairremener attacked four stock-keepers' huts within three days, killing one settler and two stockmen and wounding two others. On the third day the settlers organized a posse and chased the Larmairremener from the area, shooting two in the process. When news of the attacks reached Hobart Town, the *Colonial Times* announced that it was time the Aborigines were removed from their country, preferably to an island in Bass Strait.[6]

In 1827 the other remaining band of the Big River tribe, the Lugger-mairrernerpairrer, joined the struggle. The previous November they had killed an assigned servant on the river Shannon for attempting to fire his gun at them, but as they moved eastwards in the autumn, they were confronted by hostile stock-keepers at Michael Howes Marsh and Blackmans River. In retaliation they attacked four assigned servants hunting kangaroos and removed the catch. Finding their passage east more difficult than expected, they swung back to the Clyde and robbed huts for provisions. This was the first indication of interest by the Luggermairrernerpairrer in European goods.[7]

The Luggermairrernerpairrer possibly went to the North country rather than to the east coast for the winter, for there is no record of their movement through the settled districts. But by September they were at the Ouse and Shannon rivers, where they robbed at least five more huts, always causing panic by their sudden appearances and by their open hostility to Europeans. By the end of 1827 they were in the high country to the west. In contrast the Larmairremener spent most of 1827 in Oyster Bay country, returning to their own country by November.[8]

The summer of 1827/28 found the Luggermairrernerpairrer at the upper Clyde and the Larmairremener at the lower banks of the Ouse. The former remained at the upper Clyde from January until March, making sudden appearances at remote stockhuts, occasionally spearing sheep and creating an atmosphere of siege. At least eight huts were attacked, some twice within two days. Five Europeans were wounded and two killed, and several brace of firearms were taken. The Big River people hid these firearms in tree trunks, sometimes bartering them with the North people. Firearms became a significant item of exchange, although there is no record of their being fired at Europeans.[9]

At the same time the Larmairremener were active along the Ouse and upper Derwent rivers, where at least three huts were plundered and three Europeans wounded.[10] So in the space of three months the Big River people had attacked at least eleven huts, killed two Europeans, and wounded eight others. The bands had operated in two closely linked areas and had given the impression of combined strategy.

In April 1828 both bands moved north to the Lagoon of Islands and Regent Plains and there met up with some of the North people. Their numbers caused settlers in the area to warn the administration in Hobart Town of a forthcoming spring offensive. Military parties were sent to the frontier, but nothing materialized.[11] Both bands probably went to the North country for the winter.

By October both bands had returned to their own country. At the

Ouse the Larmairremener robbed a hut and killed an assigned servant, then moved to the south side of the Derwent where they plundered huts at New Norfolk and moved into the hills behind Hobart Town. After some skirmishes with stock-keepers in the Lakes area, the Luggermairrernerpairrer moved down the Clyde, where they speared shepherds and plundered two huts, moved east through Miles Opening to the Jordan River where they killed a shepherd hunting kangaroos, and then returned to the Clyde for the rest of the summer.[12]

Between January and April 1829 both bands were in the lower Clyde and Ouse river valleys, with a band of the Oyster Bay tribe occasionally meeting up with them. The increased numbers gave the settlers the impression of combination. But at this stage the Big River and Oyster Bay peoples preferred to move in small groups. One group plundered some stockhuts on the west bank of the Ouse at the end of March. They were immediately pursued, and in a skirmish an Aboriginal woman was severely wounded. A party of field police, aided by some stock-keepers, chased the Aborigines for several miles. They crossed the Derwent near the Cataract. On this occasion they robbed a stock hut of everything it contained, turning wool out of sacks and filling them instead with potatoes which they dug from the garden with pannikins.[13]

After the Oyster Bay people returned to the east coast in March, the Big River people went north to get ochre at Mount Vandyke and to look for some of their relatives and to confer with the North people. They returned in September, the Larmairremener to the Ouse and the Luggermairrernerpairrer to Abyssina, robbing huts and killing stock-keepers with an alacrity that horrified the district. Then the Luggermairrernerpairrer moved back to the upper Clyde, across to Blackmans River behind Oatlands, and back to Bothwell. The Larmairremener moved down the Derwent from the Ouse to Hamilton and New Norfolk and back to Macquarie Plains. At New Norfolk early in December they robbed the huts of government sawyers at Dry Creek and two settlers' huts at Sorell Rivulet. Finally they speared a settler and took his gun and two pistols. They told him, "You white . . . , we will give it to you." Both bands remained in the area for the rest of the summer. They were harassed by roving and military parties, which continually dispersed them.[14]

For the first two months of 1830, the Luggermairrernerpairrer were in the Clyde area from Hamilton to Lake Sorell, plundering huts and intimidating settlers and stock-keepers. They no longer speared cattle but burnt wheatstacks, huts, and homes. They also began to move at night, with lighted torches, to evade pursuit. This season was the worst the settlers along the Clyde River had encountered from the Big River people.[15]

In February 1830 the Larmairremener were at New Norfolk, but in March they joined forces again with the Luggermairrernerpairrer and moved through Miles Opening past Oatlands to the Blue Hills to meet with a band from Oyster Bay. This was their first meeting in Oyster Bay territory since 1828. A few Big River people joined the Oyster Bay people and they departed for the Coal River. The rest of the Big River people returned to the Clyde and stayed in their own country for the winter, which was the coldest the settlers had yet experienced. They divided into four groups, each containing five or six people to escape detection, and mounted a- sustained attack on stockhuts and houses. Their strategy was to entice the settler or stock-keeper from his hut by setting fire to the roof. In the smoke haze the stock-keeper was speared and the hut pillaged. Like the Oyster Bay people, the Big River people had become dependent upon European provisions, not to the exclusion of their own food resources but as a permanent supplement.[16]

In July two Big River people were captured, and the roving and military parties prevented a rendezvous with the Oyster Bay people from taking place. The Big River people turned west again, but so close was the pursuit that at the end of August one of the Big River men, Petelega, was captured in a bitter skirmish at the house of a Captain Wood on the upper Clyde. From there they fled north-easterly towards Blackmans River, where they fell in with a party of Ben Lomond people who had come to Big River country in search of women. It is possible the Big River people were aware of the expedition and hoped to meet up with the Oyster Bay people at Lake Tiberias to enlist their support, for without them they comprised no more than twenty. The Ben Lomond people were in a similar position. The two groups engaged in combat, but no lives were lost and no Big River women were taken.[17]

After this engagement the Big River people split in two, one group moving to Abyssina, the other towards the Clyde. In September and October both groups moved further west to avoid the Black Line. In mid-November, while travelling down the Ouse plundering stockhuts, they were overtaken by a vigilante party of stock-keepers; in the skirmish that followed, the Big River people abandoned blankets, spears, and food. On 17 November they robbed two settlers' huts, killing an assigned servant, his wife, and a constable. The stock-keepers' party quickly re-formed, and at the end of December they captured two more. After that the Big River people melted into the high country behind the Ouse.[18]

In January 1831 one group visited the North country, where they killed a female assigned servant in their search for plunder near West-

9. *The small outline of a National Picture* (The Conciliation). Designed, etched and published by B. Duterrau. July 15th 1835 Hobart Town, Van Diemen's Land. From Benjamin Duterrau, Etchings 1835–36. Mitchell Library.

bury. Then they returned to their own country and in March met up with the survivors of the Oyster Bay people at the lower Clyde. At most only thirty people remained, but this did not prevent them from splitting into small groups and continuing what had now become hit-and-run attacks on huts as they moved along the Ouse River valley until June. On their journey they killed a European woman and two stock-keepers. After a rendezvous at St Patricks Plains they again split up, one group travelling to join the Port Sorell people in the north, where in September they were involved in the killing of Thomas and Parker at Northdown. The other group remained at the Clyde, where they continued to plunder huts.[19]

This second group moved east to Oyster Bay country at the end of August, and in September and October they robbed huts on the outskirts of Pittwater and Jerusalem. Then they rejoined the other Big River people at the Ouse. At the end of November they retired to the river Dee in the high country, where, a few miles north-west of Lake Echo, Robinson met up with them on 31 December. There were twenty-six in all — sixteen men, nine women, and one child — and a hundred dogs. They were led by Tongerlongter from Oyster Bay and Montpeilliater from Big River. Tongerlongter told Robinson "that the reason for their outrages upon the white inhabitants [was] that they and their forefathers had been cruelly abused, that their country had been taken away from them, their wives and daughters had been violated and taken away, and that they had experienced a multitude of wrongs from a variety of sources".[20] They agreed to accompany Robinson back to Hobart Town, for they were exhausted by pursuit. They were in grief at the loss of so many of their people and they believed that the white man owed them compensation for the loss of their land.

This war in the settled districts brought home to the European invaders the sharp lesson that they were dealing with a formidable, courageous, and highly mobile resistance movement capable of inflicting serious losses on human life, stock, and property. Between 1824 and 1831 the Big River people killed at least sixty Europeans, plundered huts, stole firearms, speared sheep and cattle, burnt wheatstacks, huts, and homes, and laid siege to several areas where stock were grazing. Those directly affected by this successful campaign lived in perpetual fear; those in other areas not yet affected lived in apprehension, for one could never be certain when or where the Aborigines would strike next. But this struggle, successful as it was, could not match the retaliating response from the Europeans. Although the official reports suggest a much lower figure, some 240 Big River people were killed in this period; out of the three hundred living in 1823, less than sixty remained in 1831. The combination of the loss of women and shooting by Europeans was ultimately the effective cause of the dispossession of one of the Aboringal tribes in Tasmania.

NOTES

1. Plomley, *Friendly Mission*, p. 553.
2. Peter Scott, "Land Settlement", in *Atlas of Tasmania*, ed. J. L. Davies (Hobart: Dept. of Lands and Surveys, 1965), p. 43.
3. *HTG*, 23 Jan. and 16 July 1824; Rowcroft to Arthur, 16 June 1824, TSA CSO 1/316.
4. *HTG*, 10 Dec. 1825.
5. Dumaresq to Arthur, 30 Apr. 1826, TSA CSO 1/316.
6. *HTC*, 25 Nov. 1826; Wells to Arthur, 26 Nov. 1826, TSA CSO 1/316; *CT*, 6 Dec. 1826.
7. Clark to Arthur, 5 Nov. 1826, AP, vol. 28; *HTG*, 23 June 1827; *HTC*, 28 June 1827.
8. *HTC*, 1 Dec. 1827; Wentworth to Arthur, Sept. and Dec. 1827 (6 Jan. 1831), TSA CSO 1/316.
9. Worthy to Arthur, 17 Feb. 1828, and Clark to Arthur, 25 Feb. and 3, 10, and 24 Mar. 1828, TSA CSO 1/316; *HTC*, 8 and 10 Mar. and 12 Apr. 1828.
10. Wentworth to Arthur, Jan. 1828 (10 Jan. 1831), and Dumaresq to Arthur, Feb. 1828 (6 Jan. 1831), TSA CSO 1/316; Plomley, *Friendly Mission*, p. 571.

11. *HTC,* 12 Apr. 1828; *Mil. Ops,* pp. 4—5.
12. Wentworth to Arthur, 6 Oct. 1828 (10 Jan. 1831), and Hamilton to Arthur, 17 Nov. 1828, Williams to Arthur 16 Dec. 1828, TSA CSO 1/316; *HTC,* 22 Nov. 1828.
13. *HTC,* 17 Jan. and 18 Apr. 1829; Howitt to Arthur, 5 Jan. 1829, and Hamilton to Arthur 19 Jan. and 10 Apr. 1829, TSA CSO 1/329; Williams to Arthur, 12 Jan. 1829, TSA CSO 1/316.
14. Hopkins, 12 Sept. 1829, Tyrell, 23 Nov. 1829, TSA CSO 1/320; *HTC,* 26 Sept., 17 Oct., and 7 and 14 Nov. 1829; Vicary to Arthur, 29 Dec. 1829, and Dumaresq to Arthur, 6 and 8 Dec. 1829, TSA CSO 1/316; Plomley, *Friendly Mission,* pp. 87, 90—91.
15. Torlesse to Arthur, 9 Jan. 1830, TSA CSO 1/316, and 9 Feb. 1830, TSA CSO 1/328; *CT,* 19 Feb. 1830.
16. Minutes of the Aborigines Committee, 3 and 9 Mar. 1830, TSA CSO 1/332; *CT,* 16 July 1830.
17. Vicary to Arthur, 24 Aug. 1830, TSA CSO 1/320; Anstey to Arthur, 24 Aug. 1830, TSA CSO 1/324; *CT,* 1 Aug. and 3 Sept. 1830; Plomley, *Friendly Mission,* p. 262.
18. Giblin to Arthur, 21 Sept. 1830, TSA CSO 1/329; *HTC,* 30 Oct. and 13 and 19 Nov. 1830; *HTC,* 27 Nov. 1830; Wentworth to Arthur, 20 Dec. 1830, TSA CSO 1/320; Plomley, *Friendly Mission,* p. 522.
19. Smith to Arthur, 31 Jan. 1831, Dumaresq to Arthur, 9 and 21 Mar. 1831, Wentworth to Arthur, 8 and 10 May 1831, and Young to col. sec., 6 June 1831, TSA CSO 1/316; Wentworth to Arthur, 12 Aug. 1831, TSA CSO 1/322; Plomley, *Friendly Mission,* pp. 494—95, 551; Gordon to Arthur, 22 Sept. and 19 Oct. 1831, TSA CSO 1/331; Robinson to Aborigines Committee, 25 Jan. 1832, TSA CSO 1/332; J. E. Calder, "Some Account of the Country Lying between Lake St Clair and Macquarie Harbour", *Tas. Jour. Nat. Sci.* 3 (1849): 415—29.
20. Robinson to Aborigines Committee, 25 Jan. 1832, TSA CSO 1/332.

8

Robinson the Conciliator, 1829–30

While the war intensified between the settlers and Aborigines in the settled districts, Arthur appointed George Augustus Robinson to look after the friendly Aborigines at Bruny Island and to make some arrangements for the Aborigines captured in the settled districts. Robinson's appointment added a new dimension in government policy towards the Aborigines. Inside the settled districts the military conducted a guerilla war with the Aborigines, while outside the settled districts Robinson conciliated them. The next three chapters follow Robinson's career as a missionary and a conciliator between 1829 and 1834.

When Robinson arrived at the ration station on Bruny Island, 48 kilometres from Hobart Town, on 3 March 1829, he found 19 Aborigines, the survivors of the South East tribe which only six years before had comprised 160 people. They were Joe and Morley and their two children; Wooraddy, aged thirty-seven, and his wife and three sons; the females Dray, aged thirty, Truganini and Pagerly, aged eighteen and Nelson, aged forty; and the males Mangerner (Truganini's father), aged fifty, Doctor, Catherine (a man), Jack, and two others. They came from Southport, Recherche Bay, Bruny Island, and Port Esperance. Nelson had recently returned from the Bothwell district where she and her husband, Bruny Island Jack, had been guides to a roving party in search of the Big River people. There the soldiers had tried to rape her, and her husband had been shot dead while trying to escape.

Robinson drew up a plan for an "Aboriginal village", in which he was convinced the Bruny people could be Christianized and civilized.

The site [he explained to Arthur] should include fertility of soil, proximity to fresh water, contiguous to the shore and remote from settlers. . . . The establishment to form three sides of a quadrangle opening to the beach, the mission house to be situated at the upper end so as to command a view of the whole establishment, the married persons to occupy one side, the single persons the other

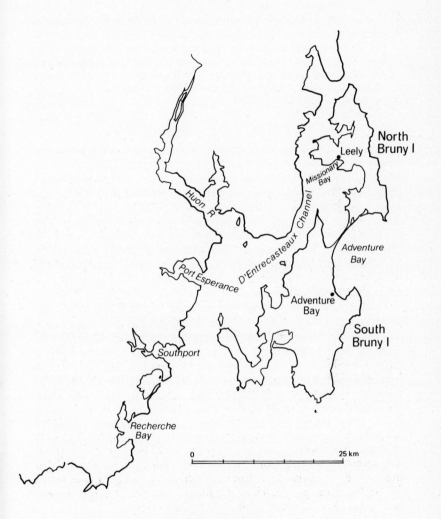

Map 33. Bruny Island

side. . . . Each family to have a log hut covered with bark, the aborigines to assist in the erection of the same. . . . Each allotment to be fenced. . . . A school to be erected with logs and covered with bark, this building to answer (in the first instance) as a church for the performance of divine worship. . . . A garden to be laid out for the general purposes of the institution.

The means: to assist the aborigine to erect his hut; . . . to assist
them in preparing a few rods of land as a potato ground; . . . to pre-
vail on them to cook their food after the manner of Europeans, to
catch fish to eat with their potatoes; the children if practicable to
eat at one table; as opportunity may occur to teach the children
trades. To instruct them in the principles of Christianity − 1st by
public worship, 2nd by public schools . . . The school to open and to
conclude with prayer. Dr Bell's system to be adopted, as far as practicable. The children to be taught the English language.[1]

Robinson had devised this model from his readings of the South Sea
missionaries, from penal settlement plans in Hobart Town, from the
writings of William Shelly, Macquarie's missionary to the Aborigines in
New South Wales, and from the report of Richard Sadlier to Archdeacon Scott in 1827 on the efficacy of Aboriginal missions in New
South Wales. Arthur approved the plan and arranged for labour and
materials to be sent to the island. Robinson selected the site for his
village at Leely, now Missionary Bay, removed the Bruny people there
on 14 May, and issued notices to Europeans at nearby farms and at the
whaling station at Adventure Bay to avoid contact with what he now
called the Aboriginal Establishment.[2]

Once at the village, Robinson removed the children from their
parents so that they could be trained in the ways of the European. He
also asked that Aboriginal children who lived with the settlers in other
parts of Van Diemen's Land be sent to the establishment to assist in
training the adults to become agricultural labourers. Then he tried to
inculcate concepts of Christian morality by clothing the Aborigines in
blankets, trousers, and shifts and then segregating them into huts.
There he instructed them in the "essentials" of the "superior civilization", a knowledge of God. He also introduced convict rations of
bread, potatoes, biscuit, salt meat, tea, and tobacco − which were lower
in protein content than the traditional diet.[3]

Within a short time illness forced most of the adults to desert the
mission, for, as they explained to Robinson, they never stayed in a
place of sickness. He was angered by this desertion, more so when he
discovered that Dray, Pagerly, and Truganini were spending most of
their time at the whaling station at Adventure Bay. When Joe and
Morley and Nelson and Woorraddy's wife died, he was faced with
the prospect of failure. So he began to formulate a plan to use the
Bruny Island people to conciliate other Aborigines, like the Port Davey
people in the south-west, to induce them to come to the mission. From
there he could press up the west coast and conciliate Aborigines on the
other side of the frontier and eventually all the Aborigines in Van
Diemen's Land.[4]

10a. *Woureddy, A wild native of Brune Island one of Mr. Robinson's most faithful attendants attached to the mission in 1829.* Designed, etched and published by B. Duterrau. August 24th 1835 Hobart Town, Van Diemen's Land. From Benjamin Duterrau, Etchings 1835–36. Mitchell Library.

10b. *Trugernana, A native of the southern part of Van Diemen's Land and wife to Woureddy who was attached to the mission in 1829.* Designed, etched and published by B. Duterrau. August 24th 1835 Hobart Town, Van Diemen's Land. From Benjamin Duterrau, Etchings 1835–36. Mitchell Library.

He was further encouraged in this plan early in July when nine Aborigines from Port Davey arrived on a seasonal visit. They included Mangerner's wife and son, who had walked from Port Davey to Recherche Bay, crossed to the southern tip of Bruny Island by catamaran, and walked to the mission. But they too abandoned the site and left Robinson pondering upon their ingratitude for his attempts to teach them Christianity. Instead they spent the rest of the winter hunting on South Bruny Island, where many died from illness contracted at the mission. By 22 September only Woorraddy and his three sons, Mangerner and his daughter Truganini, the women Dray and Pagerly, and the two orphaned children of Joe and Morley were still alive. Only three Port Davey people survived to make their way home.[5]

This first attempt to civilize the Aborigines in an artificial environment had failed. Robinson, like all his contemporaries, understood little about the nutritional properties of the rations he distributed to his charges. Nor could he know that clothes and huts produced susceptibility to European disease. Above all, he could not understand that the Aborigines were not anxious to divest themselves of their land or their culture in return for European civilization. The Bruny people had been willing to make use of the rations at the mission but saw no reason to manifest the gratitude that Robinson expected.

On 1 December Arthur gave Robinson permission to undertake an expedition to Port Davey, "for the purpose of endeavouring to effect an amicable understanding with the aborigines in that quarter, and through them, with the tribes in the interior".[6] He was to take Woorraddy and his three children; the women Truganini, Dray, and Pagerly; four Aborigines captured in the settled districts, Umarrah, Black Tom, Parwareter, and Trepanner; a "civilized" Aboriginal, Robert, and six convicts. The expedition was the culmination of Arthur's previous attempts to contact the Aborigines in a peaceful manner: in 1827, when he had unsuccessfully sought a person to undertake this task in the settled districts, and in 1828, when he had arranged for cartoon boards to be nailed on trees along the frontier depicting the government's desire for Aborigines and Europeans to live in harmony. Robinson may have got the idea of using the Aborigines as ambassadors as well as guides from the United States of America, where Indians assisted agents in visiting the major tribes to discuss treaty rights and obligations.

All the Aborigines in the party were anxious to make the journey. The Bruny Island people had no wish to return to the mission which had taken the lives of so many of their compatriots, Dray wanted to return to her own people at Port Davey, while Umarrah was ecstatic at his release from gaol. The convicts hoped to earn tickets-of-leave for

11. *Mr. G. A. Robinson* by Benjamin Duterrau. Tasmanian Museum and Art Gallery.

their exertions, and Robinson hoped to convince the Aborigines on the other side of the frontier that they could expect friendship from the government if they did not kill settlers. The party set off from Recherche Bay on 3 February 1830 to walk to Port Davey.

The Aborigines from the South West tribe were the most remote from European Tasmania, yet from their seasonal visits to the D'Entrecasteaux Channel they had been aware of European invasion from about 1804, when whalers and timber-getters paid seasonal visits to the area. Seasonal visits to the north-west brought contact with the sealers. But permanent invasion of their own territory did not take place until 1822, when a penal settlement was established at Macquarie Harbour, a pilot station was set up at Cape Sorell, and a temporary whaling station began operations from Port Davey.[7] Little was known of the level of interaction between the Europeans associated with these settlements and the four bands of the South West people — the Mimegin from the southern side of Macquarie Harbour, the Lowreenne from Low Rocky Point, the Ninene from Port Davey, and the Needwonnee from Cox Bight — but by 1830 their population had declined from between two hundred and three hundred to about sixty. Like the Bruny Island people, many were reported to have died from influenza and chest complaints.[8]

No white man had travelled the country between Recherche Bay and Port Davey before. Robinson found it dreary and cheerless. It was mountainous, with extensive marshes between the mountains, game was scarce and the rivers were bare of both scale fish and shellfish. He did not find a single Aboriginal on this part of the journey, although he travelled on the "native road" and saw nearly a hundred huts. He concluded that no Aborigines lived in that area, but made periodic, perhaps seasonal, visits, using the huts for shelter.[9]

It was not until 16 March, at Kellys Basin, that the Aborigines "descried the smoke of the natives' fire". In his first act of conciliation Robinson sent Woorraddy, Truganini, Pagerly, and Dray to make contact. He waited anxiously for a day, and eventually Woorraddy, Truganini and Pagerly returned. They had met the Port Davey people and Dray had stayed with them, for she had met her brother. Robinson was convinced that Dray had absconded and was most relieved when she returned the next morning with two young women. Leaving them at his tent as hostages, Robinson set off for the rest, taking eight of his own Aborigines and three convicts. But the Port Davey people were frightened by this large party of strangers and remained hidden. After two days of fruitless search, Robinson finally allowed Dray, her two companions, and Woorraddy to track them to their hiding place in thick scrub. Dray called to them to come out. An elderly woman

Map 34. The south-west coast: region of Robinson's expedition, February–
May 1830

emerged and was soon followed by the rest of the women and children.
They sat down by Robinson's fire and were then joined by the men,
who had been hunting. Robinson counted twenty-six in all, consisting
of ten couples and six children. He gave them biscuit and distributed
beads and ribbons, but they were suspicious of his intentions and

12. *Robinson meets Nee.ne.vuther and Tau.ter.rer* (Journal, 25 March 1830). Mitchell Library.

during the night they decamped, leaving behind three women. Thus the first encounter had met with mixed results.[10]

On 25 March, near the Giblin River, Robinson met two men, Neen-nevuther and Towterrer.

> They stood on the crown of the hill, holding in their hands a waddy with which they had been ahunting. Over their shoulders hung a kangaroo mantle. I made towards them with some difficulty, having a heavy pack on my back. . . . As soon as I came within hearing they called to the young women accompanying me who belonged to their tribe, to know if there was any NUM ("white man"), for they did not seem to heed me. A sullenness hung over their countenance and when I spoke they would not answer. As soon as the young women acquainted them that there was no NUM, they became cheerful and approached me and shook hands.[11]

The rest of the band, who had been hidden in the bush, then appeared. Among them was an old man who seemed to be the head of the tribe and his two wives and two daughters. Then one of the Port Davey women discovered three pistols in Robinson's knapsack, and he had to restrain Woorraddy, whose behaviour "had begun to excite their apprehensions". Robinson told them that he came not to injure them but to do them good. If they wished to accompany him they were welcome; if not, they would stop and he would proceed. The evening was spent in singing and dancing until a late hour.[12]

This band stayed with Robinson for four days, travelling up the coast to Little Rocky River at Elliott Bay. Then in the middle of the night they decamped. Dray said they were afraid of Woorraddy and of Black Tom and Umarrah, who had been guides with roving parties in the settled districts. When Robinson returned to Little Rocky River on 6 April with Dray he was delighted to meet some Aborigines from the earlier encounter, but they disappeared next morning, taking Dray with them.

On 18 April, at a lagoon at the mouth of the Hibbs River, he came across four more Aborigines. Timemedenene, one of the Port Davey women still with Robinson's party, knew them; one man, Treedareer, was in fact her brother. Robinson gave them blankets and beads and travelled on, with Treedareer joining them. About four miles further on they made a fire and Treedareer went in search of others from his band. He soon returned accompanied by an elderly woman named Pennerowner and her two sons. Robinson parted from them and the next day came across another family — a man named Leelinger and his wife and son and daughter. The daughter was so terrified by the presence of a white man that she plunged into the sea, and despite Truganini's attempts to reassure her, she would not come out.[13]

Robinson had now contacted about sixty Aborigines and had learnt something of the art of conciliation. He now knew he should not carry firearms, that he should travel with only a small party of people, and that he should try to live off the land to be independent of supply depots. Although the Port Davey people were wary and hostile, he considered they were unlikely to attack settlers in the settled districts and that if he returned in a year or so they would probably surrender to him. He had already formulated a plan to bring in all the Aborigines in the belief that he could save them from extinction or continued barbarousness, for he had no desire to civilize them in their own territory. Even in this remote part of the colony, Robinson believed these Aborigines were vulnerable to attack from sealers, settlers, soldiers, and stock-keepers. If the Aborigines surrendered to him voluntarily, he could remove them to an asylum where he could civilize them far from the settlers' guns; and the land the Aborigines vacated could be used by the settlers. Robinson was already convinced that only he could carry out this policy of "voluntary surrender" and thus save the reputation of the British government.

Robinson pressed on to Macquarie Harbour, where he wrote of his success to Arthur and prepared to continue his journey to the North

West tribe. On 12 May at Trial Harbour, north of the Little Henty River, Umarrah, Parwareter, and Trepanner escaped. Since they came from the Stoney Creek band of the North Midlands tribe, they knew the Aboriginal road east from Trial Harbour to Mount Vandyke back to the settled districts. Their escape indicated to Robinson his precarious relationship with the Aborigines. All three had proved helpful in making contact with the South West Aborigines, with whom they had no tribal animosities. Indeed, by the time Robinson reached Trial Harbour he placed more trust in these three than the other Aborigines in his party. So their escape was a severe blow to his prestige and control over the others.[14]

Unlike the South West Aborigines, the North West people had a long period of contact with Europeans, beginning with the sealers in 1804.[15] Their territory then supported at least eight bands and a population of four hundred to six hundred. By 1825 the sealers had hunted out most of the elephant seals as well as kangaroos on Robbins Island, forcing the band that usually resided there, the Parperloihener, to seek other places to forage, which created tension with other Aboriginal groups in the area. In December 1827 a group of sealers ambushed some Penne-mukeer people from Cape Grim opposite the Doughboys, intending to abduct the women. One of the Pennemukeer men hiding in a tree had thrown a spear at one of the sealers, who promptly shot him dead and then took seven women to Kangaroo Island.

A few weeks later, in January 1828, another group of sealers secreted themselves in a cave at the Doughboys to ambush a group of Pennemukeer women collecting muttonbirds and shellfish. As the women swam ashore the sealers rushed out with muskets, pushed fourteen women into an angle of the cliff, bound them with cords, and carried them off to Kangaroo Island. In revenge the Pennemukeer men had later clubbed three sealers to death. Most women acquired by the sealers were taken to Kangaroo Island, off the South Australian coast, or King Island at the western end of Bass Strait.

The Van Diemen's Land Company, which represented the last phase of pastoral expansion in Tasmania in the 1820s, occupied land at Circular Head and Cape Grim in 1826. When the Peerapper from West Point visited Cape Grim in November 1827 in search of muttonbird eggs and seals they found shepherds' huts and a large flock of sheep. The shepherds immediately tried to entice some Peerapper women into a hut, but the men objected and in the resulting skirmish a shepherd was wounded and a Peerapper man shot. In retaliation the Peerapper drove a mob of sheep over a cliff into the sea and speared and waddied 118 of them. Six weeks later four shepherds took the Pennemukeer

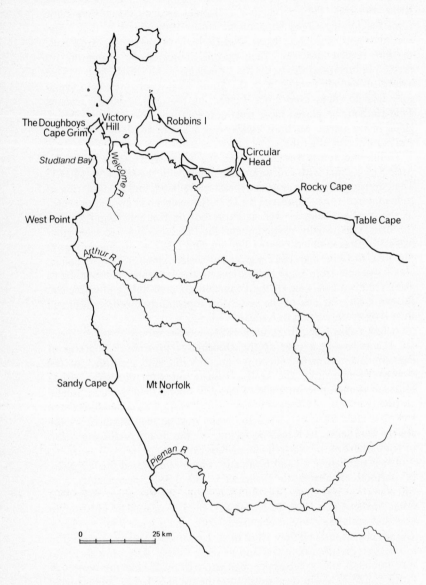

The Doughboys
Cape Grim
Victory Hill
Robbins I
Studland Bay
Welcome R
Circular Head
Rocky Cape
West Point
Table Cape
Arthur R
Sandy Cape
Mt Norfolk
Pieman R

0   25 km

Map 35. The north-west coast: region of Robinson's expedition, May–July 1830.

people by surprise while muttonbirding, massacred thirty, and flung them over that same sixty-metre-high cliff, now called Victory Hill.

After that the Pennemukeer called the white people at Cape Grim *Nowhummoe*, the devil, and when they heard the report of a gun they said that Nowhummoe had shot "another tribe of blacks". The Pennemukeer afterwards avoided the settlement at Cape Grim but plundered remote huts to obtain provisions.

In the spring of 1829 another Van Diemen's Land Company establishment was made at the Hampshire Hills which directly affected the Tommeginer people from Table Cape, the Parperloihener from Robbins Island, the Pennemukeer from Cape Grim and the Pendowte from Studland Bay. The shepherds wasted no time in acquiring women and in shooting Aboriginal men on sight. At the same time many sealers worked as boatmen and shepherds for the company.

In 1830 an Aboriginal man from the Parperloihener at Robbins Island visited the company's establishment at Circular Head for some months, having previously been with sealers. The company's manager, Edward Curr, hoped to entice more Aborigines to the establishment to employ them as shepherds, for he suffered an acute shortage of labour. The man, Nicermenic, fled when he was suspected of assisting his compatriots to raid stockhuts. By then the Pennemukeer and the Parperloihener had been forced to join larger groups like the Tommeginer from Table Cape, the Pendowte from Studland Bay and the Peerapper from West Point. Further down the coast the Manegin from the Arthur River, the Tarkinener from Sandy Cape, and the Peternidic from the Pieman River were less affected, but because their seasonal movements had been disrupted, the latter used the inland routes behind the company grants to reach Table Cape where they were in conflict with the Tommeginer. So the North West Aborigines were locked in a struggle with the Van Diemen's Land Company for control of their land.

On 23 May at the mouth of the Piemen River Robinson first saw Aborigines from the North West tribe, but they refused to meet him because they considered him an unwanted intruder. They shadowed him along the coastline until he reached the Van Diemen's Land Company establishment at Cape Grim on 14 June. Disappointed by the failure to make contact, he left gifts at their camp sites as a gesture of friendship. On 20 June, at the Welcome River, he met the sealers. With them were six Aboriginal women who had been abducted from the north-east several years before and a young man aged eighteen from Robbins Island called Pevay (also known as Tunnerminnerwait), who had come to them about a week before. Among the sealers was a Maori called Witieye, who had sold his land to Samuel Marsden to establish a

13. *The sealers' camp on the main near Robbins Island* (Journal, 20 June 1830). Mitchell Library.

mission. "He had two women and was head man among the sealers and considered the most honourable".[16] The others were an Englishman, Robert Drew, who had two sealing women; David Kelly; and Edward Tomlins, whose mother was Aboriginal and his father European. Robinson considered their activities immoral and told Witieye and Kelly that

> numerous complaints had reached the government as to the conduct of the sealers both in the eastern and in the western straits, and that numerous aggressions had been committed by them upon the aborigines of the colony. I said that I was not aware that the government had taken measures respecting them (it would perhaps depend on my report), but I assured them the government would do so should I report the necessity of such a thing, and if such an act should be passed it would make their situations very irksome.[17]

Robinson also told them he intended to make contact with every Aboriginal on the island and that if any told him of outrages by the sealers, he would bring the offenders before the courts. If they "conducted themselves with propriety", they would not be harmed. He told them that the government knew that the sealers had obtained the Aboriginal women by rushing upon them and shooting their husbands. He also said they would have to destroy their dogs because they killed too many kangaroos, which were the Aborigines' major form of subsistence. On 30 June he went to Robbins Island with Pevay and captured his brother Pendowtewer and Narrucer, a twenty-year-old woman from West Point.[18]

On 9 July Robinson set off for Emu Bay by way of Circular Head. On 27 July near the Cam River he captured Nicermenic, who had run away from the Van Diemen's Land Company not long before, and another Aboriginal man, Linermerrinnecer. He sent them to captivity in Launceston with Pendowtewer and Narrucer. Reaching Emu Bay, Robinson wrote to Arthur and told him of the success of his journey so far. But he warned that unless a plan was formulated for the quick removal of the North West people, the sealers and shepherds would exterminate them within a very short time. He also wrote to the Reverend William Bedford on the Aborigines Committee and told him that had the opportunity existed to make this kind of contact with the Aborigines some years before, cordial relations could have been reached.[19]

The North tribe, whose country Robinson was about to travel through, were struggling with the Van Diemen's Land Company — which had establishments at Emu Bay and the Surrey Hills, Hampshire Hills, and Middlesex Plains — for control of their country. The four bands — the Plairhekehillerplue from Emu Bay, the Punnilerpanner from Port Sorell, the Noeteeler from the Hampshire Hills, and the Pallittorre from Quamby Bluff — were the guardians of the ochre mines at Mount Housetop and Mount Vandyke, and also confronted the second wave of pastoral settlement moving westbound from Norfolk Plains along the Meander River to Avenue Plains.

In this second wave of pastoral expansion, settlers and stock-keepers were far less charitable towards the Aborigines than their counterparts of 1823.[20] And since the North people had experienced long contact with sealers, they too were less charitable towards the new invaders. Thus when conflict broke out in June 1827, it was more intense than in other parts of the settled districts. Between June 1827 and September 1830 the North people fell in number from two hundred to sixty. One stock-keeper shot nineteen people with a swivel gun charged with nails; another shot a group of Aborigines while offering them food; another ripped open the stomach of an Aboriginal while offering him a piece of bread at the end of a knife; others offered them poisoned flour. A party of soldiers from the 40th Regiment killed ten at the Western Marshes.

The North people resisted these assaults by killing stockmen trespassing on the road to the ochre mines at the Gog and Magog mountains, by systematically besieging their huts for plunder and firearms, and by spearing their cattle. At the Meander River in May 1830 a party of North people entered a settler's hut during his temporary absence, but while the two assigned servants were ploughing in sight of the hut, and carried off nearly all its "moveables", recognizing that only by

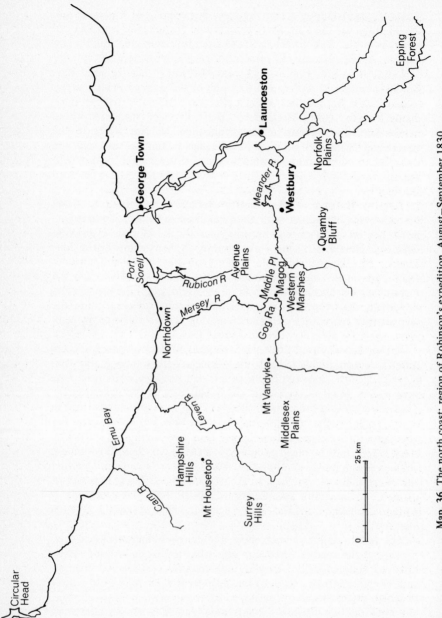

Map. 36. The north coast: region of Robinson's expedition, August—September 1830.

Circular Head

Emu Bay

Cam R

Mt Housetop

Hampshire Hills

Surrey Hills

Leven R

Northdown

Port Sorell

Rubicon R

Mersey R

Avenue Plains

Middle Pl

Gog Ra

Mt Vandyke

Middlesex Plains

Magog

Western Marshes

George Town

Launceston

Meander R

Westbury

Quamby Bluff

Norfolk Plains

Epping Forest

25 km

0

destroying the white man's environment would he leave the area. One of the North people ran from the hut with a bag of sugar, weighing about fifty-nine kilograms, while others took loaded guns. There was considerable fear that the North people would use these guns.

In July the Pallittorre disputed territory occupied by stock-keepers and successfully drove them off. A short time later their leader, Quamby, was shot. In that same month a number of stock-keepers at Middle Plain, in quest of cattle, fell in with some Plairhekehillerplue people. They drove them into a small lagoon and there shot several, then drove the rest to the foot of a mountain and shot them, except for an old man and an old woman who begged for mercy. In August a woman was shot by two Van Diemen's Land Company shepherds in the Epping Forest and at the mouth of the Leven River; another at Emu Bay was abducted, kept tied up for a month, and then shot. The Punnilerpanner from Port Sorell were harassed by military parties and picked off one by one; women were shot and burnt in fires; soldiers killed children by beating their heads with sticks; one man pursued by a soldier jumped into a lagoon, letting only his head remain above water. He was dragged out and bayoneted in the belly.

But the North people were not without leaders. At the end of 1828, the settlers were confronted by the Plairhekehillerplue led by a woman, Tarerenorerer, or as she was known by the sealers, Walyer. As a young woman she had been abducted by Aborigines from Port Sorell and exchanged for dogs and flour to the sealers. After living with them for some years she had escaped in 1828 and become the leader of the Emu Bay people, whom she taught to use firearms. Walyer was known to stand on a hill and give orders to her men to attack the whites, taunting them to come out of their huts and be speared.

On 6 August Robinson left Emu Bay for the Hampshire Hills, taking two assigned servants and the Aborigines Woorraddy, Black Tom, Robert, Pagerly, and Truganini. Pevay was his guide. At the Hampshire Hills some shepherds told him that they would shoot Aborigines whenever they found them. These attitudes, Robinson realized, provided plenty of reasons for the Aborigines to retaliate. He wrote in his journal:

> The children have witnessed the massacre of their parents and their relations carried away into captivity by these merciless invaders, their country has been taken from them, and the kangaroo, their chief subsistence, have been slaughtered wholesale for the sake of paltry lucre. Can we wonder then at the hatred they bear to the white inhabitants? This enmity is not the effect of a moment. Like a fire burning underground, it has burst forth. This flame of aboriginal resentment can and ought only to be extinguished by British benevo-

lence. We should fly to their relief. We should make some atonement for the misery we have entailed upon the original proprietors of this land.[21]

When he arrived back at Emu Bay on 5 September he learnt that the Aborigines he had sent on to Launceston had, by government order, been sent back to Cape Grim and had absconded at Circular Head. Arthur was unwilling to place in captivity Aborigines from the other side of the frontier. Robinson was angry. He considered that he now knew more about the Aborigines than anyone, and to send them back was to "subject them to the twofold dangers of being either shot by the sealers or by a stockkeeper or shepherd of the Company, or slain by some hostile aborigines".[22] Since the officials had not explained to the Aborigines why the government was letting them go, Robinson was concerned they would pride themselves in having outwitted the whites and thus lessen his authority over the Aborigines he hoped to capture.

On 13 September Robinson continued towards Launceston. On 16 September at the Mersey River he saw fresh prints of the Aborigines from the North tribe, but lost sight of them at Port Sorell. The following day he heard them on the other side of the water, where they had gathered to collect swans' eggs. Then again on 20 September he saw them at the Rubicon River. They were part of Walyer's band, and he realized that they were stalking him with the probable intention of killing him. He wanted to capture them, but since his earlier captives had been freed, he saw no point.

When he returned to the mouth of Port Sorell, Robinson found that the coxswain and the Aborigines he had left behind — Black Tom, Pagerly, and Robert — had tracked two Aboriginal youths from Circular Head who knew Pevay, William Parker, overseer of Captain Thomas's nearby property of Northdown, said he was pleased the boys had been captured because "he would have shot them had he seen them".[23] (Thomas and Parker were killed by the Aborigines the following year.) These boys had been found near Launceston a short time before, but like those captured by Robinson, had been freed by the government. The next day they absconded with Pevay.

Robinson relized that they would attempt to join Pendowtewer, Narrucer, and Linermerrinnecer. Again his authority had been challenged and he was concerned they would lead the Aborigines still in the bush in raids against the shepherds and sealers, and even against himself. At these moments he felt beleaguered, for the mission Aborigines were by no means trustworthy and preferred the uncertainties of the bush to the certainties of gaol. Yet he was learning more about the art of conciliation. Now he always carried tea and damper — the bushman's bread made from flour and water and baked in hot ashes — for the

Aborigines, and if he travelled swiftly they would stay with him. In future he would take fewer Europeans, for they were disruptive to his relations with the Aborigines and were reluctant to adopt the rigorous lifestyle. Since the convicts he took were dependent upon his recommending their tickets-of-leave, Robinson expected them to show servility, gratitude, and unquestioning obedience. In their turn the convicts saw Robinson as a lower-class upstart, intent upon making his fortune capturing blacks. His inability to work with Europeans of all classes became a feature of all the missions.

On 24 September Robinson reached Westbury on the Meander River, where he read of the proclamations announcing the forthcoming military operations against the Aborigines in the settled districts – the Black Line. At George Town and Launceston he found the colonists eagerly preparing to do battle with Aborigines and with trepidation went to Ross in the heart of the settled districts to confer with Arthur about the next phase of his mission. He wondered whether conciliation or even voluntary capture could continue.

Robinson had completed a remarkable journey. Despite lack of assistance from the commandant at the penal settlement at Macquarie Harbour, and from the manager of the Van Diemen's Land Company, and despite an acute shortage of provisions and a fearful winter, he had contacted most of the South West Aborigines, had sighted some of the North West people, and had avoided the aggressions of Walyer's people from the North tribe. He was now satisfied that relations between Aborigines and Europeans had become too fractured for the Van Diemen's Land government to allow the Aborigines beyond the settled districts to remain in their own country for much longer. He was convinced that he could entice them to surrender voluntarily at no distant future and be compensated for the loss of their land by placing them in a sanctuary arranged by the government and where they could learn the art of civilization and Christianity.

NOTES

1. Plomley, *Friendly Mission*, p. 56.
2. *HRA*, I, xiv, p. 54 ff.; R. H. W. Reece, *Aborigines and Colonists* (Sydney: Sydney University Press, 1974), chap. 2; Plomley, *Friendly Mission*, pp. 57–58.
3. Plomley, *Friendly Mission*, pp. 62–63.
4. Robinson to Arthur, 12 June 1829, ML A612; Plomley, *Friendly Mission*, pp. 63–69.
5. Plomley, *Friendly Mission*, pp. 69–77.
6. Ibid., p. 89.
7. M. D. McRae, "Port Davey and the South West", *P&P THRA* 8 (1960): 48.

8. Plomley, *Friendly Mission,* pp. 124–25.
9. Ibid.
10. Ibid., pp. 130–35.
11. Ibid., p. 137.
12. Ibid., pp. 137–38.
13. Ibid., pp. 154–55.
14. Ibid., p. 160.
15. Information in the following six paragraphs has been taken from Plomley, *Friendly Mission,* pp. 178–84, 234; Rhys Jones, "A Speculative Archaeological Sequence for North Western Tasmania", *RQVM,* n.s. 25 (Dec. 1966): 7; N. B. Tindale, "Results of the Harvard-Adelaide Universities Anthropological Expedition", *RQVM,* n.s. 2 (1953): 29–37; A. L. Meston, "The Van Diemen's Land Company 1825–1842", *RQVM,* n.s. 9 (June 1958): 29; Rhys Jones, "Rocky Cape and the Problem of the Tasmanians" (PhD thesis, University of Sydney, 1971), p. 47.
16. Plomley, *Friendly Mission,* p. 180.
17. Ibid.
18. Ibid., p. 184.
19. Ibid., p. 235.
20. Information in the following four paragraphs has been taken from Plomley, *Friendly Mission,* pp. 182, 210, 217–19, 553; Smith to col. sec., 8 July 1828, TSA CSO 1/316; Curr to col. sec., 17 Dec. 1829, TSA CSO 1/330; *HTC,* 29 May 1830.
21. Plomley, *Friendly Mission,* pp. 202–3.
22. Ibid., p. 209.
23. Ibid., p. 216.

9

From Conciliator to Captor

When Robinson met Arthur at Ross on 6 October 1830, his immediate objective was to organize an expedition to "rescue" the sealing women in Bass Strait.[1] There were two reasons for this. Robinson considered that the women would prove useful in forming a bridge between the civilized European lifestyle and the uncivilized Aboriginal. But more importantly Robinson recognized that in "rescuing" the sealing women he was raising his own prestige among the Aboriginal men and so placing them in his debt. If he rescued the Aboriginal women in Bass Strait, the Aboriginal men would be more willing to assist him in tracking down other Aborigines in Van Diemen's Land.

But Arthur wanted Robinson to participate in the Black Line, which was about to begin its great sweep across the south-eastern part of the island. Robinson had some difficulty in persuading Arthur that the mission Aborigines risked being shot by the gun-happy settlers. Besides, Robinson did not want to participate in an operation that would make the Aborigines more hostile rather than less so. So he convinced Arthur that he should move to the north-east, where he would be well placed to capture any Aborigines that might slip through the Line and could also rescue the sealing women from Bass Strait. Arthur also agreed that he should establish a temporary asylum for the Aborigines on Swan Island and explore some of the larger Bass Strait islands as a possible permanent asylum for the Aborigines. Both men estimated there were about a hundred Aborigines in the eastern part of the island. They would be surprised after a few months to find that there were only about forty.

In the following year, from October 1830 to December 1831, Robinson would search for Aborigines who were associated with the settled districts and with the sealers. They would not only prove difficult to catch; they would confront his view that it was best that they should be removed from their own country and be introduced to the benefits of Christianity. He would find that they resented losing their country and considered they had been badly treated by the government and the settlers. So in order to gain their support Robinson would have to mislead them about his intentions. The sense of adventure that permeated his first expedition to the west coast disappeared and the complexities of the role of conciliator were to test him severely.

The Aborigines that Robinson went to capture in the north-east in October 1830 had had long contact with sealers and settlers. They were remnant groups of desperadoes engaged in a tenacious war with the settlers, so they were unlikely to be friendly to an unarmed European when every other man in the colony was out hunting for them. This expedition would establish Robinson's reputation as a hunter and bagger of Aborigines.

Robinson found the north-east flat, open country, abounding in kangaroos and small animals, with river estuaries stocked with birds and shellfish and the coastline providing an abundance of muttonbirds and seals. Indeed it was the best country for Aborigines he had seen and well suited for that Aboriginal reserve Arthur had gazetted in 1828. Robinson travelled up to forty kilometres a day across open heath country between the Piper River and George Bay, sometimes hugging the coastline, sometimes taking inland Aboriginal roads. On 31 October near the source of the Anson River, sixteen kilometres from the coast, he was rewarded by signs of Aboriginal fires. The next day he found an Aboriginal hut. As he approached it, a number of very large and fierce dogs surrounded it. Bullrer, one of two women recently rescued from the sealers, called out. Soon an Aboriginal man, Mannalargenna, approached and she explained why they had come. The man embraced Robinson and then introduced him to his six Aboriginal companions, four men and two women. Another man and a woman remained hidden in the bush.

Robinson told Mannalargenna and his companions about the military expedition out against his people by tracing in the sand with a stick the nature and formation of the Black Line and told him that the military parties before long would be in the north-east. "In reply to this preamble they complained in bitter terms of the injuries to which they and their progenitors had been exposed through the medium of the whites."[2] Robinson then told them of his plan to visit the islands in Bass Strait to fetch the sealing women and that he proposed to go to Swan Island to keep out of the way of the settlers and the soldiers' guns. He made some tea and then told them that the sooner they joined him the better, for the soldiers were coming. They agreed to go with him and went to look for the other man and woman, but they would not come out.[3]

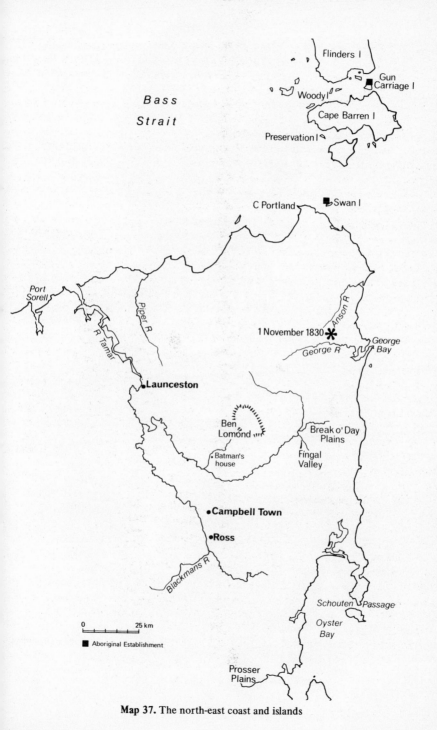

Map 37. The north-east coast and islands

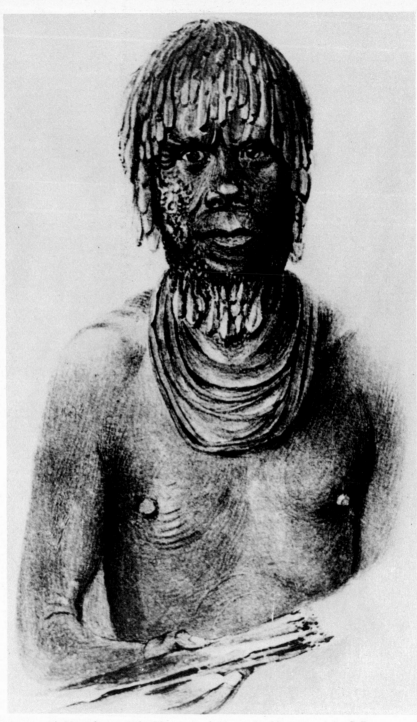

14. *Mannalangenna*, by Thomas Bock. Tasmanian Museum and Art Gallery.

Mannalargenna was a chief from north Oyster Bay. He had heard of Robinson from two Aboriginal women Arthur had released from Hobart Town some months before. Mannalargenna and his companions had recently been with about twenty other Aborigines from the Ben Lomond tribe and the Great Swanport and Stoney Creek bands to Blackmans River to fight the Big River people with whom they had been in conflict over women. On their return to the east coast across the Midlands Plain, three of their compatriots had been shot in an encounter with a military party. In revenge the Ben Lomond people had followed their assailants, waited until they were asleep beside a campfire, and killed two of them. Then to the east of Campbell Town they had met the Black Line and had to separate. Three had gone to look for more Aborigines near the Piper River, another six had gone to Schouten Passage at Oyster Bay to get swans' eggs, and Mannalargenna and eight others had gone to John Batman's house at Ben Lomond to free four Aboriginal women and a boy captured the year before. There, Mannalargenna realized that if they were to preserve their dogs and to make contact with the others who had gone to find the Port Dalrymple people, they must again separate. So he and eight others had moved towards the north-east while the other four had gone towards the Piper River. Mannalargenna's party had been in the George River area for about six days when Robinson found them.[4]

These were the first Aborigines Robinson had captured who had consistently attacked the settlers and their property. Mannalargenna had an intimate knowledge of the settled districts and was to prove a vital guide in the rest of Robinson's missions in Van Diemen's Land.

Robinson took his new captives to Swan Island on 4 November and five days later set off with the two women rescued from the sealers, Bullrer and Tib, for the Bass Strait islands to search for other sealing women. At that time there were about thirty white men and twenty-five Aboriginal women in the eastern strait, scattered in small communities from Preservation Island to the Kent Group. After brief visits to the sealing camps on Preservation and Woody islands, Robinson landed at Gun Carriage Island, where he found a substantial settlement. Only one sealer was in residence, the rest having fled after hiding the Aboriginal women among the rocks and warning them that Robinson would shoot if he found them. Despite this, Bullrer located three women and Robinson returned to Swan Island in triumph on 15 November.

In his absence an Aboriginal woman and six men had arrived at Swan Island. So within two weeks, Robinson had captured fourteen Aborigines and rescued three sealing women. Led by Wareternatterlargener, from the Piper River band, the newly arrived Aborigines had left

Mannalargenna's group in October 1830 in search of their compatriots
who had gone to Schouten Passage. At Break o' Day Plains on 1
November two had been shot. Fearing to continue south, and confront
the Black Line, they had turned north and, seeing "friendly" smoke
on Swan Island, arrived opposite it on 14 November. All the Aborigines
now exchanged stories of relatives and friends who had been killed by
soldiers and settlers while defending their country.[5]

Wareternatterlargener and Mannalargenna told Robinson that only
two groups of Aborigines remained in the north-east. One, led by
Umarrah, was in the Tamar Valley, and the other was in the Fingal
Valley. This meant that only four groups of Aborigines remained on the
periphery of the settled districts — the two in the north-east, the Big
River people, and the remnants of the North tribe at Port Sorell. The
rest of the Aborigines were beyond the frontier on the west coast.

Robinson now decided to concentrate upon organizing the asylum
on Swan Island into some form of Aboriginal establishment and to
send his coxswain, James Parish, to search for more sealing women.
Parish had immediate success and returned to Swan Island on 19
December with eleven women. The Aboriginal community now comprised about forty people, almost evenly divided between the sexes.
They plunged into new social relationships, performed ceremonial
dances, hunted birds and their eggs, and completely ignored Robinson's
attempts to move them into huts or to attend his makeshift Sunday
services.[6]

The sealing women proved the greatest disappointment. Apart from
creating their own ceremonials and lingua franca, they had developed
some immunity to European disease, adjusted to permanent habitation,
and had some form of European dress. Their familiarity with European
customs had led Robinson to believe that they would play an important
role in introducing the other Aborigines to European civilization.
Instead they became his harshest critics and consistently refused to
assist in any programme of "civilization".

One of the women, Walyer, Robinson had last seen at Port Sorell
three months before. Since then she had been captured by two sealers
and taken to an island in eastern Bass Strait. There she refused to work
for the sealers, who then decided to isolate her on Penguin Island, but
during the voyage there she had attempted to kill them and would have
succeeded had not Parish appeared. The sealers were very pleased to
give her up. At Swan Island Walyer circulated a story that a boat had
gone to Launceston to bring soldiers to shoot the Aborigines or to send
them to gaol, where they would have fetters put on their legs. Robinson
was forced to send her away with Parish on his next trip to Bass Strait
so that he could maintain order, but when she returned at the end of

December she had, within a few hours, "thrown the whole of the natives into a state of alarm by telling them the white people intended shooting them".[7] Walyer told Robinson that she liked *lutetawin*, the white man, as much as a black snake. He was relieved when she died of influenza at the end of May 1831.

When he had achieved some stability among the inmates of his fledgling asylum at Swan Island, Robinson set off for Hobart Town early in January 1831 with his most trusted Aboriginal companions, Tom and Pagerly and Woorraddy and Truganini, and one of the sealing women, Tekartee, to discuss with Arthur and the Aborigines Committee the future of his mission. Arthur was pleased with Robinson's work and increased his salary from £100 to £250 a year, with a gratuity of £100 as well as a maximum land grant of 1,036 hectares.[8] With the Black Line completed, Arthur was now anxious for Robinson to capture all the Aborigines remaining in the settled districts, particularly the Big River people. But Robinson feared to venture into Big River country so soon after the Black Line, for every settler, stock-keeper, and soldier was "extirpationist to a man" and he feared for the safety of the mission Aborigines. He managed instead to persuade Arthur of the need to establish a new asylum for the captured Aborigines, to rescue more sealing women, and to capture the other Aborigines in the settled districts, besides beginning to plan a programme for their civilization.

The problem of what to do with the captured Aborigines had bothered Arthur since 1828. In that year he had set aside the unsettled north-east of Van Diemen's Land as a reserve in the hope that the Aborigines from the settled districts would permanently retreat there and thus relieve him of any further concern for their welfare. But when this plan had failed by 1830 he set aside Tasman Peninsula as the obvious place to drive the Aborigines during the Black Line. This too had failed. Robinson now convinced Arthur that no area in Van Diemen's Land was suitable or safe for an asylum for the Aborigines from the settled districts and that the only solution was an island. So Arthur instructed the Aborigines Committee to find a suitable one.

Chief Justice Pedder, however, was not convinced that an island was a just solution. He pressed the government to negotiate with the Aboriginal chiefs for a treaty whereby their tribes would not pass beyond defined boundaries and where government agents could live among them, as with the Indian tribes in America, in order to protect both the Aborigines and the settlers. Pedder argued that if the Aborigines were sent to an island they would soon pine away "when they found their situation one of hopeless imprisonment, within bounds so narrow as necessarily to deprive them of those habits and customs which are the charms of their savage life; he meant their known love of change of place, their periodical distant migrations, their expeditions in search of game, and that unbounded liberty of which they had hitherto been in the enjoyment".[9]

Robinson's response was inadequate. While he agreed that a few years before such an option could have been possible, he now considered it was too late for a treaty. The chiefs had little influence over their tribes, government agents could never sufficiently protect the Aborigines from sealers and stock-keepers, and it was doubtful whether the Aborigines would accept whites living among them. Above all, he was convinced the Aborigines would only respond to Christianity when they had been stripped of their land and their culture. Then they would be grateful for his efforts.

Arthur agreed. While it might be possible, he wrote to the secretary of state, to send agents to the Aborigines in the west, the Aborigines in the settled districts should "be drawn by every mild excitement to resort to the Aboriginal Establishment . . . for, even if they should pine away in the manner the Chief Justice apprehends, it is better that they should meet with their death in that way, whilst every act of kindness is manifested towards them, than that they should fall a sacrifice to the inevitable consequences of their continued acts of outrage upon the white inhabitants."[10]

While the chief justice rightly saw the loss of their land as the means of the Aborigines' probable extinction, Robinson and Arthur pretended that removal from their land was the means for the Aborigines' possible survival. Arthur also did not wish to see the Aborigines dying like heroes in the face of British guns. The fate of the Aborigines of Van Diemen's Land was sealed. From now on Robinson would be the capturer rather than the conciliator of the Aborigines. Despite the failure of the Bruny Island Aboriginal Establishment in 1829 and the impending failure of the establishments in Bass Strait, Robinson never doubted that removing the Aborigines from their own country was necessary for their salvation.

In recommending a suitable island for a permanent Aboriginal establishment, the Aborigines Committee were easily persuaded by Robinson's suggestion of Gun Carriage Island, on the grounds that it had fresh water, a safe anchorage, and access to Cape Barren Island for hunting. Three kilometres long and almost two and a half kilometres wide and situated between Flinders and Cape Barren islands, Gun Carriage Island also had sealers' huts ready for immediate occupation and an abundance of muttonbirds and shellfish. It was also about thirty kilometres from the mainland of Van Diemen's Land, too far for Aboriginal escape but close enough for easy transportation of stores and supplies. Arthur appointed Robinson superintendent of the Aborigines and authorized him to evict the sealers from Gun Carriage Island and to rescue more sealing women. The capture of the remaining four groups of Aborigines in the settled districts would be undertaken by Daniel Clucas, who would search for Umarrah in the Tamar Valley, by Anthony Cottrell, who had to find the Aborigines in the Fingal Valley, and by Alexander McKay, who would locate the Port Sorell Aborigines. Robinson would search for the Big River people after he had set up the Aboriginal Establishment on Gun Carriage Island.[11]

He arrived at Gun Carriage Island on 31 March 1831 with fifty-one Aborigines. After evicting the sealers and rescuing two more Aboriginal women from their clutches, Robinson made the pretence of establishing a European style community by allocating huts to favoured Aboriginal couples in the hope that they would begin cultivating gardens, that sure sign of adjustment to European civilization. After a fruitless expedition to other islands in Bass Strait in search of more sealing women, Robinson returned to Gun Carriage Island on 30 April to find that two Aborigines had already died and fifteen others were in "a sickly state". The surgeon, Andrew Maclachlan, pointed to the "bleakness of this place and the want of proper habitation" and the insufficient water supply as possible reasons for their illness. No doubt Robinson had been more attracted by the sealers' huts and gardens than by any understanding of the need for extensive supplies of fresh water and Aboriginal food resources. An island the size of Gun Carriage could not sustain sixty Aborigines for very long. As well, they were reacting to forcible removal, enforced confinement, and the loss of control over their own lives. Robinson's favoured Aboriginal couples would not dig their gardens; nor would they sleep in their huts, for they said that "if they slept outside the devil would cure them".[12]

By the beginning of June Robinson confronted a new set of problems. Daniel Clucas proved unsuitable as a conciliator, and the sealers complained to Arthur about Robinson's appropriation of their Aboriginal wives. Arthur ordered Robinson to return a number of the women and forced him to accept the sealers' services in rounding up some Aborigines in the north-east.[13] Robinson was enraged. His prestige was immediately diminished among the male Aborigines at the establishment, while the sealers were a constant irritant to his own plans for conciliation. He did not have their activities checked until October 1831. With all these uncertainties, Robinson decided to search for Umarrah and his band himself. So he returned to Swan Island as a base camp, leaving the surgeon, Andrew Maclachlan, to oversee the increasing number of Aborigines dying on Gun Carriage Island. Robinson refused to take responsibility for these deaths, blaming Maclachlan for incompetence and the convict guards for molesting the Aboriginal women.[14] At no stage did he acknowledge the psychological or the physical surroundings or the inadequate rations as more likely causes.

The capture of Umarrah took almost as long as the expedition up the west coast the year before. For two months Robinson, with seven mission Aborigines, Tom and Pagerly, Woorraddy and Truganini, the sealing woman Tib, and the two boys Robert and Richard, criss-crossed the entire north-east from the Piper River to the Little Mussel Roe River without success. The mission Aborigines were as anxious not to locate Umarrah as Robinson was to find him. They had tasted the horrors of institutionalized life on Gun Carriage Island and were determined never to return. Instead, they used these months attempting to incorporate Robinson into their own system of mutual reciprocity, for they knew he was dependent upon their skills. So they hunted, held ceremonies, told stories, and taught Robinson new Aboriginal languages. By 1 August he realized that they would never find Umarrah.

In a desperate move Robinson fetched from Gun Carriage Island four other Aborigines to assist in the mission. They were Mannalargenna and his wife, Tanleboneyer, and a youth named Timmy from Cape Portland, all of whom knew the north-east well, and Pevay, who had been recaptured after absconding at Port Sorell and sent to Gun Carriage Island. To enlist Mannalargenna's support in his quest for Umarrah, Robinson promised him that if the Aborigines "would desist from their wonted outrages upon the whites, they would be allowed to remain in their respective districts and would have flour, tea and sugar, clothes &c given them; that a good white man would dwell with them who would take care of them and would not allow any bad white man to shoot them, and he would go about with them in the bush like myself and they then could hunt."[15]

In saying this, Robinson was not only deluding Mannalargenna into believing that he could return to his own country if he would capture Umarrah; he was also resorting to the arguments used by Chief Justice Pedder, whom he had derided some months before. Nevertheless, now that he was in the north-east, an area that had yet to attract European settlement, Robinson may have seen the possibility of the Aborigines remaining there. And Arthur had hinted at such a possibility in June when he wrote to Robinson that "whether the natives will or will not go to the establishment they should be conciliated by every possible means and promised food, clothing and protection if they will only be pacific and desist from the outrages which they have been in the habit of committing."[16] Possibly the high death rate at Gun Carriage Island may have led Robinson briefly to reconsider his opposition to agents living amongst the Aborigines. More probably Robinson, in a desperate situation, was prepared to use desperate measures to achieve his objective – the capture of Umarrah.

Robinson also realized that in their environment he was completely dependent upon the Aborigines. He quickly perceived that Mannalargenna had as much interest in finding Umarrah as his mission Aborigines. He wrote in his journal on 16 August: "it was risking a great weight of responsibility to attach this chief to my party, and every little absence by him is the occasion of painful forebodings, fully sensible it is what the evil-minded would feel pleasure in, and no doubt it would incur the displeasure of the government." [17]

It was not until 28 August, after several criss-crossings of the northeast, that Mannalargenna finally located Umarrah and his band of about fifteen Aborigines near Noland Bay. Umarrah was a most important prize for Robinson, because he was the best-known resistance fighter against the Europeans in the settled districts. Originally a member of the Stoney Creek band, he had led a series of raids against the settlers in the Campbell Town area between 1826 and 1828. Umarrah was never in any doubt that the Europeans were appropriating his country. When martial law was declared in November 1828, Umarrah and a band of Stoney Creek people had been captured near Great Swanport. [18]

Arthur had sent him to join a roving party, but he had soon escaped. When recaptured a few days later he had been sent to Richmond Gaol, where he had spent all of 1829. Then in January 1830 he had been released to join Robinson's expedition to the west coast. Robinson had found him the most articulate, diligent and useful member of his party, particularly in arranging meetings with the Aborigines from the southwest. But in May 1830 Umarrah and two other Aborigines had escaped north of Macquarie Harbour and had taken the Aboriginal road from Trial Harbour back to the settled districts. By October he had reached Launceston, where Arthur had appointed him a guide for the Black Line. But he had again escaped and joined some Port Dalrymple Aborigines along the Tamar River. They had spent the summer of 1830/31 in the Ben Lomond Tier making occasional forays into the North Esk River valley to plunder shepherds' huts for provisions. At the end of January 1831 they had attacked farms on both sides of the Tamar and North Esk rivers, spearing settlers and horses and taking provisions. Between January and July they had killed three settlers along the Tamar River, wounded five shepherds and taken four muskets, two pistols, and a bayonet. But there is no evidence that these firearms had ever been used. [19]

Robinson was under no illusions about Umarrah's propensity to

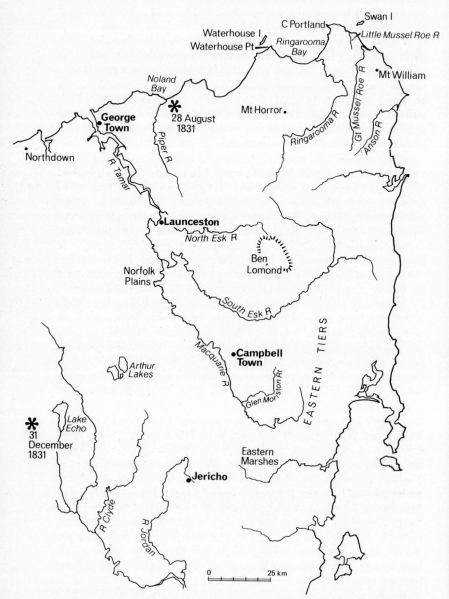

Map 38. North-eastern Tasmania: region of Robinson's expedition, August–December 1831

escape. As well, Umarrah and Mannalargenna were old enemies. Neither wanted to leave his own country, let alone go to that island in Bass Strait. Robinson spent the month of September hunting with with them and his mission Aborigines trying to devise some plan to remove them. Finally he made a second false promise to Mannalargenna: he would not be made to go to Bass Strait if he helped Robinson to put Umarrah and his band of Aborigines on Waterhouse Island. He also promised Umarrah that he would not send him to Bass Strait if he assisted in the search for the Big River people.[20] With Umarrah's capture, only one group of Aborigines, far less hostile than Umarrah and his band, remained in the north-east. Anthony Cottrell would capture them at north Oyster Bay in January 1832.

Arthur now pressed Robinson to search for the Big River people. He also accepted in principle Robinson's suggestion that Campbell Town should become a refuge for Mannalargenna and Umarrah and the mission Aborigines when the Big River people had been captured.[21] Once again Robinson was responding to pressure from the mission Aborigines for fear they would abscond. Both Arthur and Robinson knew that the settlers would not tolerate any asylum for the Aborigines in the heart of the settled districts. Once again Robinson was prepared to mislead Mannalargenna and the mission Aborigines with false promises.

Robinson set off from Campbell Town on 15 October 1831 in search of the Big River people with thirteen mission Aborigines — the youths Richard, Timmy, Lacklay, and Pevay, the couples Tom and Pagerly, Woorraddy and Truganini, Mannalargenna and Tanleboneyer, and Umarrah and Woolaytopinneyer, and the sealing woman Tib. He also had three servants, his son George, a clerk, and seven dogs and a horse.

At first they went east across the Eastern Tiers, and then southeasterly to the Eastern Marshes, thinking that if the Big River people had gone to Oyster Bay for the winter, they could be intercepted on their return to the high country to the west. Again Robinson found the country "peculiarly adapted" for the Aborigines, "consisting of thickly wooded hills and small open plains of grassy land which are surrounded with forest. There are open forest hills which abound with patches of grass, and afford shelter and food for the kangaroo."[22]

Robinson was now in the heart of the settled districts. Although he avoided the major roads and settlers' homesteads, he encountered at least six armed Europeans within a week of setting out, unlike in the north-east, where there were no armed settlers or military. Since Mannalargenna and Umarrah were at war with the Big River people, they had no desire to meet up with them. They began a series of stalling tactics which infuriated Robinson. Mannalargenna pretended to consult his "devil" to find the direction of the Big River people, while Umarrah entertained the party each evening with stories, "many of them so long as to take upwards of an hour in reciting, keeping them awake listening to his relation until twelve or one o'clock".[23] On 29 October Robinson abandoned his search in the Midlands and turned west, convinced that the Big River people were in their own country. But again the Aborigines stalled. Some said the Big River country was cold and that many devils lived there. Mannalargenna protested that he was an old man and he would soon die if he walked much.[24]

Taking the Aboriginal road through Jericho, Robinson crossed the Launceston–Hobart road on 4 November and then the Jordan and Clyde rivers, reaching Lake Echo on 8 November where he saw Aboriginal smoke. But none of the mission Aborigines wanted to pursue it. Then began a long chase of two months with the mission Aborigines using every possible means to divert Robinson from his objective. He found them "less diligent, less assiduous, less obedient than on former occasions." [25]

Tom, Umarrah, and Mannalargenna guided the party in the direction opposite to their quarry on a number of occasions. Their nightly ceremonials, their careless behaviour in killing animals, and their general contempt of the settlers and stock-keepers drove Robinson to a fury. While he was using the Aborigines to reach the Big River people, they were using him to buy time, to incorporate him into their own system of mutual reciprocity and to delay any departure for Bass Strait. Richard absconded near Norfolk Plains, where he had spent his childhood in the home of a settler, and while they were at the Arthur Lakes Woolaytopinneyer tried to abscond with the women to join the Big River people.[26] Although Robinson had accepted the departure of Dray from his party to join the South East people on the west coast the year before, he could not accept such behaviour now.

The party came upon the Big River people west of Lake Echo on 31 December 1831. The twenty-six of them represented the largest group Robinson was to capture at any one time in all his missions. Arriving at Hobart Town on 7 January 1832, they were despatched to Bass Strait ten days later. Robinson had captured the last of the Aborigines in the settled districts. He had made all the spectacular captures, at considerable personal cost. He had spent at least six months of 1831 in the bush with a group of Aborigines who were becoming increasingly disillusioned with his promises to allow them to remain in their own country. Robinson may seriously have considered other alternatives to Bass Strait when he promised the mission Aborigines some kind of asylum in Van Diemen's Land, but he also recognized that while they remained in their own country, they would fight for it and would not accept the consolation of Christianity. A mutual dependence had developed between the mission Aborigines and Robinson, and from now on a certain bitterness and ambivalence would develop.

NOTES

1. Plomley, *Friendly Mission*, p. 436 (n. 6).
2. Ibid., p. 438 (n. 44).
3. Ibid., pp. 254–55, 259–63.
4. Gray, 19 and 24 Oct. 1830, TSA CSO 1/316.
5. Plomley, *Friendly Mission*, pp. 275–76.
6. Ibid., pp. 285, 294–97.
7. Ibid., p. 304.
8. Ibid., p. 447 (n. 110).
9. *Mil. Ops*, p. 82.
10. Ibid., p. 79.
11. Ibid., pp. 76–79; Plomley, *Friendly Mission*, pp. 447–48 (n. 111).
12. Plomley, *Friendly Mission*, pp. 318–47, 456 (n. 164).
13. Ibid., pp. 457–60 (n. 166).
14. Ibid., p. 355.
15. Ibid., p. 394.
16. Ibid., p. 467 (n. 232).
17. Ibid., p. 402.
18. Report on the proceedings of Gilbert Robertson, 17 Nov. 1828, TSA CSO 1/331.
19. Stuart, 31 Jan. 1831, TSA CSO 1/321; Lyttleton, 3 Jan., Stuart, 7 Feb., Clark, 12 Mar., and Smith, 21 Mar. 1831, TSA CSO 1/316; Lyttleton, 18 Apr. 1831, TSA CSO 1/329.
20. Plomley, *Friendly Mission*, p. 415.
21. Minutes of Aborigines Committee, 6 Dec. 1831, TSA CSO 1/319.
22. Plomley, *Friendly Mission*, p. 485.
23. Ibid., p. 495.
24. Ibid., pp. 495, 496.
25. Ibid., p. 523.
26. Ibid., p. 551.

10

The Resistance of the Aborigines Beyond the Frontier, 1832–34

Elated by his capture of the Aborigines in the settled districts, Robinson was now convinced that he alone had been sent to rescue the Aborigines on the western frontier from barbarism. He offered to bring them all in for a thousand pounds, three hundred of which was to be paid in advance. So Arthur gave him sole responsibility for this task. Robinson thought there were about two hundred Aborigines in the west, but there were less than one hundred. He would spend more than three years and his mission Aborigines more than four years beyond the frontier before he could write to Arthur to announce that no more Aborigines were at large. For the Aborigines in the west were determined to fight for their country, and Robinson was more than once on the verge of defeat. But in February 1832 he was optimistic of early success. He arranged to visit the Aboriginal Establishment in Bass Strait with the new acting commandant, Lieutenant James Darling, and then with the mission Aborigines go to the west. He left Hobart on 13 February 1832.[1]

Since Robinson last visited in June 1831, the Aboriginal Establishment had moved from Gun Carriage Island to the Lagoons on Flinders Island. In that time at least twenty Aborigines had died, leaving only twenty survivors. The site at the Lagoons was exposed to the westerly gales, the soil was unfit for cultivation, and the wooden buildings lurched precariously on a sand-dune about forty-five metres from the sea. The only fresh water came from holes dug close to the beach, and the nearest anchorage for supply ships was at Green Island, nearly five kilometres away. So the new site was only marginally better than Gun Carriage Island. With the surgeon, Andrew Maclachlan, six convicts, and three sealers, the acting commandant, Sergeant Alexander Wight, had treated the Aborigines as if they were criminals. The number of Aborigines had been swelled to sixty-six by the arrival of the North Midlands, North, and North East people the previous August and the

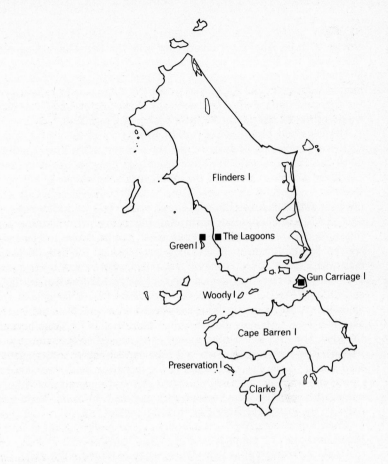

Flinders I

Green I   The Lagoons

Gun Carriage I

Woody I

Cape Barren I

Preservation I

Clarke I

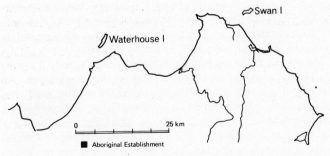

Swan I

Waterhouse I

0   25 km

■ Aboriginal Establishment

Map 39. Aboriginal establishments on the Bass Strait islands

Big River people in January. They had congregated in three distinct groups — those Aborigines identifying with the Ben Lomond people, those with the Big River people, and the third with the North, North Midlands, and western people. They had lived in separate encampments, hunted separately, and exchanged women with the convicts and sealers for dogs and flour. Before long Sergeant Wight had begun to fear they would incite the sealers to take them back to the mainland.[2]

His fears had been realized within two weeks of the arrival of the Big River people. On 22 January some men from the Big River encampment had "made a rush" for the convict boat crew for abducting two Big River women. Convinced the Aborigines were about to kill him, Wight had armed the three sealers and herded the Big River people into the boat and abandoned them on Green Island. Two weeks later he had sent the Ben Lomond and North Midlands people on a hunting trip for three days, for supplies had run short and he feared the tensions created by confinement. When they had returned a North Midlands man was missing, killed, some of the sealing women said, by two Ben Lomond men. They had denied this, but Wight had handcuffed them and ordered Maclachlan and two sealers, Robert Gamble and Edward Mansell, to take them to the place where the missing North Midlands man had been last seen. But they had been unable to find him. Still shackled, the two Ben Lomond men had tried to escape, and in the struggle that followed, Mansell had fired and wounded both men. On their return to the Lagoons, Wight had encased the men in iron hoops. Five hours later the supposed murdered man had returned, but already one of the wounded Ben Lomond men had died. In panic, Wight had removed the rest of the Aborigines to Green Island.[3]

When Robinson arrived on 25 February, the establishment at Green Island was out of supplies and the Aborigines were subsisting on muttonbird. Most were ill with dysentery and influenza. Wight and the convicts were relieved of their duties by Lieutenant Darling and eight soldiers, much to the horror of the Aborigines, who reminded Robinson that they had surrendered to him on the promise that they would be protected from the redcoats. But Robinson preferred them to the convicts and sealers. He removed the establishment back to the Lagoons and on 4 March held the first church service. The gaol-like conditions and the continuing illness and lack of provisions soon drove Robinson away. He consoled himself with the belief that Darling would introduce a civilization programme and soon turn the Aborigines from their evil ways. He was more anxious to add to this miserable group than to improve the conditions of those already captured. He would not return to Flinders Island until October 1835.[4]

By the time Robinson's ship arrived at Launceston on 13 March,

four of the mission Aborigines, Robert, Tom, Umarrah, and Woolaytopinneyer, were ill with influeza contracted at the establishment. By
24 March, Robert and Umarrah were dead. This confirmed for the
others that the establishment was a place of death and that they must
on no account return there. Robinson was also aware of their shaken
confidence and lived in increased anxiety that they would abscond, for
the success of his mission lay in their co-operation. Sixteen Aborigines
now formed the mission. Robinson planned to capture first all the
Aborigines in the country claimed by the Van Diemen's Land Company
on the west coast, from Cape Grim to West Point, then push south to
the Arthur River and to Macquarie Harbour. Then he hoped to capture
those south of Macquarie Harbour. Later he realized he would need a
further expedition to capture those in the high country behind the
Hampshire Hills. For the first stage of the expedition he employed
Anthony Cottrell and four Sydney Aborigines to assist him. He also had
his son George and his black convict servant from Hawaii, John
McLean. On 14 June 1832, in the middle of a wet, cold winter,
Robinson moved south from Cape Grim in search of the western
Aborigines. It was to prove one of the most hazardous journeys he
had yet undertaken.

On 19 June at Bluff Hill Point near the mouth of the Arthur River,
the Aborigines saw smoke, and Robinson sent the two mission
Aborigines from this area, Pevay and Kit, to look for their compatriots.
Kit returned that afternoon with the news that they had located them.
Pevay had remained with one man, Pannerbuke. The rest had gone to
Robbins Island, and when they returned they expected to fight the
Tarkinener Aborigines from Sandy Cape over the abduction of women.
On 22 June, Robinson went to the Arthur River to intercept the return
of the West Point Aborigines from Robbins Island. When he saw smoke
from their fire the next day, he again sent Pevay and Kit after them.
They returned with about eleven of their kin, including their chief,
Wymurrick. Later, five more West Point people joined Robinson, and
Wymurrick went to find others. On 13 July Wymurrick and his people,
twenty-two in all, appeared at West Point and surrendered. Robinson
decided to return to Cape Grim with his catch and put them on Hunter
Island until a ship was available to take them to Flinders Island.[5]

Two difficult months followed. Robinson set up encampments on
each side of Hunter Island. The Sydney Aborigines erected huts and
hunted kangaroos on the mainland to provide an adequate supply of
food. Then a woman, her infant son, and an old man died, which
created uneasiness among the rest. Robinson was anxious to return to
the Arthur River to capture the Sandy Cape Aborigines, but with few
provisions, windy and cold weather, and no prospect of a ship arriving

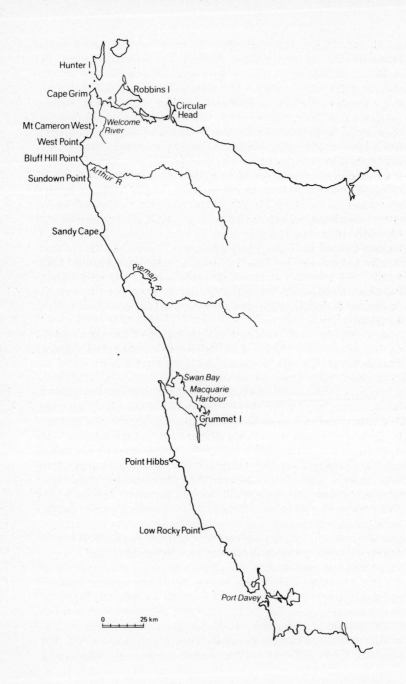

Hunter I

Robbins I

Cape Grim

Circular
Head

Mt Cameron West
Welcome
River

West Point

Bluff Hill Point

Sundown Point
Arthur R

Sandy Cape

Pieman R

Swan Bay

Macquarie
Harbour

Grummet I

Point Hibbs

Low Rocky Point

Port Davey

0   25 km

Map 40. The north and west coasts: region of Robinson's expeditions, June–October 1832, May–August 1833, February–July 1834

to take the Aborigines to Flinders Island, he was forced to stay at Hunter Island.

In correspondence to his friends George Whitcomb in Launceston and the Reverend William Bedford in Hobart, Robinson recognized that the Aborigines had full rights to their land. "Las Casas — to his dying hour maintained the right of the native Indians to make war upon their oppressors for the purpose of obtaining the restitution of their property and their freedom." He also remembered that John Locke had said that "no body has a right to take away a country which is the property of the Aboriginal Inhabitants without their own consent — that if they do, such inhabitants are not free men but slaves under the force of war."[6] By what tenture, Robinson argued, did Europeans hold Van Diemen's Land? The colonists had neither conquered nor purchased it; they had illegally occupied it. However, while admitting that the Aborigines in the west were rightfully fighting for their land, Robinson was also convincing his friends that his method of removal was the most humane gesture the colonial government could offer as compensation. This remarkable logic sustained him for the rest of his journey.

At the end of August he set out again for the Arthur River. His party consisted of two Sydney Aborigines to assist with the baggage, the mission Aborigines, and some Aborigines captured in June. He reached the Arthur River on 31 August and sent Wooraddy and Truganini, Timmy, Lacklay, and Pevay, and three of the newly captured Aborigines, Pannerbuke, Penderoin, and Heedeek, across the river in the hope of meeting their quarry. On 3 September, having heard nothing from his scouting party, he crossed the Arthur on a raft, ferried by four Aboriginal women. Shortly after, one of the women called "that plenty of blackfellows was coming" — all men. They came to Robinson's fire with the mission Aborigines and all had spears. Despite his presents of beads and bread, Robinson observed "that something was suspicious about them. They were shy and sullen, yet bold and full of bravado."[7]

The men went to hunt and Robinson visited their camp and "conversed freely with the women". There were twenty-nine in the party, consisting of Port Davey, Pieman River, and Sandy Cape Aborigines. Among them was Narrucer, who had been with Robinson two years before. Robinson spent the night in great anxiety. He got up at dawn, put on his clothes and packed up his knapsack, expecting an attack. He told Pevay that if these people did not wish to join him, they could go away, for he would not use force. Scarcely had he spoken when the strangers surrounded Robinson holding spears. His own Aborigines fled. Somehow Robinson escaped. As he ran through the scrub he overtook Truganini, who was fearful of capture, for she had relatives among these people, and they had a shortage of women. On reaching the river,

Robinson fashioned a makeshift raft out of two spars of wood tied together with his garters at first and then, when they broke, with his cravat. He lay on this raft and urged Truganini to push him across, for he could not swim. Arriving safely at the other side, they made for their own camp and alerted the others.[8]

When he returned to the river, Robinson found that most of the mission Aborigines had crossed, with his tent and knapsack. Four young women also joined them. On the other side of the river the Sandy Cape people were goading the mission Aborigines to join them. Eventually they enticed Heedeek back across the river. Robinson was then told that Heedeek had played a major part in the plot to kill him. After offering dogs in return for their women, the Sandy Cape people then disappeared into the bush.

Robinson was shaken by the experience. He later learnt that the Sandy Cape people had gone first to the Welcome River, then to Mount Cameron West, and finally to West Point in search of Wymurric and his people, with whom they were at war. When they found Robinson's huts they assumed he had captured them. They told the mission Aborigines when they met up with them that they would not go to Hunter Island but would take the women and dogs in his party. Unable to accept that these people were fighting for their lives, Robinson would in future carry firearms and use belligerent methods to force surrender. He beat a hasty retreat to Hunter Island, where he found the West Point Aborigines in a state of rebellion. There was still no sign of a ship.[9]

Existence at Hunter Island was now worse than in the winter. Wooraddy become so rebellious that Robinson had to threaten him with a gun, Mannalargenna feared the West Point people planned to abscond, the Sydney Aborigines complained of insufficient rations, and one of the sealing women absconded to the sealers camped at the southern tip of the island. When more women visited the sealers' camp on 22 October Robinson knew it was time to go.

He decided to return to Hobart to arrange for a ship to take the Aborigines to Flinders Island. The mission Aborigines were to remain on Hunter Island with his son and Cottrell and the Sydney Aborigines until he sent word to meet him at Macquarie Harbour. But the long-awaited ship from Flinders Island, the cutter *Charlotte,* containing Darling and two soldiers, intercepted Robinson at Circular Head on 28 October. He decided not to accompany the cutter to Hunter Island, for he wished "to avoid the unpleasant feeling at removing the aborigines", knowing that force would be used. He waited for the ship to return to Circular Head and sailed in her to George Town and then dispatched it to Flinders Island. Robinson then went overland to Hobart. He had captured twenty-seven Aborigines on this mission and had barely escaped with his life. The western Aborigines were becoming more difficult to conciliate than he had imagined.

He remained in Hobart Town until April 1833. Meanwhile, from Hunter Island Cottrell, Robinson's son, the Sydney Aborigines, and the mission Aborigines proceeded on 20 November down the west coast towards Macquarie Harbour. On 26 November they again met the Sandy Cape people at the Arthur River. The following morning the Sandy Cape people called to Cottrell and he beckoned them across, promising them blankets. They refused, insisting that Robinson was with them and that he had surely planned revenge. Cottrell assured them that Robinson was in Hobart. A short time later two men crossed.

They explored the camp and, satisfied there were no firearms, beckoned the rest across. But the Aboriginal chief, Wyne, insisted that Cottrell's people make the rafts for the women and children, for the Arthur was a swift-flowing stream. Three men, one woman, and a female child crossed, but the rest refused to go. In the evening one of the Sydney Aborigines took across a canoe, but he was greeted with a shower of spears. By next morning the Sandy Cape people had gone, so Cottrell returned to Hunter Island with the seven who had joined him. From there they were taken to George Town and put in gaol to wait for a ship to Flinders Island.[10]

Cottrell returned to the west and on 10 January 1833 again fell in with the Sandy Cape people, about fifty kilometres from the heads at Macquarie Harbour. They remained with Cottrell's party all night and agreed to accompany him to Macquarie Harbour, but when they had proceeded about six kilometres they disappeared into the scrub. The Sandy Cape people were not yet ready to surrender.

Undeterred, Cottrell continued south-west and on 5 February met with some Port Davey people. He succeeded in inducing five women, two men, and a boy to join him, and these he took to Macquarie Harbour to wait for a ship to take them to Flinders Island. By the time Robinson arrived at the end of April, all Aboriginal groups in the west had been contacted and they knew that Robinson intended to bring them in. But it had been a costly exercise. Two convict servants had drowned while crossing the Pieman River, three Sydney Aborigines had absconded north of Macquarie Harbour, and three of the Port Davey women had escaped from the settlement. Before returning responsibility to Robinson, Cottrell warned him that the only way to capture the remaining Aborigines was to use force.[11]

Desperate to accomplish his task as fast as possible, Robinson ordered his four convict assistants to carry firearms and warned the mission Aborigines that they would probably have to bring in the west coast people by force. He moved south and on 19 May discovered traces of the Port Davey people near Low Rocky Point. He sent the mission Aborigines in pursuit. They returned the next day with twelve Port Davey people; force had been used to bring them in, and three had escaped.[12] The period of voluntary surrender was over. Robinson justified his actions in his journal that night:

> Patriotism is a distinguishing trait in the aboriginal character, yet for all the love they bear their country the aboriginal settlement will soon become their adopted country and they will find that protection which they cannot find in their own land, not only against the attack of the whites but also against the tribes in hostilites with them. With these views I purposed acting accordingly and trusted to the goodness of providence for wisdom to direct me in what I had to do.[13]

But the Port Davey Aborigines refused to go to Macquarie Harbour and began to sharpen their spears. Robinson then ordered, for the first time, the four white men in his party "to uncover their fusees", and the Port Davey people then surrendered. But Robinson did not breathe freely until he reached Macquarie Harbour and embarked them on the *Shamrock* for Flinders Island on 5 June.

On 17 June the mission Aborigines located more Port Davey people, including Dray, who had disappeared with the Aborigines at Little Rocky River in April 1830, and the chief, Towterrer. They too resisted capture, and Robinson had to use another show of force to prevent their escape. He sent all of this group except Dray to Flinders Island on 23 June. Now only sixteen Aborigines remained south of Macquarie Harbour, and Robinson captured these on 12 July. On the return journey to Macquarie Harbour one man temporarily escaped, and for the third time Robinson had to order the white men in his party to display their guns as a show of force.[14]

Leaving this group on Grummet Island in Macquarie Harbour, Robinson turned north, hoping for the same quick success in capturing the Sandy Cape and Pieman River people. On 21 July he found traces of the Aborigines at the Pieman River. He hastily dispatched the mission Aborigines to surround their huts for the night to prevent escape, and they returned next morning with nine captives. Among them was the chief of the Pieman River people, Wyne, who was one of the group that had attempted to spear Robinson at the Arthur River the previous September. They were soon joined by two other men. The Pieman River people were unwilling to go to Flinders Island, but they were anxious to see their relatives and friends. Robinson noted proudly: "Providence had certainly crowned my labours with abundant success and I remarked that with me the motto, *veni, vidi, vici,* was applicable."[15]

Upon his return to Macquarie Harbour Robinson found the sixteen Port Davey people on Grummet Island had succumbed to chronic chest complaints. One woman had already died and two men and another woman were dangerously ill. By 27 July two more were dead. The mission Aborigines sought sanctuary at Swan Bay on the north side of Macquarie Harbour, while the sick Aborigines were placed in the hospital. Robinson asked Dray why they cried, and she retorted, "Why black man's wife not to cry as well as white man's?" The next day they left the hospital and Robinson returned them to Grummet Island. He had no idea what to do. No ship arrived to take them to Flinders Island, and he could not even countenance their returning to the bush to die. He considered that these sadnesses had been sent to try his patience and diligence. But he did not falter in his belief that he had removed them for their own good.[16]

On 31 July Wyne and another man died and another seven became critically ill. Robinson blamed the doctor, the hospital, and the settlement for the calamity. He could not see that confinement, the dramatic change in diet, and the loss of their land were more responsible for Aboriginal deaths than the erratic behaviour of a doctor. When the Aborigines pleaded with Robinson to take them away, he refused because he was afraid they would escape and all his work would be lost. It was not until 6 August, when twelve of the twenty-seven Port Davey and Pieman River people had died, that Robinson removed them to the pilot station at the heads.

Robinson was distressed by the deaths. He suffered bad dreams, became depressed, and despaired of the ship *Tamar* ever returning to rescue them. When the ship finally arrived in the middle of August, the master, Captain Bateman, told him that a further nineteen Aborigines had died at Flinders Island. Undeterred, Robinson embarked his party on the *Tamar,* arrived in Hobart on 12 October, and dispatched his captives to Flinders Island.

Each mission was becoming more hazardous and unbearable for Robinson. Ready supplies were difficult to sustain, his servants were unruly, and the mission Aborigines were becoming more rebellious. The spirit of adventure had long since died. His work was now largely a mopping-up operation which in other colonies at a later date would be carried out by military and native police parties. No one was again to spend so much time in the bush bringing in the last few.

On 20 February 1834 Robinson set out from Cape Grim in search of the rest of the western Aborigines. Two days later he reached the Arthur River. On 28 February his Aborigines brought in eight Pieman River people, two men, two women, a twelve-year-old boy, two little girls, and an infant. They had five dogs. They told Robinson they had fought the Tommeginer a short time before and that one of their people had been killed as well as a Tommeginer. He hastily took these people to Hunter Island and on 6 March set off to find the two remaining families. He crossed the Arthur River again, camping at Sundown Point. The next morning the mission Aborigines set off, and on 14 March found one family near the Arthur River. On 7 April they found the other family at Sandy Cape. They were pleased to see Robinson. There were four men, three women, and two children. Robinson afterwards recorded what they had told him:

> They had declared their intention was never to be subdued, that as they had plenty of dogs they would retire to the mountains and live on Quoiber, i.e. badger. They had formed a plan to kill me and my aboriginal attendants by laying in ambush, and had stuck sharp pointed sticks in their pathways to wound the feet of my native attendants, some of which we discovered. My natives were averse to follow after or look for them from an apprehension that they could not be found and that if we did they would assuredly kill us.[17]

They all returned to Cape Grim on 12 April, and Robinson had the satisfaction of farewelling the last of the west coast people to Flinders Island on 24 April. He now turned towards Circular Head to find the Tommeginer.

For the next two months he followed the Aboriginal roads at the back of the Hampshire Hills and across the high country to the east of Mount Roland and Mount Vandyke without success. At the end of July Robinson went to Launceston, leaving his two sons, George and Charles, in charge of the mission Aborigines at the Mersey River. They proceeded along the Aboriginal track in the high country to the river Ouse, which they reached in October. On 28 December, while on the Black Bluff Range, they saw the smoke of the Tommeginer and a day or so later succeeded in meeting them. There were eight of them — one man, four women, and three boys, the eldest of whom was eight years old. They were in "a sickly state" and were anxious to join their compatriots on Flinders Island "but had been afraid to give themselves up".[18]

Robinson reported to the colonial secretary on 3 February 1835: "The entire Aboriginal population are now removed." But in February 1836 reports were received from the Van Diemen's Land Company that some Aborigines had visited their grants. The following month Robinson, now at Flinders Island, dispatched nine mission Aborigines and his two sons to search for them. On 20 November they met a family of Aborigines — wife, husband, and four children — near Cradle Mountain. The family refused to go to Flinders Island because they said they were frightened by some of their compatriots there who had previously

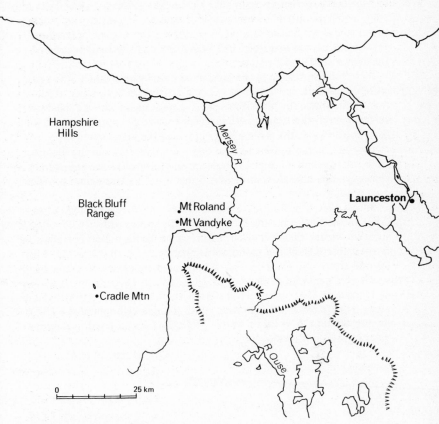

Map 41. The central north: region of expedition by Robinson's sons, 1834–36

been hostile to them. Neither Robinson's sons nor the mission Aborigines tried to change their minds, for they possibly envied their continued association with their country. The party returned to Launceston and resumed their search in January 1837, but it was broken off
in the winter.

This experience behind the frontier had subtly changed Robinson's
view of conciliation. Convinced that he was capturing the Aborigines
for their own good, he was able in all conscience to use the threat of
firearms to achieve his objective. He interpreted their hostility not as
resistance in defence of their land and their lifestyle but as a response

to previous experiences from sealers, shepherds, and convicts. He was also unable to attribute their rapid deathrate in captivity at Hunter Island and Macquarie Harbour to anything more than a temporary adjustment on the long road to Christianity or to incompetent care by the doctor at Macquarie Harbour.

Yet Robinson saw on the west coast a relatively intact Aboriginal society. Until his experience at the Arthur River in September 1832, he was sympathetic to the Aborigines' commitment to the land and suffered momentary pangs of conscience when he captured them. But their resistance at the Arthur River provided the justification he needed to continue to capture them. Like their counterparts from the Big River tribe, the western Aborigines were too dangerous to leave undisturbed. He convinced himself that he was bringing in the Aborigines for their own good.

In his journal Robinson revealed the extent of the Aboriginal resistance in the west. Like the Europeans in the settled districts, he refused to acknowledge their behaviour as a response to his presence. Robinson refused to confront the moral consequences of his own behaviour. By an odd irony the Van Diemen's Land Company ceased to graze sheep south of Cape Grim at the end of 1832, and in 1833 the penal station at Macquarie Harbour was transferred to Port Arthur. After that the area attracted very few Europeans until the mining boom of the 1870s. So the western Aborigines would probably have survived if Robinson had not captured them.

NOTES

1. Plomley, *Friendly Mission,* pp. 588–89.
2. Ibid., p. 682 (n. 13).
3. Statement of Capt. Bateman to Aborigines Committee (Feb. 1832), TSA CSO 1/319; James Bonwick, *The Last of the Tasmanians* (London, 1870), p. 248; Plomley, *Friendly Mission*, pp. 681–82 (n. 8); statement by Maclachlan, 27 Feb. 1832, TSA CSO 1/318; draft letter, Arthur to Darling, (Feb. 1832), TSA CSO 1/316.
4. Plomley, *Friendly Mission,* pp. 685 (n. 17), 592.
5. Ibid., pp. 618, 622.
6. Robinson to Whitcomb, 10 Aug. 1832, ML A612, pp. 155–6.
7. Plomley, *Friendly Mission,* p. 647.
8. Ibid., pp. 647–52.
9. Ibid., pp. 652–56.
10. Ibid., pp. 672–76, 802–3 (n. 6).
11. Ibid., pp. 804–5 (n. 7), 717.
12. Ibid., p. 724.
13. Ibid., p. 725.
14. Ibid., pp. 743, 754.

15. Ibid., p. 769.
16. Ibid., pp. 771–72.
17. Ibid., p. 875.
18. Ibid., p. 926.

11

The Reckoning

It was a fatal error in the first settlement of Van Diemen's Land, that a treaty was not entered into with the Natives, of which Savages will comprehend the nature, — had they received some compensation on the territory they surrendered, no matter how trifling, — and had adequate Laws been, from *the very first*, introduced, and *enforced* for their protection, His Majesty's Government would have acquired a valuable possession, without the injurious consequences which have followed our occupation, and which must forever remain a stain upon the Colonization of Van Diemen's Land.[1]

In 1823 the estimated population of the Big River, Oyster Bay, North Midlands, North East, and North tribes was about a thousand. By 1832, 156 had been captured, 50 lived with sealers, and 27 lived with settlers. Of the remainder, 280 were recorded shot, which leaves some 480 unaccounted for. It seems that even on the Tasmanian frontier only about one-third of the Aborigines killed were recorded and that a more realistic total would be about 700, or nearly four times as many as the 176 Europeans killed by the Aborigines.

In south-east Queensland between 1834 and 1853, 250 Europeans were reported killed by Aborigines, but no record was kept of the Aborigines killed. In the Liverpool Plains area of New South Wales between 1832 and 1838, fifteen Europeans were reported killed by the Aborigines, while at the Port Phillip district between 1836 and 1846, forty Europeans were reported killed. Although records in these areas were not kept as strictly as in Tasmania, researchers have estimated that the ratio of European to Aborigines killed on the frontier of mainland Australia was probably 1:10. In Tasmania the ratio was probably 1:4. This is an indication of the successful tactics of the Tasmanian Aborigines in the settled districts and an indication of the inability of the white population to understand Aboriginal resistance.[2]

Robinson's journeys through the settled districts in 1830 and 1831 revealed the extent of the fear in which the Aborigines were held. Most Europeans, settlers and convicts alike, were armed. Even if only half the stories Robinson heard were true, then it is possible to account for seven hundred shot. This is about three-quarters of the Aboriginal population in the settled districts. So how did the rest of the Aborigines die?

In many areas of Australia, Aborigines were recorded dying from European disease long before they were captured. But aside from the Aborigines at Bruny Island who were decimated by influenza in 1829, only one reference was found of an Aboriginal in the settled districts who suffered from disease before he was captured. The European population of Tasmania enjoyed good health during the first fourteen years of settlement, and the records suggest that the only deaths were from old age or misadventure.[3] The temperate climate of Tasmania was better suited to the European population than the humid, sub-tropical climate of Sydney, where a smallpox plague wiped out a large proportion of the Aboriginal population in 1788 or at Melbourne, where an outbreak of influenza in 1836 had a similar impact upon the Aboriginal population there.

But the good health of the Europeans alone would not normally have prevented the transmission of the common cold and chest complaints to the Aborigines. Part of the answer may lie in the nature of the Aboriginal diet in Tasmania, which by most mainland Aboriginal standards had a high protein and vitamin C content. The Aborigines in Tasmania had access to vast resources of shellfish rich in iron and thiamine which may have assisted them for a time to combat the common cold. Another factor may have been their adjustment to a climate that was cold by mainland standards and their custom of smearing themselves with ochre and charcoal as protection from the cold winds. A further factor may have been the slow growth in the European population, from 480 in 1804 to 3,114 in 1817.[4] The seasonal visits of the sealers along the north-east and north-west coasts may also have been significant in enabling the Aborigines to develop a resistance to chest complaints while they could continue their traditional lifestyle, for a similar resistance to external disease has been noted among the Aborigines in Arnhem Land as the result of long contact with the Macassans.[5] But the most puzzling factor of all is the apparently low level of venereal disease among the Aborigines in Tasmania before capture, for it was noted among the stock-keepers and sealers, and at least one prominent settler, John Batman, who had contact with the Aborigines, had syphilis. Even after capture, the

Aboriginal Tasmanians had a far lower rate of venereal disease than Aboriginal groups in other parts of south-eastern Australia.

The other major cause for decline in the Aboriginal population of mainland Australia is the addiction to alcohol. During the first period of settlement in Tasmania, there was a shortage of European provisions, including alcohol, which continued until the 1820s, and although illicit distilleries were found at New Norfolk and Pittwater, they were never as numerous as in New South Wales. Since alcohol was scarce, it was unlikely to have been "wasted" upon the Aborigines. The first inebriated Aborigines were not recorded until 1823. During the guerilla war, Aborigines did not plunder alcohol from stock-keepers' huts; indeed, it was noted as late as 1823 that they openly rejected the one form of alcohol that was readily available — rum. Robinson had no difficulty in "protecting" the mission Aborigines from alcohol during his travels around the island, although he noted a number of "inebriated" sealing women. Thus alcohol, like disease, does not appear a factor in the decline of the Aboriginal Tasmanians until they were in captivity.[6]

But one other factor was significant — the loss of women through exchange with the sealers and stock-keepers. The demand for Aboriginal women by the convict society in Tasmania was considerable during the first twenty-five years of settlement, owing to the shortage of European women. Even in 1828 there were still three males for every female in the colony, and most conflict between Aborigines and stock-keepers took place over women and kangaroos.[7] Aboriginal society faced its first major upheaval with Europeans over the "gift" of women to the stock-keepers in return for European provisions as a means to incorporate the stock-keepers into the obligations of Aboriginal society. While some tribes were anxious to develop strong ties of obligation with the Europeans, others found themselves with only a small number of women, having lost many to neighbouring bands who appropriated them for exchange with the Europeans. The loss of women led to an immediate decline in the birthrate.

The Aborigines in the settled districts were attacked from two sides — from the stock-keepers in the hinterland and the sealers on the coast. Had not the two prongs of European invasion taken place, the Aborigines would have survived in greater numbers. This perhaps is where the Tasmanian experience is different.

By September 1832 Arthur had formulated a policy relating to the Aborigines for the British government to follow in the establishment of any new colony in Australia. He now believed that the Aborigines could be civilized, but for this to take place they would have to be removed from their traditional environment. This did not necessarily mean that the Aborigines would lose all their land. Reserves or protectorates would be set up at the outset of European settlement. Eventually it would be possible for the Aborigines to be absorbed into the lower strata of European society. However, treaties would have to be signed with the Aborigines to legitimate the appropriation of their best land and missionaries would be needed to bring in the Aborigines to the reserves, to protect them from the excesses of the settlers, to educate the young Aborigines into European culture, and to devise special codes of law to protect the adult Aborigines until they learned to live within the framework of British law.[8]

The Colonial Office responded to this suggested policy in 1834 by instructing Governor Hindmarsh and the commissioners of the Wakefield Scheme in South Australia to sign a treaty with the Aborigines there, but this was never implemented. The commissioners probably never had any intention of carrying out these instructions and only made promises in this direction to gain approval for their project. They did appoint a protector in 1837, but by then relations between the settlers and Aborigines had deteriorated to such an extent that by 1840, four Aborigines were hanged for violating British law and the first punitive expedition had taken place.[9]

In 1835 John Batman set off for Port Phillip and there signed a treaty with the Aborigines, possibly at the instigation of Arthur, but this treaty was not ratified. In 1839 the Port Phillip Protectorate was established with G. A. Robinson as chief protector. By the time Robinson took up his duties, the Aborigines at Melbourne had succumbed to disease. By then too Robinson was in poor health, while his lack of diplomacy and tact in relating to his fellow Europeans made it difficult for him to undertake the arduous task of co-ordinating sub-protectors, placating angry squatters, and establishing ration stations. In 1849 the protectorate was abolished.

In New Zealand in 1840 a treaty was signed with the Maoris at Waitangi which guaranteed them rights to certain areas of land. But the settlers and the Colonial Office simply regarded this treaty as a legitimate means to appropriate Maori lands as needed, not as a guarantee of Maori rights.[10]

In the 1840s in the Australian colonies Arthur's three-pronged plan of civilization, appropriation of land by treaty, and establishment of reserves and protectors was ignored and replaced by a simple removal policy. The question of treaties with Aborigines never arose again in the nineteenth century. After the termination of the Port Phillip Protectorate in 1849, no new reserves were established in the eastern colonies until the 1880s. The removal policy proceeded not through the employment of a person like Robinson to "entice" the Aborigines from their land but by native mounted police forces who moved among resisting

Aboriginal groups and soon developed a speedy reliability in bringing in Aboriginal groups and individual "troublemakers". The survivors clustered around country towns or on pastoral properties, dependent on the fluctuating generosity of Europeans for their survival. Robinson's personalized removal techniques were not used again until government agents in Queensland went in search of tribal remnants in the 1890s and government patrols brought in isolated Aboriginal groups in Central Australia in the 1950s.

While Arthur's policy smacked of racism in his assumption that Aborigines were inferior to Europeans and thus could be removed from their land, he was concerned that they should survive. This latter concern was abandoned by most colonial governments between 1850 and 1880. During this period the Aborigines sustained assaults from police parties and from disease. By the time concern was renewed about their fate, there was widespread belief that they would soon die out. Thus Arthur's policy of removing Aborigines from their land for the highest of moral reasons was distorted by colonial governments into a policy of wholesale slaughter of the Aborigines in eastern Australia until the 1880s.

The removal of Aborigines from land coveted by settlers continued well into the twentieth century. C. D. Rowley, in *The Destruction of Aboriginal Society* recalls the rounding up of Aborigines from the stations of the hinterland in Queensland after 1918 and their removal to Palm Island, the arrest and removal of the Aborigines from Northam and the Moore River in Western Australia in 1933, and the removal of Aborigines from valuable gold-mining areas of Tennant Creek in the Northern Territory in 1935.[11]

Having failed to secure a treaty with the Aborigines in Van Diemen's Land, but having succeeded in removing most of them from their traditional lands, Arthur set about devising a programme for their Christianization and civilization in captivity. The programme came from four sources: from Arthur himself, from Robinson, from the members of the Aborigines Committee, two of whom were clergymen, and from the Quaker missionaries James Backhouse and George Washington Walker, who visited the Australian colonies between 1832 and 1838 and spent three years in Van Diemen's Land. They all passionately believed that in the artificially created environment at Flinders Island the Aborigines would discard their own cultural beliefs in favour of the European form. When Lieutenant Darling replaced Sergeant Wight at Flinders Island in February 1832, Arthur had already put some thoughts on paper about the future of the Aborigines. He wrote to Darling:

Your first duty will be effectually to provide for the security of the Natives and to afford their protection, and as the great design of the Government in forming this Establishment is with a view to their civilisation, His Excellency places the fullest reliance on your exertions to accomplish this great and important object. In order to effect this, it will be therefore necessary in the first instance that you carefully study their peculiar habits, and by kind treatment endeavour to gain such a knowledge of their desires, as will enable you by gratifying them to the fullest allowable extent to acquire that influence over them, which will eventually tend to promote the great object in view. Restraints will not be imposed upon them more than is consistent with their perfect security on Great Island and at the same time that they will be permitted to indulge in their favourite amusements, it is hoped that by the example of good order and unanimity maintained amongst the white people belonging to the Establishment, and by constant encouragement to a friendly intercourse, they will by degrees be familiarised to a more civilised mode of life and gradually be induced in great measure to relinquish their wild propensities.[12]

Darling was convinced that he could "foster an interest in civilization" among the Aborigines. By withholding or proliferating tobacco, for example, he could induce the women to wash their clothes, to bake bread, and to clean out their wattle-and-daub huts. He could also persuade them to wear coats and to refrain from using ochre at scripture readings on Sundays. Thus began a tug of war for their hearts and minds. They had to fulfil certain requirements before they could return to their own lifestyle. The Ben Lomond and Big River people competed for status and prestige as the oldest inhabitants of the establishment, controlling ceremonial activities, the exchange of women and dogs, and the organization of hunting parties. Their greatest need was a regular supply of ochre, for the island had only small deposits, so they were dependent upon new arrivals to continue ceremonial life. The songs and dances brought by the new arrivals were eagerly copied. Soon they developed a lingua franca, and the men sought attachments with the women from the North West who were still imbued with the values of traditional society, while the sealing women formed sexual relationships with the sealers, military, and convicts.[13]

It was unusual to find the total Aboriginal population at the establishment at any one time. One group would be absent hunting, a smaller group absent because of illness, another group of women shellfishing up the coast, and another group searching for ochre. Although they could not be away from the settlement long and were often accompanied by a military officer, and although they were disunited in themselves, the Aborigines individually and in small groups were able to develop a pattern of resistance to institutionalization. Sometimes they feigned an interest in European civilization by attending religious services and listening with zeal and patience, but they promptly returned to their own ceremonies as if to demonstrate their independence. Sometimes they ate all their European rations in one day, so that they had to leave the establishment to hunt for more food. Then they had to suffer a few days in gaol for disobedience. They also divided their European keepers by creating conflict between the soldiers, the convicts, and the sealers, making it more difficult for them to insist upon the more onerous duties like gardening, sweeping, cleaning, and learning to read and write. [14]

In June 1833 a catechist, Thomas Wilkinson, was appointed to the establishment. To show his natural superiority in "understanding native peoples" he translated the first four chapters of Genesis into the language of the Ben Lomond people, who saw this as recognition of their superior status among their own people. But in response to the message of Christianity, they told Backhouse and Walker in December 1833 that black people worshipped the devil, who told them what to do — that his spirit lived in their breast and that when they died they went to some of the islands in the straits where they were reincarnated as white people. [15]

In 1833, 43 Aborigines arrived at the establishment to join the 78 already there. But 37 died, leaving 84. In 1834, 42 arrived, but 14 died, leaving 112. Had the opportunity existed to continue their lifestyle in adjustment to European society on their own terms, the Aborigines would have increased their number, as there were almost equal numbers of each sex. Several children were born, but most died within a few days. No European expressed concern or alarm at this stage at this infant mortality rate; it was seen as evidence of their inevitable extinction or the loss of their will to live. Since the establishment already cost over two thousand pounds a year to maintain, a high death rate and a low birth rate were to European advantage.

While the Aborigines failed to accept the "blessings" of civilization in not adopting agriculture, it was reasoned they should not be given superior rations or share poultry and green vegetables from the officers' store. [16] In December 1834 the daily rations were, for each adult, one pound (450 g) of salt beef, one pound (450 g) of flour, half a pound (225 g) of biscuit, quarter of an ounce (7 g) of sugar, quarter of an ounce (7 g) of soap, quarter of an ounce (7 g) of salt, and half rations for children. Since the Aborigines would not eat salt meat, to stave off malnutrition they were forced to hunt, even though they were often too ill to hunt, or forbidden to hunt, or had nothing to hunt. An uneasy pattern familiar to all institutional existence prevailed. The repression was sufficient to discourage, control, and divide the Aborigines but not sufficient to provoke open and united rebellion.

By the time Robinson arrived in October 1835, the establishment had become a gaol. He would turn it into "the prototype of the multipurposed institution, asylum, hospital, training centre, school, agricultural institution, rationing centre, pensioners' home, prison — which was for so long to be assumed suitable" for dispossessed Aborigines in all parts of Australia.[17]

NOTES

1. Arthur to Hay, 24 Sept. 1832, PRO CO 280/35.
2. John C. Taylor, "Race Relations in South East Queensland, 1840–1860" (BA thesis, University of Queensland, 1967), p. 30; R. H. W. Reece, *Aborigines and Colonists* (Sydney: Sydney University Press, 1974), pp. 217, 219–20; Peter Corris, *Aborigines and Europeans in Western Victoria* (Canberra: AIAS, 1968), pp. 155–57; Henry Reynolds, "The Unrecorded Battlefields of Queensland" (Typescript, Townsville, 1974).
3. Van Diemen's Land, Register of Deaths 1803–20, ML C190.
4. R. W. Giblin, *The Early History of Tasmania,* vol. 2 (Carlton, Vic.: Melbourne University Press, 1939), p. 137.
5. C. C. Macknight, "Macassans and Aborigines in the Northern Territory" (typescript, Department of Prehistory, RSPS, ANU, 1968), p. 11.
6. Horton, 3 June 1823, BT, pp. 1268–74; *HTC*, 23 Oct. 1828.
7. Arthur to Huskisson, 1 May 1828, PRO CO 280/16.
8. Arthur to Hay, 24 Sept. 1832, PRO CO 280/35.
9. D. A. Dunstan, "Aboriginal Land Title and Employment in South Australia", in *Aborigines in the Economy,* ed. Ian G. Sharp and Colin M. Tatz (Brisbane: Jacaranda Press, 1966), pp. 314–16; C. D. Rowley, *The Destruction of Aboriginal Society* (Canberra: ANU Press, 1970), pp. 77–79.
10. H. Merivale, *Lectures on Colonization and Colonies,* 2nd ed. (London, 1861), pp. 497–98.
11. Rowley, *Destruction of Aboriginal Society,* p. 47.
12. Draft letter, Arthur to Darling (Feb. 1832), TSA CSO 1/316.
13. Darling to Arthur, 4 May 1832, AP, vol. 28; James Backhouse, *A Narrative of a Visit to the Australian Colonies* (London, 1843), p. 83.
14. James Backhouse and C. Tylor, *The Life and Labours of G. W. Walker* (London, 1862), pp. 97, 148–49; Arthur to Goderich, 7 Jan. 1832, *BPP*, 1834, vol. 44, no. 617, p. 163.
15. Backhouse, *Visit to the Australian Colonies,* p. 175.
16. RP, vol. 11, 7 Nov. 1835.
17. Rowley, *Destruction of Aboriginal Society,* p. 52.

12

Flinders Island 1835–39: False Hopes and Broken Promises

> In my conferences with them I have been scrupulously tenacious in keeping my word. The tribes knew when in their own districts they would be sent to an island, where they would be secure from the attack of the depraved portion of the white population and where they would enjoy uninterrupted tranquility in the society of their kindred and friends, their wants and necessities were to be amply supplied in addition to which they were to enjoy their native amusements. Moreover their customs were to be respected, and not broken into by any rash or misguided interference. [1]

When Robinson set off for the Flinders Island Aboriginal Establishment in October 1835 with the mission Aborigines and several children from the Orphan School, he expected to remove it to the Australian mainland within a very short time. Arthur's suggestion to the Colonial Office in January 1832 that the "native inhabitants" of any new colony in Australia should be conciliated before settlement actually took place had been accepted in principle. With new areas of settlement opening up at Swan River in 1829 and Portland Bay in 1834 and proposed free settlements at South Australia, Port Phillip, and Moreton Bay, it was inevitable that Arthur and Robinson should play a vital role in shaping Aboriginal policy in some of these areas.

Already in February 1835 the colonial secretary in Hobart had written to Robinson about the possibility of "opening a friendly communication" with the Aborigines at Portland Bay and taking all the Aborigines at Flinders Island there with him, if they could be trusted not to abscond or create tension with the Aborigines living on the mainland. Robinson thought the scheme would give the Tasmanian Aborigines something to live for, as Flinders Island had already taken too many Aboriginal lives. Nothing came of the Portland Bay venture, but Arthur was then requested to recommend the appointment of a chief protector of the Aborigines in the new province of South Australia.

Arthur was anxious for Robinson to accept the appointment, and Robinson planned to move the establishment as soon as the details had been completed.[2]

The hundred or so Aborigines who met him at the jetty at Flinders Island were the survivors of the three hundred he had originally captured. Most had died in the various transit camps set up to process them upon capture. On paper Robinson was committed to allow the Aborigines to pursue their own culture, but in practice he intended to use the artificial environment of Flinders Island to prove that his captives wished to advance towards civilization, which consisted of an appreciation of the main tenets of Christianity and a disposition to adopt European standards of personal cleanliness, dress, and housing, develop a desire to accumulate money and material possessions, and pursue agriculture. To achieve all this Robinson not only needed a willing Aboriginal community but also regular supplies of European food, reasonable living conditions, a sympathetic European staff, and an awareness of the psychological dislocation that this would create among his victims. That he had none of these did not deter him. Robinson was determined to prove wrong the natural inference drawn by the colonists that the Aborigines possessed certain "anti-civilizing properties" which prevented change. He was better equipped than most to carry out such a programme, but he would prove unequal to the task.

At the Aboriginal Establishment, now called Wybalenna, meaning black man's houses, Robinson found a settlement consisting of living quarters for civil staff, two cottages for the military, and huts for the convict labourers. There were nine double huts for the Aborigines, a large provision store, cultivated land, and flourishing vegetable gardens for the Europeans. There was a military detachment of one captain and four privates and their families, a civil detachment of a catechist, a storekeeper, and a coxswain and their families, a medical officer, and sixteen convicts. In all, forty-six Europeans supervised 123 Aborigines. The settlement was in a most unsatisfactory condition, with inadequate food, water, clothing, and shelter for the Aborigines, the staff unruly, and the dissatisfied Aborigines wanting to return to their old tribal lands. In the previous two years twenty-eight Aborigines had died.[3]

On 7 November Robinson celebrated his arrival with a gala fete at which the civil officers were forced to serve the Aborigines with fresh mutton, rice, and plum pudding.[4] After dinner the Aborigines played cricket and in the evening were entertained by a fireworks display. A few days later, under the direction of the surgeon and Robinson's sons, the Aborigines cut a road from the commandant's house to the jetty, a distance of three-quarters of a mile. A few weeks later they were reaping barley. Robinson was convinced that these activities were signs that the Aborigines wanted to become civilized.

He had already encouraged the men to cut their hair, prevented the women from cohabiting with the convicts, and isolated the mission Aborigines from the communal atmosphere of the large huts in the hope that they would set a good example to the others by building fences and digging gardens for their own use.

When Mannalargenna died early in December Robinson insisted upon burial rather than cremation in order to deprive the women of his bones to use as relics. He knew that Mannalargenna would never have converted to Christianity, and would have strongly opposed his civilization programme, but this did not prevent Robinson in the funeral oration from depicting him as the last of the great chiefs who had encouraged his people to learn the blessings of civilization.

When he changed the names of the sealing women, this proved so popular that all Aboriginal names were changed. Woorraddy became Count Alpha because he was the first Aboriginal Robinson encountered at Bruny Island in 1829. Truganini was renamed Lalla Rookh because she was the daughter of a chief and last survivor of her people from Recherche Bay. Tongerlongter, the chief of the Oyster Bay people was renamed King William, after the reigning king of England. Robinson did not attempt to disrupt the existing authority system in name changing; rather, he wanted the Aborigines to understand that their authority structure was very similar to the European. By calling the tribes nations and their leaders kings, he hoped they would understand more readily the nature of his programme. By March 1836 they were part of a rigid daily routine designed to expunge their traditional life.

The fourteen children, aged between six and fifteen, were the most regimented of all. Most were orphaned or parted from their parents, and the girls lived at the storekeeper's house and the boys with the catechist, Robert Clark. They rose at half-past six, washed and said their prayers, and at seven o'clock assembled with the catechist and his family to read the Bible. At half-past seven they had breakfast with Robinson. Then they went to school until noon, when they had lunch and returned to school at two o'clock, where they remained until tea at half-past three. At six o'clock they helped the adults at the evening school until eight, when they returned to the catechist's house for family worship, and at nine o'clock they went to bed.[5]

The eldest boy, Walter George Arthur, aged fifteen, had spent most of his childhood at the Orphan School and was expected to become the future leader of his people and lead them to salvation. Robinson hoped the rest of the boys would become skilled tradesmen. The girls were already serving as housemaids to the civil officers. They fared poorly at school and were considered a bad influence upon the boys, encouraging them to lie and steal. They also refused to teach the women to sew and cook.

The next regimented group were the fifty Aboriginal women, whose average age was thirty and who were placed under the charge of Mrs Clark. At nine o'clock each morning they were inspected by Mrs Clark on their general appearance. She would then examine their huts and windbreaks to check whether their grass-filled mattresses had been aired or washed, the floors and tables swept, and the crockery and cutlery cleaned. Then they went to the store for rations of meat and vegetables. At midday they cooked damper and stew on open fires outside the huts and attended sewing classes for two hours in the afternoon. On Fridays after dinner, they washed their own clothes and the men's, and on Saturdays they cooked a second damper for Sunday. In the evenings between six and eight o'clock on Mondays, Wednesdays, and Fridays and between seven and eight on Tuesdays and Thursdays they went to evening school to learn their letters and to hear stories from the Bible. Few learnt to read and most fared poorly in examinations. The promises of rewards were the only effective means of ensuring regular attendance.

Unlike the women and children, the fifty-six men had no specific routine devised for them. Apart from attending evening school, they were expected to cultivate the gardens, build roads, clear forest land, erect fences, and shear sheep. But they spent most of their time playing marbles, cricket, and rounders. On Sunday mornings at half-past ten all the men and women stood outside their huts to await Robinson's inspection. The women wore checked gingham petticoats with handkerchiefs about their necks and heads and the men wore canvas trousers with tail coats buttoned to the waist. After breakfast they proceeded to chapel from eleven o'clock to one o'clock. After lunch they had hymn singing.[6]

After five months Robinson was encouraged by the Aborigines' initial response to this routine. But beneath this veneer of change they adhered to their own traditions. Their continuing susceptibility to chest complaints and the increase in ophthalmia, created largely by their poor diet as well as the impure water supply and insanitary accommodation, ensured their continued use of relics. They hoarded ochre and performed ceremonial rites in secret. Conflict still took place among the three tribal groupings — the western, the Ben Lomond, and the Big River — over the possession of women and dogs, and sometimes Robinson had to send a particular group hunting to forestall violence. The intermittent arrival of ration ships forced Robinson to rely more upon traditional food sources, but by 1837 these had largely been hunted out.

The adult daily ration, now one pound (450 g) of salt meat, a pound and a half (675 g) of flour, two ounces (57 g) of sugar, half an ounce (14 g) of tobacco, half an ounce (14 g) of soap, and one ounce (28 g) of tea, was still nutritionally inadequate. Damper, tea, and stews made from salt meat, cabbage, and turnips were the staple diet. Apart from what they obtained from hunting and muttonbirding when in season, the Aborigines never tasted fresh meat.[7]

When the commandant at Launceston, Major Thomas Ryan, visited the settlement in March 1836 he found the Aborigines suffering from malnutrition and physical infections. He found that the Aboriginal women prepared meals by boiling the vegetables in the same pot with the salt beef and pork, reducing any nutritional properties and producing cutaneous disease. Experience in India had taught Major Ryan that a salt diet not only produced disease but also reduced the ability of people to procreate. The impure water supply could only exacerbate an already distressing state of affairs. He wrote:

> If it is the wish of the Government to propagate the species it is our bounden duty to provide all the means that are in our possession for the accomplishment of so desirable an end — if not, I tremble for the consequences, the race of Tasmania, like the last of the Mohicans will pine away and be extinct in a quarter of a century. [They live in] an artificial society where most of their traditional food resources have been hunted out, and living in damp, poorly ventilated huts with impure water and inadequate provisions.[8]

Ryan found it hard not to draw the conclusion that the Aborigines were being deliberately exterminated in a manner that involved considerable pain and suffering. He recommended that a new site be found for the establishment and that vastly improved rations, including fresh meat, be provided. Arthur ordered Robinson to construct an aqueduct to bring fresh water from the near-by hills and to arrange for fresh mutton to become part of the rations. But the aqueduct was never built and fresh meat did not become part of the rations until 1838.

Despite Robinson's zeal, the civilization programme was carried out in piecemeal fashion. He made three trips from the establishment in 1836 and in March sent the mission Aborigines back to the mainland to search for the family from the North tribe who had been reported by the Van Diemen's Land Company as being still at large. He was glad to see the mission Aborigines go, for they had accused him of breaking his promise to respect their customs, not eradicate them. Robinson also found the daily routine, after years on the move, as much a drudge as did the Aborigines. Indeed, Wybalenna had become yet another transit camp where, while awaiting to move to the Australian mainland, the officers enjoyed reasonable accommodation and the Aborigines suffered in their vermin-infested huts which in their traditional environment they would long ago have abandoned.[9]

On 21 September Robinson returned to Hobart expecting to complete arrangements for the transfer to South Australia. Arthur offered him the appointment on condition that he left at once, that he took only a clerk and ten Aborigines, and that he left his family and the rest of the Aborigines on Flinders Island. When Robinson discovered that the secretary of state had offered only half the expected salary and had queried his claims for reward for his previous work, he decided that neither Arthur nor the secretary of state had any concern for him or the Aborigines. So he refused the appointment. Arthur was disconcerted and believed that if Robinson took the appointment then a reasonable salary would follow and that the rest of the Aborigines could join him in due course. But Robinson was so disappointed that he even boycotted the official farewell for Arthur, who was leaving the colony after twelve years.[10]

He returned to Flinders Island on 24 November in the hope that he would be offered the position of chief protector to the Aborigines at Port Phillip. The belief that Melbourne would become the base of his future operations gained credence a month later when he paid an official visit there as the guest of the Port Phillip Association. The six Aborigines he took with him were "highly pleased with the country and want[ed] to leave Flinders and fix their abode [t]here".[11]

When he returned to Flinders Island in January 1837 Robinson realized it would be at least eighteen months before an appointment could be offered and he was still uncertain that he would be allowed to take all the Aborigines. So he embarked on a European housing programme and produced the *Flinders Island Weekly Chronicle,* written by the adolescent boys "to promote christianity and civilisation and learning amongst the Aboriginal Inhabitants [and] be a brief but accurate register of the events of the colony moral and religious".[12] In 1837 the *Chronicle* appeared every Saturday in manuscript, priced twopence, with the profits distributed among the writers. The paper was really a public relations exercise to convince the authorities that the Aborigines could be civilized. Most of the articles were addresses the boys delivered at the evening school and revealed Robinson's need to evoke gratitude from his charges and respect from the government:

Now my friends you see that the Commandant is so kind to you he gives you everything that you want when you were in the bush the Commandant had to leave his friends and go into the bush and he brought you out of the bush because he felt for you he knowed the

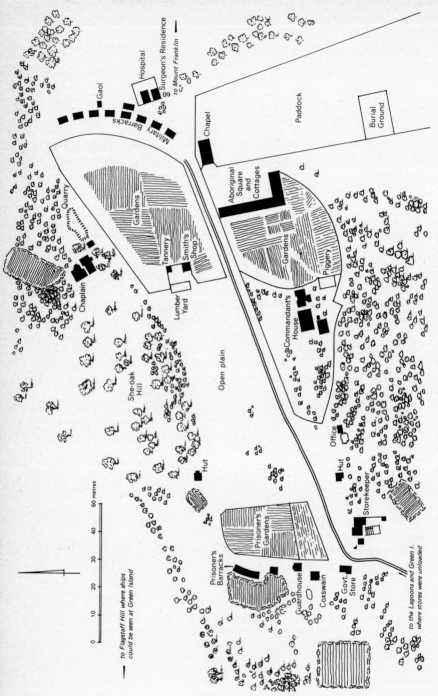

Map 42. Plan of Flinders Island Aboriginal Establishment

to Flagstaff Hill where ships
could be seen at Green Island

to the Lagoons and Green I.
where stores were unloaded

Surgeon's Residence
to Mount Franklin

Hospital

Gaol

Military Barracks

Chapel

Quarry

Gardens

Tannery

Smith's Shop

Chaplain

Lumber Yard

Aboriginal Square and Cottages

Gardens

Piggery

Paddock

Burial Ground

Commandant's House

She-oak Hill

Open plain

Hut

Office

Hut

Storekeeper

Prisoner's Gardens

Prisoner's Barracks

Guardhouse

Coxswain

Govt. Store

0 10 20 30 40 50 metres

white man was shooting you and now he has brought you to
Flinders Island where you get every things and when you are ill tell
the Doctor immediately and you get relief. [13]

Next was the weekly market. Between ten o'clock and noon every
Thursday the Aborigines sold to the Europeans shell necklaces, wallaby
skins, feathers, waddies and spears, and some of their needlework. The
Europeans sold them clay pipes, sugar plums, fishing lines, crockery,
shirts, beads, belts, buckles, and marbles and cricket bats. But there was
no trading between the Aborigines. Robinson used old English coins
as a medium of exchange with *FI* (Flinders Island) marked on one side
and *AE* (Aboriginal Establishment) on the other. From time to time
the Aborigines sent articles like shell necklaces and salted muttonbirds
to Launceston for sale, and the money earned went into an Aboriginal
fund with which tobacoo and other European luxury items were
bought. Market days continued until the end of 1838. [14]

Despite these innovations, the Aborigines still resisted Robinson's
programme. In these circumstances they reacted like any group under
restraint in an artificial environment. They reverted to their "secret"
life by maintaining tribal relationships, adjusting their kinship structure,
raiding each other for women, and performing ceremonial dancing
which represented their conflict with Europeans on the mainland. The
horse dance, which originated from the Big River people, concerned
the outrunning of a European on a horse by an Aboriginal. Their
"secret" life also involved the keeping of relics, hunting two or three
times a week, acquiring dogs, searching for shells, and developing
relations with convicts and sealers. They paid lip service to the obligations of their gaolers but refused to accept the attitudes foisted upon
them. They saw the dichotomy between Robinson's teaching of the
gospel and its fruits − the flogging of soldiers and convicts, the
wrangling between the storekeeper and the catechist, the insolence of
Robinson's sons towards their father, and the liaison between one of
Robinson's daughters and the medical officer.

Robinson's one redeeming feature was his refusal to use physical
force on the Aborigines, but he used moral and coercive force with
devastating results. He isolated groups, denied rations to others, prevented some from hunting, and encouraged spying − all the usual forms of
behaviour that the superintendent of any asylum or institution can
resort to in his need to keep control. He could not see that moral
coercion was contrary to voluntarism.

At the beginning of 1837 Robinson appointed salaried constables
among the men, remunerated those who attended evening school
regularly, and offered one shilling for every dog they killed. But these
actions served only to reinforce their determination to resist his pro-

gramme. All spirit of co-operation from the adult Aborigines disappeared. That summer they suffered a fresh outbreak of chest complaints, and one by one temporarily deserted the establishment for the hinterland in the hope that a change of location would restore their health. During the previous year there had been comparatively few deaths and four children had been born. Robinson had to face the chilling prospect that 1837 would be in marked contrast to that.

That winter Robinson saw his programme disintegrate. Formal instruction was abandoned as supplies failed to arrive, and most Aborigines moved to the bush to fend for themselves. Twenty-nine people died. The *Flinders Island Chronicle* reported:

> The brig Tamar arrived this morning at Green Island. . . . Let us hope it will be good news and that something may be done for us poor people. They are dying away. The Bible says some or all shall be saved but I am much afraid none of us will be alive by and by and then as nothing but sick men amongst us. Why don't the blackfellows pray to the King to get us away from this place.[15]

Robinson was now desperate about the future. His chances of obtaining the position at Port Phillip had brightened, but the future of the Aborigines had not. He wrote to the colonial secretary in Hobart Town:

> Should . . . His Majesty's Government still object to their removal, and continue the settlement where it now is, I have no hesitation in stating that the race in a very short period will be extinct; and although it might be urged that the same results would occur were the translation permitted, still it would be found that by the admixture of the Flinders' Island aborigines with the aborigines of the country, the declension would not be observed, consequently the excitement not felt.[16]

The fear expressed by the press at Port Phillip and by the government in Sydney that the Aborigines at Flinders Island were desperadoes who would excite other Aborigines into "wanton acts of violence" dismayed Robinson. Rather than turning them into aggressors, Flinders Island had transformed them into "social nuisances". He could not conceive the British government would let them die.

In the midst of this despair the nine mission Aborigines — Woorraddy, Truganini, Fanny, Pevay, Dick, Timmy, Lacklay, Jenny, and Edward — who had been in the bush in northern Tasmania since March the previous year in search of the remaining Aboriginal family from the North tribe returned. They were critical of the deaths that had taken place, and Truganini predicted "there would be no blackfellows to live in the new houses".[17] They openly defied Robinson's authority, wore ochre, incised their bodies with bottle glass, and performed ceremonial rites.

He had even worse problems with the fourteen sealing women. Their better health, familiarity with European customs, and readiness to dispense with some of the more "distasteful" traditional ceremonial dances had led him to believe that they could form the vanguard of his new society. But he soon discovered that they performed the equally distasteful dances they had developed in cohabitation with the sealers, that their knowledge of English was liberally stewn with epithets, the lingua franca they introduced to the establishment was a powerful weapon of ridicule, and their religious view of the world was controlled not by God but by the devil. In the second half of 1837 they emerged as a significant dissident group, critical of the establishment and resisting both Robinson's authority and that of the Aboriginal men.

In August 1837 Robinson organized "marriages" for four of them, Matilda, Emma, Flora and Rebecca, because they refused to live with men. Once "married", Robinson believed, they would become more tractable and bear children. But within a week they left their husbands for the bush, warning that they would not return until they could live as they chose. Robinson refused them rations, so they robbed the camp at night. Then he sent the boys who wrote the *Flinders Island Chronicle* to visit them. They "told the women if they did not clean the houses and clean themselves they would put them in the paper. [The women] said they may speak but not write — They seemed to have a great abhorrence of being put in newspapers."[18] Then he sent the men:

> Women you are still continuing to do what is improper — when you go into the bush — God may take away your lives very soon for your wickedness. You go about the settlement some of you living like dogs — God does not like that — bad people will be sent to Hell — bad people are the Devil's people.
>
> Every woman should mind her own house and not be going to other people's houses — keep your blankets clean — carry plenty of wood to your houses for your fires take care of your clothes and sew them when they are old and torn — do not throw them away when you go to the bush hunting as you used to do.[19]

At the end of October the Aborigines moved into their new houses. Built of brick, the twenty apartments formed an L-shaped terrace facing east to keep out the cold westerly winds. Each house had one room with two beds sufficient for four persons. There were two cupboards on either side of the fireplace and one latticed window and a small yard partly enclosed with a picket fence. The roofs were thatched with grass. The terrace formed part of a square, with the newly constructed chapel, designed to hold two hundred people, occupying the opposite corner. After living in couples for a few weeks, the Aborigines soon returned to their preferred mode of communal living. They cooked outside and allowed their dogs to sleep with them. But by then Robinson had abandoned his demand for a European family lifestyle.

Earlier that month he had found his prize pupil, Walter George Arthur, in bed with Mary Ann Cochrane, the daughter of the Aboriginal woman Sarah and a sealer. He abandoned the idea to train Walter as a catechist and prepared the pair for marriage. In drinking the toast, the Aborigines appeared to say "Go to hell" instead of "Good health". When Truganini found her tobacco pipe missing, she asked the culprit, Dawunga (Leonidas), whether "God tell him to steal lubra's pipes?" When Moultelargine (Ajax) called a woman black, she was most offended and wanted to know if he was a white man. Robinson was embittered by this "careless indifference and ingratitude", but he never faltered in his belief that the course of all human history was progress towards what he believed himself to be, and that there was nothing unreasonable in persisting with this barren harvest. But he was concerned to move the Aborigines. When the new governor, Sir John Franklin, visited the establishment in January 1838 he agreed that they must go to the Australian mainland if they were not to die out. But Franklin's support came too late. The dispatch from the secretary of state for the colonies in London, Lord Glenelg, leaving the decision for removal in the hands of the governor of New South Wales, Sir George Gipps, in whose jurisdiction Port Phillip lay, had already been sent.[20]

In August 1838, armed with Franklin's support for removal and a promise that the Van Diemen's Land government would continue financial aid once the Aborigines were at Port Phillip, Robinson set off for Sydney. But there the first trial of the perpetrators of the Myall Creek massacre had just concluded. In March 1838, twelve stockmen had killed a party of Aborigines at Myall Creek, a tributary of the Gwydir River on the Liverpool Plains in northern New South Wales. Eleven stockmen were arrested and brought to trial. The stockmen were acquitted, but immediately afterward seven of the men were retried, found guilty, and hanged. The press and community became deeply divided over the issue, and Gipps was in no mood to promote further press antagonism by permitting the Aboriginal "desperadoes" from Van Diemen's Land to go to Port Phillip to "subvert" the Aborigines there. Gipps offered Robinson the position of chief protector of the Aborigines at Port Phillip at a salary of five hundred pounds a year and a pension on condition that he went to Melbourne at once. He could take the mission Aborigines, but no others.[21] Robinson accepted the appointment, for he planned to take the children as well as the mission adults and hoped to transfer the others in a short time. Franklin was also convinced that once the public hysteria of the Myall Creek trials had subsided the transfer of the rest could take place.

Robinson returned to Flinders Island in January 1839, selected fifteen Aborigines, and departed for Port Phillip on 25 February. The Aborigines were Truganini, Woorraddy, Pevay, Walter George Arthur and his wife Mary Ann Cochrane, Lacklay, Timmy, Fanny, Harriet, Matilda, Woorraddy's sons Peter and Davy Bruny, the sealing woman Charlotte and her son Johnny Franklin, and another boy, Tommy Thompson. Only six would return to Flinders Island in 1842. Robinson's last gift to the establishment was the Spanish influenza he had contracted in Sydney and from which eight Aborigines died. Robinson's eldest son wrote in his diary in March:

> It would be impossible to describe the gloom which prevails . . . from the bereavement of so large a portion of their kindred and friends, and the anxiety they evince to leave a spot which occasions such painful reminiscences is hourly increasing. . . . the males . . . attenuated forms . . . proves them to be the greatest suffered, and that the island has been a charnel house for them.[22]

Robinson's departure deprived those who remained of a chance for survival, since he took with him the few Aborigines who were articulate and strong enough to voice outrage at their treatment. His efforts to take the rest of the Aborigines to Port Phillip failed. Neither Lieutenant-Governor Charles La Trobe at Melbourne nor Sir George Gipps in Sydney was prepared to countenance them on the mainland of Australia.

From the time of Robinson's arrival at Flinders Island in October 1835, when there were 123 Aborigines living there, to his departure three and a half years later, 59 Aborigines died, 11 were born or arrived separately, and 15 accompanied him to Port Phillip. Only 60 remained. Robinson had failed to perceive that the Aborigines saw their own culture as more important than his. They had lost their land and wanted to cling to every vestige of their traditional life that remained. Nor did he offer them any viable economic existence. He had the opportunity to develop their sealing and sailing skills, but the only acceptable occupation was agriculture. Robinson himself had no farming experience, so with poor soil, lack of organizational experience, and uninterested Aborigines, agriculture was bound to fail.

The Aborigines on Flinders Island were not without ability or initiative; these attributes were simply never exploited. As a traveller and explorer, Robinson was singularly unsuited to administering a supervised camp. In retrospect, the survival of any Aborigines after three and

half years of broken promises, disease, a restricted existence, and poor
rations must be seen as a triumph of endurance. But they had to pay
the price for surviving the wars with the settlers by incarceration in a
place far from their homeland.

NOTES

1. Plomley, *Friendly Mission*, p. 941 (n. 28).
2. Ibid., pp. 928–29, 938.
3. Flinders Island Papers, 30 Apr. 1836, ML A573.
4. Information in the following four paragraphs has been taken from Robinson's Flinders Island Journal (RP, vol. 11, pt 1) for 7 and 18 Nov. and 2, 3,
4, 7, 10, 16, and 28 Dec. 1835.
5. Clark to Robinson, Dec. 1835, RP, vol. 24.
6. Robinson, Flinders Island Journal, 10 Feb. 1837.
7. Report of Major Thomas Ryan upon the Aboriginal Establishment, Mar.
1836, RP, vol. 24.
8. Ibid.
9. Plomley, *Friendly Mission*, p. 932.
10. Robinson, Flinders Island Journal, 21 and 25 Sept., 26 Oct., and 18 Nov.
1836.
11. Ibid., 20 Dec. 1836.
12. *Flinders Island Weekly Chronicle*, 17 Nov. 1837, in the papers of William
Thomas, ML uncat. MSS, set 214, item 1.
13. Ibid.
14. Report of the Aboriginal Establishment at Flinders Island, 24 June 1837,
BPP, 1839, vol. 34, no. 526, p. 7.
15. *Flinders Island Weekly Chronicle*, 17 Nov. 1837.
16. Report of the Aboriginal Establishment, p. 7.
17. Robinson, Flinders Island Journal, 10 Oct. 1837.
18. Ibid., 17 Oct. 1837.
19. Encl. in Robinson to col. sec., 4 July 1838, RP, vol. 24.
20. Ibid., 26 Jan. 1838; Franklin to Glenelg, 12 Feb. 1838, PRO CO 280/93,
pp. 171–72; Glenelg to Gipps, 31 Jan. 1838, *BPP*, 1844, vol. 34, no. 6, p. 4.
21. Gipps to Glenelg, 10 Oct. and 10 Nov. 1838, ML A1219, pp. 450–51, 611–
16, 619–20.
22. Journal of George Robinson, jun., RP, vol. 50, 28 Mar. 1839.

13

Flinders Island 1835-39: A Push for Independence

> The remainder of my country people are desirous of doing all we can to support ourselves upon Flinders without our being any more expensive to the Government. . . . the Blacks would all petition the governor to get land to earn for themselves but they are afraid and when they will not work for other people they are called Idle and Lazy, altho' we are paid but very little.[1]

With Robinson's departure Franklin set up a board of inquiry, the first of three that were to take place during the next six years. Its findings set the tone for the succeeding ones — the establishment was not paying for itself, and the Aborigines were so ungrateful, lazy, and indolent that they should be sent to the mainland of Van Diemen's Land to work as agricultural labourers. But there was no opportunity to leave Flinders Island. There was no native police work to absorb their restless energies, the settlers were still fearful of reprisal, and the British government was reluctant to scatter a people they had so zealously captured. Franklin reduced the European staff to a commandant, a medical officer, a storekeeper, a catechist, a coxswain, five convicts, and six soldiers and decreased annual expenditure from four thousand to two thousand pounds. But the European staff all had such large families that there were more Europeans at the establishment than in Robinson's time.[2]

The new commandant, Malcolm Laing Smith, formerly police magistrate at Norfolk Plains, arrived in April 1839. He saw the Aborigines as possible cheap labour on his own farm which he planned to lease from the government on another part of the island. He settled his large family into the commandant's house and left the supervision of the Aborigines to his sons. So long as they co-operated in basic tasks such as collecting wood, digging gardens, and attending church, the Aborigines were left alone. But upon any sign of insubordination they were gaoled.

This policy of indifference was certainly an improvement upon Robinson's administration. In the more relaxed atmosphere the Aborigines enjoyed better health and produced more children. They were permitted to use ochre, to perform ceremonial dancing, and to take frequent hunting trips. But this relative freedom was simply another manifestation of the government's belief that they were an abandoned people, destined to perish. For Flinders Island was now a ration station to a remnant group of people from whom the most able and the most healthy had been removed. Supply ships still failed to arrive at regular intervals, many of the Aborigines still could not stomach salt meat, and on a clear day a number of women would sit on Flagstaff Hill and look across to the north-east coast of Van Diemen's Land sixty-five kilometres away and lament the loss of their country.

In May 1841, when another epidemic ravaged the establishment and Van Diemen's Land was suffering an economic slump, Franklin appointed a second committee of inquiry to suggest a means for further reducing expenditure. The cost of European salaries was nearly double that of Aboriginal rations, so the commandant was dismissed and the staff reduced to eight. Eight Aboriginal children were sent to the Orphan School in Hobart in the hope that they would lose their Aboriginal identity. The committee again noted the indolence among them: "Having everything provided for them, having for the most part, all things in common, they shew no inclination to employ themselves in gardening or other light work." In an attempt to reorder their lifestyles to that of a subsistence agricultural community, the committee recommended the Aborigines should be forced to live in family rather than communal groups, with separate enclosed gardens to control their livestock of pigs and dogs. But the Aborigines were still angered by the loss of their land and had no desire to earn another chance to join European society as self-supporting farmers. [3]

Smith was replaced first by Peter Fisher, who had previously conducted the medical supervision of the convict hulks at Chatham, and then by Henry Jeanneret, a brilliant medical officer who had a vast knowledge of the treatment of dysentery. When Jeanneret arrived at Wybalenna with his family in August 1842 he found fifty-two Aborigines, consisting of twelve "married couples", eleven single men, six single women, and eleven children in various stages of ill-health. One man, Leonidas, could plough a little; two women, Bessy Clark and Daphne, could sew "tolerably"; and the rest could drive carts when asked to do so. Their dogs, which were central to their social relationships, were a menace to attempts at tidiness and destroyed crops and stock with impunity. Indeed, the Aborigines were indifferent to Jeanneret's position. At night they performed ceremonial dancing and by day they went hunting for muttonbirds and shellfish without his permission.[4]

Jeanneret's difficulties were increased by the unexpected arrival of two new groups of Aborigines – one from Port Phillip, the other from Cape Grim. They were to have a profound effect upon the establishment.

The first group comprised Walter George Arthur and his wife Mary Ann, Truganini, Fanny, Matilda, and Davy Bruny, survivors of the fifteen Aborigines Robinson had taken to Port Phillip over three years before, and Jack Allen, formerly with John Batman. At Port Phillip Walter George Arthur and Timmy had become stockmen and made at least two overland trips to Adelaide, while Mary Ann and Woorraddy had spent most of their time in Robinson's household. Robinson had made no attempt to use these Aborigines to make contact with the Victorian Aborigines, although Walter George Arthur and Truganini had joined him on at least one expedition to the interior. Five others had quickly removed themselves from his care and become the desperadoes Gipps and La Trobe and the Sydney press had predicted: in August 1841 Truganini, Matilda, Fanny, Timmy, and Pevay had begun a series of raids in the Western Port–Dandenong districts, looting shepherds' huts and wounding four stock-keepers. Their tactics had all the marks of sustained guerilla resistance to white settlement. Then at Western Port on 6 October they shot dead two whalers. At their trial the two men, Timmy and Pevay, admitted shooting the whalers and were sentenced to hang on 20 January 1842, the first public execution in Melbourne. Truganini, Matilda, and Fanny were acquitted and bundled back to Flinders Island with the other Tasmanian Aborigines.

Woorraddy, perhaps dreading the indignity of the return to the establishment, died as the ship docked at Green Island, within sight of Flinders Island. He had been the first Aboriginal Robinson had met at Bruny Island in 1829 – a proud warrior with three young children. In that year his wife died, and before Robinson set off on his first journey to the west coast in 1830 Woorraddy had become associated with Truganini. He had been a faithful companion to Robinson in all his missions, providing him with much information about the customs, languages, and religious beliefs of his compatriots. At the age of fifty he represented the last of the traditional Aborigines. He never learned to read or write, never wore European clothes, and never ate European food. His belief in his Aboriginal identity remained unshaken through the years of dispossession.[5]

The second group of Aborigines arrived from Cape Grim in December 1842 and consisted of William Lanney, aged seven, his parents, and four brothers. This was the family that had remained in

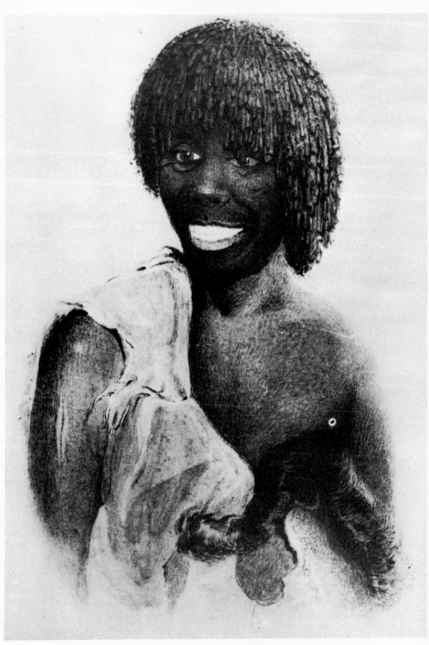

15. *Pevay*, by Thomas Bock. Beattie's Photographs, Hobart.

16. *Aboriginal Establishment at Flinders Island, 1845.* View from Mt. Franklin, by Simpkinson de Wesselow. Tasmanian Museum and Art Gallery.

the bush after refusing to surrender to the mission Aborigines led by Robinson's son in 1836/37. The family had lived in the hills behind Cape Grim until 1841 when they had begun to rob huts belonging to the Van Diemen's Land Company. They "gave themselves up" near the Arthur River — because, they said, they were lonely. By the end of 1847 both parents and three of the children would be dead, leaving only William Laney and his brother, Barnaby Rudge.[6]

The arrival of these two groups created a new interest and incentive for survival. The Aborigines from Port Phillip had a greater understanding of their rights and privileges, and Walter George Arthur and Mary Ann, Jack Allen, and Davy Bruny soon became the leaders of the establishment. Even before their arrival they had heard stories of Jeanneret's "rigid and severe" regime. The women immediately sought out the sealers, introduced new forms of ceremonial dancing, and produced fresh supplies of ochre and new relics to reinforce ritual. The men amazed and delighted their compatriots by refusing to dig the gardens unless they were paid and refusing to unload the stores unless they were given extra rations, while Mary Ann refused to clean her house unless she had better clothes. This new state of affairs distressed Jeanneret, who had envisaged a different programme of Aboriginal improvement designed to make them more dependent on him. He believed the Aborigines should give considerable labour in return for normal rations, while they regarded rations as bare compensation for the loss of their land. They told him that Wybalenna had been created not for their benefit but for the benefit of the Europeans who had taken their country. In an attempt to restore control, Jeanneret removed three more of the children to the Orphan School at Hobart. [7]

But Jeanneret's blustering behaviour also irritated his superiors in the civil and military establishment in Hobart. He was accused of insubordinate conduct towards the colonial secretary at Hobart and of ill-treating a soldier at the establishment. He was suspended in December 1843. [8]

His successor was Joseph Milligan, also a surgeon, who had previously been attached to the Van Diemen's Land Company at Circular Head. A favourite of Governor Franklin's circle, he had a scientific as well as humanitarian interest in the Aborigines, and during his time at Flinders Island he studied their languages and customs. His vocabulary, published in 1857, became an influential guide in giving Aboriginal Tasmanian names to newly settled areas of Tasmania after 1880. He also encouraged prominent artists like John Skinner Prout and Francis Guillemard Simpkinson de Wesselow to visit Wybalenna in 1845. Their drawings reveal the grim conditions of the site and of the Aborigines, most of whom wear blankets for clothes, while their faces are stricken with the fear of illness. [9]

The fifty-seven Aborigines at Wybalenna in 1844 still kept large numbers of dogs, lived communally in the Aboriginal terrace, and performed ceremonial dances which the Europeans thought had become more "depraved". There were now more women than men. They lamented the loss of their children to the Orphan School, where they could not learn the traditions of their parents. The policy of removing Aboriginal children as a means of expunging Aboriginal identity and of controlling the parents had begun with Governor Macquarie in New South Wales in 1810 and still continues as government practice in all parts of Australia.

Shortly after Milligan's arrival, Jeanneret appealed to the secretary of state for the colonies about his suspension, and in December 1845 it was upheld. Milligan suggested to Walter George Arthur that if he did not wish Jeanneret to return he should write to that influential Quaker in Hobart, George Washington Walker. Walter George Arthur wrote that his people did not want another commandant, for they could grow their own wheat and potatoes and use muttonbirds and their eggs for provisions, together with the mob of sheep that still remained from a bequest made by Arthur in 1832. The catechist Robert Clark could provide for their spiritual needs. But above all they wanted land so

17. *Taking a break from the hunt, Grass Tree Plains, Flinders Island, 1845.* By Simpkinson de Wesselow. Tasmanian Museum and Art Gallery.

they could be entirely independent. In February 1846 they all petitioned Queen Victoria not to allow Dr Jeanneret to return. They accused him of threatening to shoot them, putting them in gaol, forcing them to work without remuneration, and withholding rations for disobedience. This was the first petition sent to a reigning monarch from an Aboriginal group in Australia. But before the petition could be sent, Jeanneret returned to Flinders Island. When he learned of their move against him he blamed Milligan and Clark and accused Davy Bruny and Jack Allen of "inciting the others to riot and to set the authorities at naught. [Walter had] wantonly seized a musket, with intent to besiege my house at night."[10]

But the Aborigines fought back. They wrote to the lieutenant-governor in Hobart. Jack Allen wrote: "We want to tell you we do not like the man you sent down here for superintendent. We have to work for the clothes on our backs." Washington, one of the Big River people, wrote: "Dr. Jeanneret is a very bad man to me and my countrypeople – Please let me and my wife come to Hobart Town to see you. Dr. Jeanneret had put me in jail for speaking out for my rations which he stopped for two days." Walter George Arthur wrote: "We black people are threatened by Dr. Jeanneret to be hanged if we write any more about him we want a Protector, we are threatened to be put into Jail. . . . we are threatened to have our rations stopped if we do not work." Davy Bruny wrote: "Dr. Jeanneret says we must work for our clothes – Governor, I like work very well for white man when he pay me, but

Dr. Jeanneret want to make me and my wife work at his own garden
. . . and then pay me out of the government stores with the clothes you
send down to us. He growl at us too much for we blackfellows no like
work in his garden." And Mary Ann wrote: "Dr. Jeanneret wants to
make out my husband and myself very bad wicked people and talks
plenty about putting us into Jail and that he will hang us for helping
to write this petition to the Queen from our countrypeople . . . Dr.
Jeanneret does not like us for we do not like to be his slaves nor wish
our poor countrypeople to be treated badly or made slaves."[11]

The letters of petition were sufficient to provoke yet another
inquiry, by the port officer at Launceston, Matthew Friend, who was
instructed to check the validity of the petition and the complaint by
Jeanneret that Clark and his family had ill-treated the children, to
investigate the imprisonment of Walter George Arthur for seventeen
days, and to ascertain the need for building materials. Friend found
that the Aborigines were aware of the purport of the petition, that
Clark had not intentionally ill-treated the children, but that he had on
several occasions chained and flogged Fanny Cochrane, Mary Ann's
sister, for disobedience. In retaliation she had attempted to burn down
Clark's house. Finally, Friend found that Jeanneret had no legal right
to imprison Walter George Arthur.[12]

But the letters of petition provoked a different response from the
Colonial Office in London. The under-secretary, James Stephen,
recommended the abandonment of the establishment in favour of a site
on the Tasmanian mainland: "Why we should persevere in a policy at
once so costly to the author, and so fatal to the objects of it, I cannot
imagine, particularly as the establishment had been created not so much
with a view to any benefit to [the Aborigines] as from a regard to the
interests of the Colonists."[13] In Hobart the lieutenant-governor, Sir
William Denison, agreed. He was perturbed that the Aborigines' continued relations with the sealing community on the surrounding islands
in Bass Strait would contaminate the remaining "fullbloods" and feared
that their offspring would become a future charge upon the colonial
government. So he chose an abandoned penal station at Oyster Cove, in
the D'Entrecasteaux Channel, about thirty kilometres from Hobart, as
the Aborigines' "final" home. He dismissed Jeanneret on 5 May 1847
and appointed Milligan to conduct the removal of the establishment to
Oyster Cove the following October.[14]

The Aborigines now had fewer means to resist their institutionalized
environment. Had they remained on Flinders Island they could possibly
have increased their number by interaction with the Aboriginal sealing
community which had adapted to the realities of the Bass Strait

environment and provided a positive alternative to the artificial society at Wybalenna.

The move was not achieved without public protest. In Launceston the leaders of the anti-transportation movement called a public meeting on 30 September to protest against the return of "these savages to their primitive home". Many respectable settlers, clouded with memories of the guerilla war twenty years before, told the meeting that the Aborigines were still savage beasts, and that if they escaped from Oyster Cove, as they would try to do, they would again place the security of the island in jeopardy. The anti-transportationists saw the return of the Aborigines as an attempt by Denison to forestall the clamour for self-government, for the British government not only bore financial responsibility for both convicts and Aborigines, but also provided costly military protection for the settlers. Unless transportation were abolished and the Aborigines placed in a cheap gaol beyond the fears of the settlers, the colony could not afford self-government. They also argued that since the Aborigines had no proved potential as labourers, it would be cheaper to leave them at Flinders Island rather than indulge in an expensive removal to Oyster Cove, which had the potential to become valuable farming land.[15]

But for the Aborigines the removal was a release from the "charnel house" that had incarcerated them since 1833. Only forty-seven made that journey to Oyster Cove — fifteen men, twenty-two women, and ten children. Their average age was forty-two. Most suffered from chronic chest complaints, four had become enormously fat, one was blind, another was senile, while another suffered from acute arthritis. Between March 1839 and October 1847, thirty Aborigines had died, thirteen had arrived either from Port Phillip or Cape Grim, at least one woman had come from the sealing community, and at least five children, all part-Aboriginal, had been borne. There was not one expression of sorrow or regret as they packed themselves, their dogs, and their few possessions into the ship on that blustery day in October. They thought they were returning to their own country and escaping the deaths that had made their lives at Wybalenna so miserable. Oyster Cove represented the hope of new hunting grounds, better provisions, and restored health.

In administrative terms Flinders Island had been a success. It had been cheap to run, remote from white settlement, and hidden from the public eye. It became the model for all other Australian colonies to follow when disposing of their own unwanted indigenes. It was only the complaints from the Aborigines themselves that had brought change, and after self-government these complaints would be ignored.

NOTES

1. Walter George Arthur to G. W. Walker, 31 Dec. 1845, ML A612, pp. 221–23.
2. Report of the Board of Inquiry, 25 Mar. 1839, RP, vol. 50; Flinders Island Papers, ML A573.
3. Report of the Board of Inquiry, 10 June 1841, encl. no. 7, Franklin to Russell, 6 Aug. 1841, PRO CO 280/133, pp. 165–67.
4. Henry Jeanneret, *Vindication of a Colonial Magistrate* (London, 1854), p. 38; *ADB*, vol. 4, p. 472; Plomley, *Friendly Mission*, p. 1020; Plomley, *"Friendly Mission*: A Supplement", p. 28; Jeanneret to col. sec., 21 Feb., 31 Mar., and 20 May 1843, TSA CSO 8/157/1166.
5. Jeanneret to col. sec., 16 July and 15 Sept., 1842, TSA CSO 8/157/1166; see encl., Gipps to Stanley, 11 Mar. 1842, ML A1227, pp. 1309 *et seq*; Robinson, 20 July 1842, RP, vol. 18.
6. G. W. Walker to Harriet Jeanneret, 16 Sept., and Jeanneret to col. sec., 20 Dec. 1842, TSA CSO 8/157/1166; Plomley, *Friendly Mission*, pp. 926–27.
7. Jeanneret to col. sec., 16 Nov. 1842 and 31 Mar. 1843, TSA CSO 8/157/1166; Jeanneret, *Colonial Magistrate*, p. 54.
8. *ADB*, vol. 4, p. 472.
9. Report of the Aboriginal Establishment, 31 Mar. 1847, TSA CSO 11/26; "J. B." (John Broadfoot), "An Unexpected Visit to Flinders Island in Bass Straits", *Chambers' Edinburgh Journal*, 20 Sept. 1845, pp. 187–89; Clive Turnbull, *Black War* (Melbourne: Cheshire–Lansdowne, 1965), pp. 224–25; Joseph Milligan, "Vocabulary and Dialects of Aboriginal Tribes in Tasmania", *J&P LC Tas.* (1856), paper 7; John Skinner Prout, *Tasmania Illustrated* (Hobart Town, 1844).
10. W. G. Arthur to G. W. Walker, 31 Dec. 1845, ML A612; encl. in Wilmot to Gladstone, 13 Aug. 1846, PRO CO 280/195, p. 312; Jeanneret to Milligan, 17 Mar. 1846, PRO CO 280/195, p. 337; Jeanneret to col. sec., 12 June 1846, PRO CO 280/195, p. 352.
11. John Allen, Washington, Walter George Arthur, and Davy Bruny to governor, 16 June, and Mary Ann Arthur to governor, 10 June 1846, PRO CO 280/195, pp. 319–28.
12. Denison to Grey, 27 May 1847, PRO CO 280/209, p. 151 *et seq.*; Report on Flinders Island, 31 Oct. 1846, TSA CSO 11/27/658.
13. Remarks by James Stephen, 30 Jan. 1847, on dispatch of Wilmot to Gladstone, 13 Aug. 1846, PRO CO 280/195, p. 302.
14. Denison to Grey, 7 Dec. 1847, PRO CO 280/215, p. 3 *et seq.*; Robert Clark to col. sec., 30 Mar. 1847, TSA CSO 11/27/658; P. E. de Strzelecki, *Physical Description of New South Wales and Van Diemen's Land* (London, 1845), pp. 344–46.
15. *Examiner*, 20 Oct. 1847.

14

The Fragments

The Oyster Cove Aboriginal Station was divided into two sections. The central part of about forty hectares, which contained the original convict buildings, the superintendent's house, and the school, was situated at the mouth of the Great Oyster Cove and Little Oyster Cove rivulets. The other section of 688 hectares, which was set aside to provide sufficient game to supplement European provisions, was about a kilometre and a half west of the main settlement, along the Little Oyster Cove Rivulet. In layout it differed little from the Aboriginal terrace at Wybalenna. The buildings formed a rectangle with a church and school house at one end and living quarters at the other. Lieutenant-Governor Denison considered that Oyster Cove had advantages over Wybalenna in terms of climate, proximity to Hobart Town, exposure to official scrutiny, and the availability of new areas for hunting and fishing. But Oyster Cove was built on a mudflat with poor drainage. The buildings, made of wood instead of brick, offered no protection from the biting southerly winds. They were subject to damp and vermin and for much of the year were a repository for the waste water from farms further up the creeks. In later years malaria infested the area. The original penal station, built in 1843 for female convicts and later used for male convicts, had been abandoned in 1847 when it failed to meet convict health standards. So the Aborigines were removed to a settlement that had already proved insanitary for Europeans.[1]

When they arrived at Oyster Cove the Aborigines plunged into ceremonial dancing, much to the delight of the surrounding settlers and astonished visitors. Then they moved into their apartments, freshly painted and furnished with chairs and tables, cupboards and beds, and glass windows. The eleven couples lived on one side of the square and the fifteen single people occupied the other; the ten children were sent to the Orphan School in Hobart Town. The Aborigines were supposed to cook in big round pots inside their apartments, but when they found

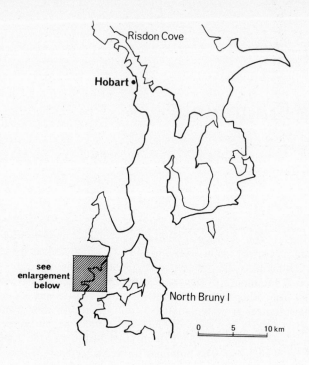

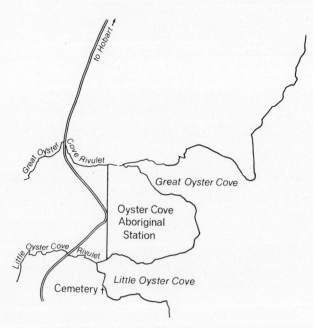

Map 43. Oyster Cove Aboriginal Station

18. *Oyster Cove.* An old convict station now inhabited by the few remaining Aborigines of Tasmania. [c. 1849]. By Charles Edward Stanley. National Library of Australia.

the floors too damp to sit on, they lit fires outside. Their rations were increased to two pounds (900 g) of meat a day, two ounces (57 g) of tea, quarter of an ounce (7 g) of tobacco, and two ounces (57 g) of sugar. Although they had few vegetables, they took advantage of the abundant shellfish in the D'Entrecasteaux Channel and hunted wallabies and wombats in the Aboriginal reserve. For a short time the Aborigines maintained their health.[2]

Denison was determined not to repeat the administrative mistakes of Flinders Island. To ensure that the station was efficiently managed, a visiting magistrate made weekly inspections of the Aborigines' clothes, houses, treatment and behaviour, and the quality and condition of the rations. Apart from the catechist Robert Clark, the only other Europeans at the station were a storeman and bullock-driver and their families. The station was budgeted at £1,120 a year, two-thirds the annual expenditure at Wybalenna.

Denison sent the children to the Orphan School in the hope they would "adjust" to European society and arranged for Robert Clark to provide regular religious instruction at the station, for he believed that everyone should have the opportunity to die in God's grace. At Christmas in 1847 Denison invited a party of Aborigines to government house at New Norfolk to share in the celebrations. Their infectious good humour and delight at everything they saw confirmed his view of their harmlessness and timidity.[3]

19. *Aborigines at Oyster Cove, 1847.* By Fanny Benbow. [c. 1900]. W. L. Crowther Library, State Library of Tasmania.

But for the Aborigines, the struggle for a different kind of acceptance continued. In an attempt to prove their equality with whites, the unofficial leaders of the community, Walter and Mary Ann Arthur, bought a three-hectare block of land near the station, constructed a three-room bush hut, and began to live as humble European farmers. Walter was later granted eight hectares of land and applied to the government for an assigned servant. He was refused on the grounds that none was available, but it was whispered that the government had no intention of allowing a white man to become the servant of a black.[4]

By 1849 the period of "initial co-operation" common to the inmates of new institutions had passed. On a visit to the station in April of that year, Denison found the Aborigines had developed a "tense recklessness", not so much for survival but in a desperate rush for life. The women found it more "exciting" to prostitute themselves for alcohol than to listen to the catechizing of Robert Clark. The men found it easier to escape their sorrows in a public bar in Hobart Town than hunt in the bush, where they risked being starved or shot. They no longer took care of themselves or their houses, they openly flouted Denison's authority by absenting themselves when he visited, they complained of damp and cold, and they regretted the move from Flinders Island, for they were now in worse misery and despair. Denison retreated to Hobart Town enraged that these people, for whom he considered he had done so much, now manifested only base ingratitude.[5]

When the visiting magistrate reported a "decline" in the Aborigines' "moral behaviour", distinguished visitors no longer came to the station. They feared that "scenes of depravity" might offend them. It was the same with the Anglican Church. The first Anglican bishop of Tasmania, Francis Russell Nixon, had often visited the station in its early days, but when he too felt the lash of the Aborigines' "ingratitude" he sent proxies in his place.[6]

In April 1851 Robinson paid a brief visit to the station before his return to England. He found only thirty Aborigines there, thirteen having died since 1847, and four children were at the Orphan School. They told Robinson they wanted to return to Flinders Island or Cape Barren Island, because Oyster Cove was "unhealthy, too low, damp". He noted that they were no more elated at seeing him than any other old friend, but characteristically considered this was probably due to the pernicious influence of Robert Clark and other Europeans in the area. After accepting some shell necklaces from Mary Ann Arthur and her sister, Fanny, he departed for England and never saw them again.[7]

By the time Denison departed from Van Diemen's Land at the end of 1854, the population at Oyster Cove had fallen from forty-seven to seventeen. He never bothered to investigate the reasons for this decline, nor the increase of disease. Nor did he inquire into the whereabouts of the ever-diminishing rations, the absence of vegetables, and the decrease in traditional food sources such as shellfish and wallabies, which had originally abounded in the area. Milligan reported that the only labour the Aborigines performed was the "procurement of their own firewood". He despaired of what he called "their natural indolence and love of ease characteristic of the Aboriginal races of these islands". They usually huddled in their "close overheated apartments" like "hot house plants". They had stopped cultivating their gardens. In keeping with previous attitudes, Milligan considered that since all their "wants" were supplied, the Aborigines had nothing to do. He blamed their illness upon their indolent behaviour and their association with nearby settlers. By 1854 the Aborigines had lost their health and their hope.[8]

The achievement of self-government for the colony of Tasmania in the following year reduced the fortunes of the Aborigines even further. The local government considered the "absence" of Aborigines in the colony an indication of its maturity. This attitude was shared by the newly responsible governments of Victoria and New South Wales, which also had "remnant" Aboriginal populations. Thus from 1855 to

1869 Tasmanian government policy towards the Aborigines at Oyster Cove was based upon minimal expenditure and neglect, in the hope that they would die out. Indeed, so anxious was the Tasmanian government to get rid of the Aborigines that at the beginning of 1856 they nearly accepted an offer by the former commandant Malcolm Laing Smith to take charge of the Aborigines at a cost to the government of thirty pounds a year each. Had Smith tendered a lower price, the government would probably have accepted.[9]

By the end of 1855 expenditure at Oyster Cove had been reduced to nearly half that of the previous year. The government then decided that the able-bodied should be removed from the station and "put to work", while the part-Aborigines should be expelled. Three of the men, William Lanney, Adam, and Jack Allen, were apprenticed to whaling ships. The part-Aboriginal woman Fanny Cochrane was married to a European named Smith; she brought with her a dowry of twenty-four pounds a year to remove to Nicholls Rivulet. Walter and Mary Ann Arthur abandoned their attempt to cultivate the land so that Walter could become an overseer, but he was dismissed for subversive conduct. The weekly magistrate's visit became a monthly visit, rations were further reduced, and building repairs were curtailed.[10]

These "economies" made the Aborigines even more dependent upon surrounding settlers, who provided them with alcohol, tobacco, and tea in exchange for blankets. An attempt by the authorities to issue specially marked blankets to prevent trafficking in these items proved abortive.[11]

By 1859 the Oyster Cove Aboriginal Station had become "a miserable collection of huts and outbuildings . . . profoundly dirty and swarming with fleas . . . the sides . . . in a ruinous condition, roofs not waterproof, windows broken, the furniture gone". Of the nine women still alive, Dray, now called Sophia, was constantly in tears, and another one, Caroline, spoke only to her dogs, while the rest suffered severe respiratory complaints. Of the five men, one, Tippo Saib, was senile and nearly blind, and two others, Jack Allen and Augustus, Bessy Clark's husband, were alcoholics. The women most admired William Lanney, aged twenty-four, whom they saw as "a fine young man, plenty beard, plenty laugh, very good, that fellow".[12]

In the midst of this squalor, James Bonwick, evangelical lay preacher and schoolmaster in the colony of Victoria, visited the station. He was deeply grieved at his findings: "No means are adopted by Government to provide any religious instruction or emulation and no effort made to protect them from the vicious influence of the bad white man or to keep them from the destructive effects of strong drink. The remnant

20. *Tasmanian Aborigines at Oyster Cove, 1860.* Beattie's Photographs, Hobart.

should at least be prepared for death and eternity."[13] But the government believed otherwise and blamed their misery and squalor upon the Aborigines themselves: "There are five old men and nine old women living at the Oyster Cove Station — uncleanly, unsober, unvirtuous, unenergetic, and irreligious, with a past character for treachery, and no record of one *noble* action, the race is fast falling away and its utter extinction will be hardly regretted."[14] Photographs of the Aborigines taken a year later by J. W. Beattie revealed their wretchedness, their defiance, and their hostility. Comforted by their dogs, they eschewed the outside world, clinging to the few remaining threads of traditional society.[15]

In 1860 Tippo Saib, Augustus, Flora, and Caroline died, followed in 1861 by Dray and Walter George Arthur. The death of Walter George Arthur was one of the more sorrowful aspects of the European invasion of Tasmania, for he was the one "fullblood" Aboriginal Tasmanian who tried to conform to European mores. Captured with his father's people, the Ben Lomond, in 1830 at the age of ten, he had first been placed in the Orphan School at Hobart Town until taken to Flinders Island by Robinson in 1835. There he had been under the care of the catechist, Robert Clark. Both Robinson and Clark had hoped that Walter George Arthur would become a catechist, but his "immoral" behaviour with Mary Ann Cochrane in 1838 had prevented this. While he was at Port Phillip with Robinson he had worked as a stockman and drover. He had also been introduced to alcohol, which seemed to quench the passionate outrage that he secretly felt in the presence of all white men. On his return to Flinders Island in July 1842 he and Mary Ann and their five compatriots from Port Phillip, by having the audacity to question the quality of the rations and by refusal to do any unpaid work, had become the unofficial leaders of the community. At Oyster Cove Walter and Mary Ann had been exhorted to set an example in docility, cleanliness, and gratitude. They had lived in their three-roomed bush cottage surrounded by the trappings of European civilization, gifts from clergymen and well-wishers. But they had preferred the communal warmth of the station, where they could relax and share a bottle with their own people. It was Walter's particular regret that he and Mary Ann produced no children. He had developed a schizophrenic personality: sometimes he was a resistance leader demanding better conditions for his people; at other times he was a desperate conformist aching for the acceptance of white society. But he was never "good enough". One blustery evening in May 1861, returning to the station by boat from a waterfront pub in Hobart Town, he fell overboard and was never seen again.[16]

By 1864 Jack Allen and Emma had died, followed in 1867 by Patty

21. *Walter George Arthur and Mary Ann.* Oyster Cove, 1860. Beattie's Photographs, Hobart.

and Wapperty, the last of the sealing women, and Bessy Clark. In 1868 only three remained — Truganini, William Lanney, and Walter George Arthur's widow, Mary Ann, who had remarried in 1865, this time to a European named Adam Booker. However, she remained at the station.[17]

At this time there was a renewed interest in the Aboriginal Tasmanians from the scientific world, based upon the conviction that they were the missing link between ape and man. As the last "full-blood" male Aboriginal, William Lanney aroused considerable scientific attention. He had arrived at the age of seven at Flinders Island in 1842, one of five children of the last family of Aborigines captured near the Arthur River at the end of 1842. He had attended the Orphan School in Hobart Town between 1847 and 1851 and then had gone to sea as a whaler. He had found more acceptance from his seafaring friends than any of his compatriots experienced from the rest of European society. His proudest moment came in 1868 when during the visit of the duke of Edinburgh in Hobart Town, he was introduced as the "king of the Tasmanians". From 1851 Lanney had rarely been at Oyster Cove and had not been exposed to the disease and despair that overtook the rest of his compatriots. It was a great disappointment to the Aboriginal women that he never married and produced a child. But he took his responsibilities as the last male "fullblood" Aboriginal very seriously. At the end of 1864, he had lodged an official complaint with the colonial secretary that the women were receiving inadequate rations. He had explained, "I am the last man of my race and I must look after my people." An official investigation had revealed that when the supply vessel for the area failed to arrive from Hobart Town, the settlers bought or borrowed stores from the Aboriginal station. As a result the Aboriginal women were sometimes starved.[18]

On 2 March 1868, while in Hobart Town on leave from his ship, Lanney became ill at the Dog and Partridge Hotel at the corner of Goulburn and Barrack Streets. He died at one o'clock the following afternoon.[19] His friends, the banker George Whitcomb and the solicitor J. W. Graves, concerned to save his body from the clutches of science, immediately visited the premier, Sir Richard Dry, and persuaded him to agree that the body should be buried. The premier then ordered the corpse to be removed from the Dog and Partridge to the morgue at the Colonial Hospital, where it was believed a guard could more readily keep watch over it. But placing the corpse in the Colonial Hospital was tantamount to throwing it into a lion's den. The chief house surgeon at the hospital, Dr George Stokell, was a leading member of the Royal Society of Tasmania, while one of the honorary medical officers, Dr W. L. Crowther, MLC, was a member of the Royal College of Surgeons.

22. *Truganini, William Lanney and Bessy Clarke, 1866.* Beattie's Photographs, Hobart.

Both organizations had already expressed an interest in Lanney's skeleton, and both men were quick to support their interests.

When Lanney's body arrived at the morgue, the premier ordered Stokell not to allow anyone into the morgue. At six o'clock that afternoon, 3 March, Stokell received an urgent invitation to take tea with Mrs Crowther in Davey Street. He locked the morgue and, leaving the keys in the charge of the house steward, set off. At half-past seven Dr Crowther and his son visited the hospital and summoned the gatekeeper, Charles Williams, and asked him to find the hospital barber, John Shakerow. Then having obtained the keys from the house steward, Crowther, his son, and the barber entered the morgue. The gatekeeper, suspecting treachery but fearing punishment, looked through the keyhole and saw three men attending the bodies of William Lanney and a schoolmaster named Ross. At nine o'clock the gatekeeper saw Crowther and his son leave the hospital, the former carrying a parcel under his arm.

When Stokell returned a short time later, he realized that "something was up"; he entered the morgue to find that William Lanney's head had been removed and replaced by that of the schoolmaster's. He alerted the Royal Society of Tasmania, and with their agreement Stokell cut off Lanney's hands and feet at nine o'clock the next morning. At the same time a search was made for the head, for there were rumours that it had been thrown over the hospital walls into the rubbish dump.

At two o'clock that afternoon between fifty and sixty gentlemen presented themselves at the morgue to carry the coffin to the funeral service. But already rumours of mutilation had spread. An inspection of the body was demanded. The coffin was opened and Lanney's mutilated body was exposed to public view. After the cries of horror had subsided, it was decided that nothing could be done, for both Whitcomb and Graves realized that the premier, in placing the body in the hospital in the first place, was as much responsible for the mutilation as were any of the individual mutilators. The coffin was sealed and draped with the Union Jack, some native flowers, and a possum skin. The procession then moved to St David's Church, where the service was read by the Reverend Mr Cox. On leaving the church the procession, numbering about 120 mourners, many of whom were Lanney's shipmates, went to St David's Cemetery in Davey Street, where the second half of the service was read. Then the grave was closed over William Lanney, died 3 March 1869, aged thirty-four years.

But science had yet to finish with William Lanney. That evening Dr Crowther arranged for a small group of men to assemble in Harrington Street, while in Salamanca Place another group awaited the arrival of Dr Stokell and members of the Royal Society. This time Stokell reached the cemetery first. About midnight he and his party dug up the body of William Lanney and took it to the rear of the hospital, where he and a Dr Judge and Messrs Burbury, Sheehy, and Weir, all members of the Royal Society of Tasmania, examined it. Then they placed it in the morgue once again.

Having missed his opportunity the evening before, Dr Crowther hurried to the hospital the next morning, Sunday 5 March. Finding the morgue locked, he broke the door down with an axe, but found nothing except a few particles of flesh. Stokell had removed what remained of Lanney's body early that morning into the house steward's garden. From there it was put in a cask on the Sunday night and later buried in the Campbell Street Cemetery.

There was not much left. Dr Stokell had a tobacco pouch made out of a portion of the skin, and other worthy scientists had possession of the ears, the nose, and a piece of Lanney's arm. The hands and feet were later found in the Royal Society's rooms in Argyle Street, but the head never reappeared.

When news of further mutilation filtered through to the press, a public inquiry was urged. But both Stokell and Crowther were men of considerable public influence. The premier supported Stokell's efforts on behalf of the Royal Society; however, he feared Crowther as a political enemy and so relished suspending him from his duties at the hospital. Crowther's supporters rallied in the columns of the *Mercury*. At the inquiry both men protested their innocence, while emphasizing the importance of Lanney's body to the study of mankind. Crowther was never reinstated.

Now only two Aborigines remained at Oyster Cove — Mary Ann and Truganini. The government decided to place them in the direct care of James Dandridge, the last superintendent at Oyster Cove, and his family for ninety pounds a year. In July 1871 Mary Ann had a seizure and was removed to the hospital in Hobart where she died in August. Only Truganini remained.[20]

Truganini, the daughter of Mangerner, chief of the Recherche Bay people, was born in 1812. By the time she met Robinson at Bruny Island in 1829, her mother had been stabbed by a party of sealers, her sister Moorinna had been abducted to Bass Strait by another sealer and there accidentally shot, and her fiance, Paraweena, had drowned while attempting to save her from abduction by sawyers. In July 1829 Truganini had "married" Woorraddy. With him she had accompanied Robinson on all his missions to the Aborigines between 1830 and 1834. By the time she and Woorraddy arrived at the Aboriginal establishment on Flinders Island in October 1835 Truganini had become a firm critic of Robinson, and he had been relieved to send her with the other mission Aborigines to search for the last family of the North people on the Tasmanian mainland in March 1836. When she and the other mission Aborigines had returned empty-handed to Flinders Island in 1837, Robinson had realized his authority had been flouted.

In 1839 Truganini had again escaped the horrors of Wybalenna by going to Port Phillip, where she had been expected to assist Robinson in conciliating the Aborigines there. But she had absconded with four of the others and begun raiding and looting shepherds' huts, which culminated in the shooting of the two whalers, Yankee and Cook, one of whom may have been the man who abducted her sister in 1828. Truganini and her two female companions had been acquitted on condition that they returned to Flinders Island.

So at the age of thirty Truganini had returned to Wybalenna, her husband Wooraddy dying *en route*. At the Aboriginal Establishment she had lived with an Aboriginal from the Big River named Alphonso, but had produced no children. Although she had formed a close liaison with the sealing women, she had taken no role in the struggle for independence led by Walter George Arthur in 1846. She had been delighted with the removal to Oyster Cove a year later, for it lay in her own country, the D'Entrecasteaux Channel. There she was able to visit Bruny Island and other places in the area of significance to her childhood. Such excursions probably helped to prolong her life.[21]

In 1872 Lucy Beedon, one of the leaders of the community in Bass Strait, asked Truganini to join them. But she was already living with her dreams and had removed herself spiritually from the European world.[22] She used to visit what she called her own country, the isthmus and Adventure Bay on Bruny Island, wandering the beaches, gathering shells and seaweed, and calling upon those of her old friends who were still alive, particularly Fanny Cochrane Smith's family at Nicholls Rivulet. She frequently expressed fears that upon her death she would be "cut up" like William Lanney and placed in the museum. She preferred burial in the deepest part of the D'Entrecasteaux Channel.[23]

Floods in the winter of 1874 so ravaged Oyster Cove that the Dandridge family moved to Hobart. There Truganini was to be seen about the streets dressed in a red turban, serge dress, and knitted cardigans and scarves, always accompanied by her dogs. She died in Hobart, in the house of Mrs Dandridge in Macquarie Street, at two o'clock in the afternoon of 8 May 1876 at the age of sixty-four. She had been ill for some weeks.[24]

The two doctors in attendance conveyed Truganini's body to the Hobart Hospital. Mrs Dandridge wrote a note to the colonial secretary to inform him of the death. The *Mercury,* suspecting impending foul

23. *Truganini, 1876.* Photo by H. H. Baily, Hobart Town. From the copy in the Mitchell Library.

play, thought that Truganini would have been safer in Mrs Dandridge's house. But the colonial secretary sent a memorandum to the surgeon superintendent of the hospital ordering him to allow no one to view the body. At this stage the government was undecided about the disposal of the body. Many members of government were also members of the Royal Society of Tasmania, so the *Mercury*'s suspicions were well founded.[25]

On 9 May the secretary of the Royal Society wrote to the colonial secretary asking for the corpse of Truganini, since she was the last "fullblood" and a valuable scientific specimen. Whatever the government originally had in mind, and from earlier correspondence with the Royal Society it had envisaged Truganini ending up in the museum, it felt unable to accede to the request at this stage. Instead, the government ordered a "decent interment" at the old Female Factory at the Cascades, in a vacant spot immediately in front of the chapel.[26]

The funeral took place privately at midnight on 11 May with the premier, the colonial secretary, and the Reverend Mr Parsons in attendance. The *Mercury* suggested that the private funeral was held not to forestall potential body-snatchers and mutilators but to make it easier for her body to be exhumed at a later date. As a consolation, the government intimated that a monument would be placed over the grave and J. W. Graves asked to write an epitaph.[27]

But this never took place. The museum of the Royal Society of Tasmania acquired Truganini's skeleton in 1878. Apart from two short visits to Melbourne, in 1888 and 1904, it remained there and was on public display from 1904 to 1947. Then in response to press agitation claiming the public display was in bad taste, the skeleton was stored in the vaults of the museum, where only scientists could view it. In 1971 the only anatomical study of the skeleton was carried out. In 1974, after a successful application to the government by the Aboriginal community in Tasmania, the cabinet agreed that Truganini's skeleton should be cremated in the centenary year of her death. But the trustees of the Tasmanian Museum were reluctant to part with it and started legal proceedings to determine ownership of the skeleton. This was cut short when legislation was passed in 1975 making Truganini's skeleton the property of the Crown. The skeleton was removed from the museum and placed in the vaults of the Reserve Bank in Hobart. On 30 April 1976 it was cremated. The next day the Aboriginal Tasmanian community scattered her ashes on the D'Entrecasteaux Channel. Truganini had finally gone to rest.[28]

Truganini was not in fact the last "fullblood" to die. On Kangaroo Island, Suke, a woman taken from Cape Portland and living with the old sealing community, died in 1888.[29] Nevertheless, for Aborigines Truganini has become a symbol of struggle and survival; for Europeans she has become a useful scapegoat for the extermination of the Tasmanians. With her death most Europeans considered the Aboriginal problem in Tasmania finished.

NOTES

1. J. E. Calder, *Some Account of the Wars, Extirpation, Habits, etc. of the Native Tribes of Tasmania* (Hobart, 1875), p. 112.

2. Denison to Grey, 7 Dec. 1847, PRO CO 280/215, p. 3 *et seq.*
3. Sir William Denison, *Varieties of Vice-Regal Life* (London, 1870), vol. 1, pp. 69–70.
4. James Bonwick, *The Last of the Tasmanians* (London, 1870), p. 353; Calder, *Wars, Extirpation, Habits,* p. 75; Dandridge to col. sec., 4 June 1868, TSA CSD 4/77/231.
5. Denison, *Varieties of Vice-Regal Life,* vol. 1, p. 104.
6. F. R. Nixon, *The Cruise of the Beacon,* (Hobart, 1854).
7. Robinson, 26–28 Apr. 1851, RP, vol. 67, pt 2; Milligan to col. sec., 31 July 1851, TSA CSO 24/284/6314.
8. W. E. L. H. Crowther, "The Final Phase of the Extinct Tasmanian Race 1847–1876", *RQVM,* n.s. 49 (1974): 29.
9. Smith to col. sec., 5 Dec. 1855, J. Knox to Dandridge, 14 Jan. 1856, Dandridge to Knox, 22 Jan. 1856, TSA CSD 1/76/2029.
10. *J&P LC Tas.,* (1864), "Statistics of Tasmania"; visitors book, Oyster Cove Visitors' Book, 28 Apr. 1858, TSA 4/1692.
11. Visitors Book, 2 Sept. 1859 and 8 July 1860.
12. Bonwick, *Last of the Tasmanians,* pp. 276–85.
13. Visitors book, 21 May 1859.
14. H. M. Hull, *Royal Kalendar, and Guide to Tasmania for 1859* (Hobart, 1859).
15. J. W. Beattie, *Photographs of Aborigines at Oyster Cove* (Hobart, 1860).
16. Bonwick, *Last of the Tasmanians,* p. 284.
17. Dandridge to col. sec., 14 Feb. 1867 and 20 Dec. 1865, TSA CSD 4/77/231.
18. Bonwick, *Last of the Tasmanians,* p. 395; Complaint by Aboriginal "Billy", 5 Dec. 1864, TSA CSD 4/77/231.
19. The following account of the disposal of William Lanney's body is taken from: "Statement made by Charles Williams, gatekeeper at the General Hospital, Hobart, Tasmania, giving an account of the death of 'King Billy' or 'William Laney' – 1869", Alex Morton MSS, ML A612; *Mercury,* 3, 4, 18, 20, and 27 March and 21 May 1869.
20. Dandridge to col. sec., 29 Sept. 1869, TSA CSD 7/33/450, and 12 Oct. 1871, TSA CSD 7/26/215.
21. La Trobe to Robinson, 15 Jan. 1842, RP, vol. 55, pp. 5–6; Jeanneret to col. sec., 31 Mar. 1843, TSA CSO 8/157/1166.
22. M. B. Brownrigg, *The Cruise of the Freak* (Launceston, 1872), p. 8; col. sec. to Dandridge, 11 Mar. 1872, TSA CSD 7/33/450.
23. Dandridge to col. sec., 31 July and 21 Aug. 1873, TSA CSD 10/31/488; *Mercury,* 9 May 1876.
24. Mrs Dandridge to col. sec., 8 May 1876, TSA CSD 10/31/488.
25. *Mercury,* 9 May 1876.
26. Sec. of RST to col. sec., 9 May 1876, TSA CSD 10/31/488; col. sec. to RST, 19 July 1864, TSA CSD 4/77/231, and col. sec. to RST 10 May 1876, and memo to col. sec., 10 and 11 May 1876, TSA CSD 10/31/488.
27. *Mercury,* 12 May 1876.
28. Lyndall Ryan, "Report to the Australian Institute of Aboriginal Studies on Truganini" (typescript, Canberra, AIAS, Oct. 1974); *Mercury,* 1 and 3 May 1976.
29. N. B. Tindale, "Tasmanian Aborigines on Kangaroo Island, South Australia", *Records of the South Australia Museum* 6 (1937): 29–37; Herbert Basedow, "Relic of the Lost Tasmanian Race: Obituary Notice of Mary Seymour", *Man* 14 (1914): 161–62.

15

The Islanders: Emergence of a New Aboriginal Community

With the death of Truganini in 1876, white Tasmanians firmly believed that their island had lost all its original inhabitants. But there were survivors — the community of Aboriginal women and sealers on the islands in eastern Bass Strait. By 1847 this "Islander" community had consisted of thirteen families totalling about fifty people.

On Gun Carriage Island there was Thomas Beedon, who lived with a woman from Cape Portland, Emerenna (Bet Smith), and their four children, Thomas Tucker, who lived with an Indian woman, Maria Bengally; David Kelly with his Aboriginal son; and John Riddle and his children. On Woody Island lived James Everett and Wottecowidyer (Wot, Wotty or Harriet), also from Cape Portland, and their four children. Richard Maynard also lived there with an Aboriginal Tasmanian, Margaret or Pollerwottelterkunne, from Piper River, by whom he had two children, and an Aboriginal Australian woman, Elizabeth, by whom he had four children. An earlier inhabitant, Andrew Armstrong, and his Aboriginal Australian wife, Jane Foster, and two of their children had recently left the island for the west coast of Tasmania to engage in sealing, but later returned to Clarke Island. On Long Island lived Edward Mansell and Julia (Black Judy) from St Patricks Head and their child. On Tin Kettle Island lived John Smith and his three children by Sarah (Mother Brown, or Pleenperrenner) from Cape Portland. On Cape Barren Island lived John Thomas and Nimerana, (Teekoolterme) a daughter of Mannalargenna, and at least three children, as well as Robert Rew and his part-Aboriginal wife, Frances Anderson. On Preservation Island was the Aboriginal Australian Margery, who had lived with James Munro until his death in 1845, and two of her children. On Hunter Island, at the western end of the strait, lived William Proctor and the part-Aboriginal Tasmanian Mary Ann Brown, and two of their children. There were other families on Kangaroo Island, but those associated with the Furneaux Group remained in sufficient contact to form the Islander community. Three

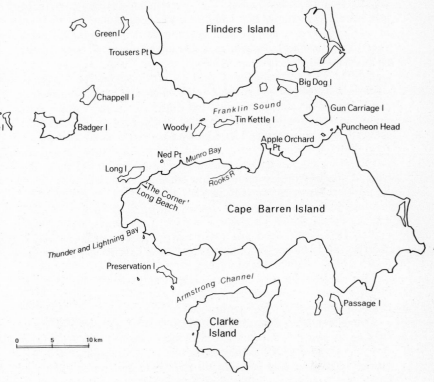

Map 44. Cape Barren Island

other European men entered this community in the succeeding twenty years — William Richard Brown, John Summers, and George Burgess. After that the Islanders Married within their own community, forming the basis of the present-day grouping.[1]

The community in the 1840s was seen by the outside world in sharply different ways. Some observers found the elders "hale, rubicund fellows, hearty and joyous", and the children "sharp and intelligent". Others found them "barbarous", "literally half-savage and half-civilised; half black and half white". Having survived eviction and harassment, they now began to seek recognition as a separate community.[2]

In February 1848 Thomas Beedon, of Gun Carriage Island, applied to the Van Diemen's Land government for the lease of Badger Island, but was refused on the ground that the island could be needed for the construction of a lighthouse. The government was not anxious to legitimize a community that had long evaded regulation. But the Bass Strait islands were beginning to attract other settlers, so in the following year the government decided that the surveyor-general should make an official visit, to make recommendations on future occupation. He found the Islander community scattered throughout the Furneaux Group. They ran pigs and goats and grew wheat and potatoes to supplement catches of kangaroos, seals, and muttonbirds; they visited each other's establishments, sometimes for months at a time, to exploit seasonal food resources; and they pursued a lifestyle based on elements from both traditional Aboriginal and nineteenth century European society. He said the Islanders were "kind and gentle; and upon the whole I consider them a primitive and amiable people, and believe that the greatest harmony prevails amongst them. The men are excellent boatmen and possess a capital description of whaleboat. . . . every encouragement should be given to a class of men most invaluable as Pilots." He recommended that a nominal rent of one shilling a year be paid by the Islanders for occupation of their existing places, on the understanding that the Crown possessed the right of resumption at six months' notice. The government, too, recognized that "the occupation of the Islands by acknowledged Tenants is better by far than having them occupied without leave or licence".[3]

Two years later the community applied to Lieutenant-Governor Denison for the appointment of a missionary-catechist to educate their children. They suggested that by virtue of their Aboriginality the salary of such a person should be paid from the Land Fund, which also maintained the Aboriginal station at Oyster Cove. Denison refused their application on the ground that they "could not fairly be termed Aborigines", although there were at least seven "fullblood" Aboriginal women in the community. In his view there was only one official Aboriginal community in Van Diemen's Land — the Aboriginal station at Oyster Cove. But he suggested that Bishop Nixon might take an interest in the Islanders' welfare.[4]

The geographical remoteness of the Islander community proved an attraction to the Anglican Church in Tasmania. In contrast to the inhabitants of the Aboriginal station at Oyster Cove, the Islanders in their comparative isolation appeared sober and industrious, sheltered from the "pernicious influences" of the "lower orders" of white society. The newly established missionary society for the diocese of Tasmania wrote of the Islanders: "The young men are prepossessing in their manners and address, and of athletic frame; the girls are modest in their demeanour and can make themselves useful in domestic affairs."[5] The society considered that these people should have some claim on any projected missionary enterprise.

In September 1854 Bishop Nixon paid his first visit to the Islanders, accompanying the surveyor-general, Robert Power. At Gun Carriage Island, still the centre of the community, he baptised some children and married Edward Mansell and the Aboriginal Tasmanian Julia Thomas, who had lived together for twenty-five years. Lucy Beedon, aged twenty-five, the daughter of Thomas Beedon and Emerenna, had become the teacher. She had received an education in Launceston and was already involved in the business interests of the community. Like the surveyor-general in 1849, the bishop was impressed with the Islanders' air of "quiet domestic union" and apparent innocence of drunkenness and theft. The Islanders, however, took the opportunity to protest about the harassment they received from Europeans illegally occupying nearby islands, who interfered with their muttonbirding.[6]

This visit persuaded the government to lease other islands to the community. Between 1855 and 1860 the Maynards and the family of James Everett's son George moved to Cape Barren Island, and the Beedons to Badger Island. By 1861 the Waste Lands Amendment Act had made available for lease islands or parts of islands for periods up to fourteen years, and in 1865 the community received permission to lease up to 222 hectares. The rapidly increasing numbers of the community severely tested their established decision-making processes, which depended upon reciprocal arrangements. It was no longer possible for John Riddle to depasture his sheep on Thomas Beedon's lease on Gun Carriage Island in the dry season, in exchange for Beedon's "birding" on Riddle's rookery. Some of the older members of the community, like Margery Munro, were left destitute on Preservation Island. But the long-established seasonal visiting patterns had survived, with a private season in family groups and a public season with the general congregation at the end of the muttonbird season.[7]

The outside world was almost completely excluded from their proceedings. They operated their leases according to their needs, often incurring the wrath of the Lands Department, which found their lack of co-operation infuriating. One officer wrote in 1861, "I . . . hardly think . . . any of the Straits inhabitants can be relied upon as I have most conflicting accounts given me by them of different matters. In fact they seem reluctant to give any information — they are evidently a most indolent, shiftless race of beings."[8]

But they were concerned to educate their children. When Thomas Beedon died in 1862, his daughter Lucy found that her business responsibilities precluded her from continuing to teach, so she invited Archdeacon Thomas Reibey and the Reverend George Fereday to the islands

24. *The Islanders, 1868.* Tasmanian State Archives.

to discuss the appointment of a teacher, after agreeing that the Islanders would raise a portion of the salary. Reibey photographed the Islanders and reported to the Tasmanian parliament but was unable to produce a teacher. Lucy Beedon later appointed two teachers from Melbourne. Concerned that the Islanders should not become alienated from the Anglican Church, Reibey launched an appeal to raise £500 for a missionary boat to make regular visits to the Islands. At the same time Fereday agreed to act as the Islanders' agents on the Tasmanian mainland.[9]

In 1866, following a misunderstanding over the renewal of licence fees, some Islanders lost the opportunity to renew their leases of the major muttonbird islands. Taking advantage of this, a recently arrived outsider leased four sixteen-hectare blocks on Chappell Island, which contained the largest muttonbird rookery in Bass Strait, as grazing land for his sheep. The surveyor-general dismissed the Islanders' protest that sheep disturbed the rookeries even though they were removed during the muttonbird season. In desperation the Islanders pursued the only avenue available to them as an Aboriginal community — they petitioned Governor Du Cane for exclusive rights to muttonbirding on Chappell Island and requested that an island be granted to them, to serve as the focal point of their life and identity. [10]

In August 1871 the governor held a meeting with the Islanders at Goose Island. Du Cane sympathized with their grievances and pressed their claims upon the government. The government, reluctant to grant land in Bass Strait, offered the Islanders (under the Waste Lands Act of 1870) two- to ten-hectare blocks for homestead and agricultural land, on the western end of Cape Barren Island. It also gazetted Chappell and Big Dog islands as muttonbird rookeries under the Game Preservation Act. The government had thus accepted the Islanders as a separate community and had protected the major rookeries from further incursion. But it had denied the Islanders ownership of land and exclusive rights to the rookeries by virtue of their Aboriginal descent.[11]

Cape Barren Island, at the western end of Bass Strait and part of the Furneaux Group, is about thirty-seven kilometres long and twenty-seven kilometres wide. It is separated from its larger neighbour, Flinders Island, by Franklin Sound. Named for its barren appearance by Tobias Furneaux in 1774, it has granite peaks and low-lying scrub. The land, though "quite unfit for cultivation",[12] can graze sheep and cattle. With few trees to afford protection against the westerly gales, dependence is placed upon coves to provide shelter, particularly the area known as the Corner on the western side of the island. Its immediate marine environment abounded at that time in crayfish and seals. The area between Thunder and Lightning Bay and Ned Point had been inhabited at various times by the Islanders from about 1810. Apart from white families at Apple Orchard Point on the northern side and at Puncheon Head opposite Gun Carriage Island, it had attracted few "outsiders", although there were 143 European settlers in the Furneaux Group in 1872.[13]

By the end of 1872 seven Islander families consisting of thirty-two adults and fifty-two children had settled on Cape Barren Island. George Everett and his family were at Thunder and Lightning Bay in the south, John Smith and family at Long Beach, young John Maynard and Thomas and James Mansell at the Corner, Thomas Rew at Rooks River, and William Brown at Munro Bay. Each household was about three kilometres away from the next. They made up for this separation by constant visiting, meetings, and expeditions. With old John Maynard on

25. *The Islanders, 1868.* Tasmanian State Archives.

Long Island, the Beedons at Badger Island, and old Edward Mansell at Passage Island, the community had become closer physically than at any period since the 1830s. The appointment of a schoolmaster, Henry Collis, who taught at Badger Island in the winter and at Long Beach in the summer, had given the community a recognition and stability never previously experienced.[14]

The community had retained many traditions from its Aboriginal and European founders. Most families spent the summer on Cape Barren Island and, at the end of the muttonbird season in May, travelled to Badger Island for the winter. In July many collected shells for stringing, and in November there was a further congregation for "egging". It was still common for a number of families to visit each other until "the neck of the flour bag became a little long".[15] The celebratory gatherings at the end of the muttonbird season were as important as the season itself, for the Islanders drew no distinction between work and leisure. Singing was as important as muttonbirding, curing kangaroo and seal skin as important as sharing the flour bag.

The women continued the traditions of their mothers, such as stringing shell necklaces. At certain times of the year a range of shells the Aboriginal Tasmanian women had traditionally used for stringing, were washed ashore. The young women combed the beaches, selecting with great care the types of shell needed for the painstaking process of stringing. In the evenings they would string the shells into delicate, intricate patterns. One present-day resident recalls that as a child she had to string for several hours each evening, taking months to complete one necklace. For this woman, stringing is still an important aspect of her existence.[16]

With the concentration of the community in one area, Canon Brownrigg of Launceston began regular missionary visits to conduct baptisms and marriages and to inspect the schools. From the start, Brownrigg wanted the leasehold land on Cape Barren Island converted to a reserve, and for the next fourteen years, through his articles in the Launceston *Examiner* and *Church News,* he pursued his view that the Islanders needed "guidance" in order to acquire "civilized" habits. This was reinforced by the visit of the Anglican bishop of Tasmania, Charles Henry Bromby, in 1876. In the bishop's view the Islanders were a godless community, addicted to drunkenness and sloth. He had no doubt that their Aboriginal ancestry was responsible for this "moral weakness" which was further manifested by the fact that they did not cultivate the land. He wanted a settled community which would relinquish the pursuit of muttonbirds, properly attend to the soil, and receive tuition in the "sober virtues" of respectable white society.[17]

The Islanders wanted protection from harassment in the muttonbird industry and from the threatened loss of land for debt. Some Islanders had not paid leasehold rent because they considered the land theirs by occupation or by virtue of their Aboriginal ancestry. So, for different reasons, the Islanders and the Anglican Church sought to have the leasehold area of Cape Barren Island legally associated with the Islanders.

In February 1881 the administrator of the colony of Tasmania withdrew from lease 1,416 hectares of land on the western end of Cape Barren Island, from Thunder and Lightning Bay to Munro Bay, together with a further 202 hectares of Crown land. The government intended the land for the exclusive use of the Islanders but did not wish to name them or officially extend to them any rights or privileges by virtue of their Aboriginality. The Islanders had lost the right to lease land in favour of right of occupation but had no control over the land and no security of tenure. The proclamation represented a confused if well-intentioned attempt to protect them, but it fell short of their needs.[18]

At first the Islanders thought they had been granted land and set about planning a township. But when they learned that they had no security of tenure and that the government could revoke the proclamation at any time, some families departed for Flinders Island. Only Brownrigg's assurances that revocation was unlikely brought some back. By 1884 some families at the Corner had built cottages, launched boats, and erected fencing. Brownrigg was optimistic that the means had been established for their eventual transformation into agriculturists.[19] He did not understand that the Islanders' relationship to the land rested on their Aboriginal heritage, their pursuit of muttonbirding, and their descent from a sealing community. Agriculture had never been a significant part of their existence.

To the outside world the Islanders were now a separate community whose lifestyle placed them beyond government assistance. If the Islanders were to achieve lasting recognition, it would only take place through the "protectionist-development" policies of the Anglican Church.

In 1889 the Right Reverend H. H. Montgomery arrived in Hobart as the fourth bishop of Tasmania. He was deeply committed to help the "unfortunate sable people of the earth" in their struggle to receive the Christian faith and learn the rudiments of European civilization. He attacked the "problem of the half-castes" with the enthusiasm of someone who was able to lose himself entirely in the joys of the unfamiliar. He noted that, unlike their "fullblood" counterparts at Flinders Island sixty years before, the Islanders were increasing in numbers. Since they already lived in an isolated environment and were seeking assistance for a new schoolteacher, he believed it possible to undertake a programme of instruction in the principles of Christianity and agriculture.[20]

Montgomery persuaded the minister for education to appoint to the community a "missionary schoolteacher" who would exemplify Christian standards of behaviour, instruct the children and their parents in horticulture and agriculture, and combine the functions of postmaster and governmental representative. The island would take on the air of a training institution with the habits of the Islanders under constant scrutiny.

The missionary schoolteacher appointed was Edward Stephens, then aged forty-seven. He arrived with his family at the Corner in August 1890 to find a community of 110 people, consisting of 30 adults and 80 children, who earned a livelihood from muttonbirding, piloting stores, sealing, whaling, fishing, itinerant labouring, and snaring animals.

For four months of the year, from February to May, the community was absent muttonbirding. In July some of the women went shelling at Thunder and Lightning Bay, and in November many of the men visited the rookeries for muttonbird eggs. Most families contained about ten people, housed in wooden cottages of two to four rooms surrounded by small gardens, with goats, pigs, poultry, some sheep, and a few horses. With no shop, church, school, police station, or post office, the jetty was the focal point for the community. Having been without a schoolteacher for some time, the Islanders hailed Stephens's arrival with enthusiasm.[21]

Stephens had known Aborigines since his childhood in South Australia. He had turned to missionary work because he wanted to control his desire for alcohol. During eight years on the island, Stephens operated a repressive system of law and order in conformity with the reserve system then developing in other parts of Australia. The Islanders were at first impressed by his concern for their welfare, but as they became aware of his own failings and his determination to control their lives, they withdrew their friendship and retreated into non-cooperation. Finally they were forced to resist in more positive fashion to protect themselves.

Six months after Stephens's arrival, Montgomery paid his first visit. He listened to the Islanders' requests for more favourable muttonbird regulations and their pleas for land ownership, baptised a number of their children, inspected the new school, decided to build a church and to consecrate a cemetery, and departed a week later, promising to present their grievances to the premier.[22]

Montgomery had quite different ideas for their advancement. Rather than pressing their claim for communal ownership of land, he recommended to the premier that each Islander family be allocated a block of land near the school under the watchful eye of the schoolmaster and that if they did not farm their land, then the lease should be withdrawn. Instead of pressing for the communal lease of muttonbird rookeries, he recommended the introduction of a family licence system where the Islanders would compete rather than co-operate during the muttonbird season. For Montgomery was determined that the spirit of private ownership and individual achievement should replace the Aboriginal communalism, which he considered had been responsible for their moral decline. He was now confident that if the Islanders were "kept from drink, encouraged to become farmers by judicious grants, prevented from intermarrying too much, these islands would be a very happy region, famed for its salubrity and out of reach of the greater temptations".[23]

On his second visit in 1892 Montgomery was deceived by Stephens

26. *Boatharbour "The Corner", Cape Barren Island.* Views in Norfolk Island and Bass Strait from negatives taken by the Rt. Rev. Dr. Montgomery, Bishop of Tasmania during his visit in 1892. Mitchell Library.

into believing that the Islanders had made "steady progress" towards "civilization". In the address written by Stephens and signed by the Islanders, he was told they observed the sabbath, regarded the school-teacher and his family with reverence and respect, and manifested gratitude for Montgomery's interest in their welfare. But Stephens was again wrestling with his craving for alcohol and a few weeks earlier had written in his diary: "This has been the most horrible year I can ever remember. I have not touched a drop of intoxicating liquor the whole year."[24]

Stephens's difficulties were exacerbated in June 1892 with the appointment of a constable to supervise the new muttonbird regulations. Stephens insisted that his second white official should attend Sunday services and refrain from drink and the use of bad language. The constable, who displayed his own eccentricities of character, eventually manifested his wrath by firing shots at the schoolhouse where Stephens was conducting Sunday service.[25]

By 1894, tensions at the Corner had become so intolerable that some Islanders departed for Flinders Island while others kept their children from the school. The climax came in October 1895, when the ketch *G.V.H.* was wrecked off the west coast of the island with the loss of three lives. Stephens accused the Islanders of displaying false lights to cause the ship to founder, intending to loot its cargo. In retaliation the Islanders accused Stephens of adultery and attempted murder, of

27. *Cape Barren Islanders.* Views in Norfolk Island and Bass Strait from negatives taken by the Rt. Rev. Dr. Montgomery, Bishop of Tasmania during his visit in 1892. Mitchell Library.

appearing before the children in a "beastly state of intoxication", and of locking their children out of the school. Driven to the limits of endurance, Stephens fired shots at two Islanders entering the boat harbour and, it was reported, threatened to "shoot all the half-castes or any other caste be damned if he wouldn't".[26]

Stephens was summoned to Hobart to explain himself. There Montgomery learnt for the first time how Stephens had become the butt of the Islanders' mockery, a common pattern of Aboriginal defensive behaviour. For a moment Montgomery faltered, but then determined that Stephens's work must continue. Reprimanded for drunkenness, Stephens was sent back to the island. But the Islanders had had enough. If he was not replaced, they informed the director of education, all the children would be removed from the school. In September 1896 they accused Stephens of threatening them with a pistol. He accused them of incest and adultery. In Hobart Montgomery explained his disillusionment to the minister for education: "All that Stephens says about the Half-castes is just what I believe to be true. They are not improving except in some families. No one will ever keep their goodwill long. When they have tired of one man and they know he knows too much about them, they will try to get rid of him."[27]

By the time the director had admonished the Islanders for their ingratitude, Stephens had suffered a nervous collapse and surrendered his position to his son, Charles. During his convalescence, Stephens wrote of his difficulties with the Islanders:

> As liars I do think the men are peerless. I will give one instance at my own expense. It went the round of the islands, and was believed to be a fact, that Bishop Montgomery, on one of his visits, found me sitting on the roof of the water closet; and I had only my nightshirt on, and was singing the national anthem! He asked me what I was doing and I told him "I was showing my loyalty to the Queen". He said, "Oh, come down and come inside and we will make a night of it". And we did so. They said they knew I was a drunkard but the Bishop was a "bloody sight worse!"[28]

He concluded that if such stories were commonly believed, then the life of a civil servant was "an ever-increasing torment from which there was no escape, but by resignation or suicide".

Stephens had no understanding of the Islanders' need to pursue their lifestyle on their own terms. He saw their defensive behaviour as another example of their perversity and lack of intelligence, also manifested by the failure of any one of them to announce his conversion to "civilized society" or even to wish to become a catechist.

The Islanders considered Stephens's retirement their victory. In 1897 they formed an Islander Association, which initiated petitions to

28. *Islander Children, Cape Barren Island.* Views in Norfolk Island and Bass Strait from negatives taken by the Rt. Rev. Dr. Montgomery, Bishop of Tasmania during his visit in 1892. Mitchell Library.

government concerning muttonbirding and land tenure and attempted to establish a newspaper and a health benefit organization. But neither Montgomery nor Charles Stephens could tolerate any display of Islander independence and saw the existence of the association as a threat to their authority. In 1898 Montgomery took the chief inspector of education to the island; in the following year, the minister for justice. A meeting called with the latter attracted only four Islanders. The presence of such authority figures had driven many into the scrub, for they had been threatened with the loss of their leasehold land on the ground that it had not been cultivated.[29]

To further undermine the Islander Association, Montgomery recommended to the commissioner of police in August 1899 that a committee of inquiry should investigate the condition of the "reserve" and the muttonbird industry and that a police magistrate should visit the island to hear some cases that had been outstanding for years. He wrote: "I believe the terror of the proceedings in the eyes of these natives would be such that the evils now existing would be checked. At present I believe every known sin short of murder is rife here, and no evidence can be obtained. . . . Nothing would do more than the stern hand of the law at this time." He now believed it had been a mistake to concentrate the " 'half-castes' into a township which had brought its own special evils". They had developed a "settled hatred" for himself, the schoolmaster, and the constable, and had expressed a wish not to become "like white people".[30]

By October 1899 Islander resistance to Charles Stephens had reached its peak. "They will give the Government more trouble than the Boers are giving Great Britain," he wrote in despair to Montgomery. He decided to concentrate on Bible history in the school curriculum, in the hope that they would be terrorized into submission. He now believed that the second- and third-generation "half-castes" were of weaker character than the first and needed more rigid instruction. But the Islanders could still make life very difficult. "They actually stand on the bank out of my sight, with a clock and check my time of going into school with theirs," Stephens wrote, "then they lie in the sun until it is time for the children to go home, when they look at the clock to see if it is exactly to the minute. If a little before, they would bring a charge of neglect of duty, if a little over, they would get up a petition saying that the teacher was overtaxing the brains of the scholars."[31]

In May 1900 the report of the committee of inquiry recommended an annual licensing fee for muttonbirding and proposed that the land originally withdrawn from lease in 1881 be thrown open to Islander selection with fourteen years to pay. Those Islanders not wishing to cultivate the land could lease a homestead block of two hectares at the rental of one pound a year; the remainder of the land could then be leased to outsiders.[32] Fortunately only the muttonbird licensing system was enacted. But with the land ownership issue unresolved, the Islanders found their occupation of the "reserve" was as insecure as at any time since 1881. This insecurity was exacerbated in 1902 when Chappell Island was leased for grazing in the "off season". The Islanders were constantly aware of covetous settlers seeking to alienate their land.

Montgomery departed Tasmania after a final visit to the Islanders in August 1901, no more aware of the Islanders' needs as a separate community than he was on his arrival twelve years before. His successor, Bishop John Edward Mercer, hardly bothered about their existence. In Hobart the view was taken that since Montgomery had failed to earn their gratitude, it was unlikely that anyone else would. In 1902 a debate in the Tasmanian parliament on the future of the Islanders lapsed for want of a quorum. [33]

The attempt by church and state to bring "civilization" to Aboriginal communities in eastern Australia between 1880 and 1900 was part of the campaign for egalitarian conformity which swept the Australian colonies at that time. The fortunes of these communities, of which the Cape Barren Islanders are an example, oscillated between regulation and indifference. If they did not conform to accepted "standards of civilization" they became outcasts in their own country. There was no opportunity for self-determination.

NOTES

1. See notes, Bladon to premier, 30 Nov. 1911, Bladon Papers, U. Tas. Lib.; "Report of the Surveyor-General on the Islands of Bass Strait, 1849", TSA CSO 24/66; Plomley, *Friendly Mission,* p. 1015; B. C. Mollison, *The Tasmanian Aborigines: Tasmanian Aboriginal Genealogies* (Hobart: Psychology Dept., U. Tas., 1977), vol. 3, pt 1, notes on Armstrong and Proctor families; N. B. Tindale, "Results of the Harvard-Adelaide Universities Anthropological Expedition", *RQVM,* n.s. 2 (1953): 10–15.
2. J. Milligan to R. C. Gunn, 17 Nov. 1844, Gunn Papers, ML A316; "J. B." (John Broadfoot) "An Unexpected Visit to Flinders Island", *Chambers Edinburgh Journal,* 20 Sept. 1845, p. 188; John Lort Stokes, *Discoveries in Australia* (London, 1846), vol. 2, p. 451.
3. "Report of the Surveyor-General"; col. sec. to Denison, 7 Jan. 1850, TSA CSO 24/93/3033.
4. *Tasmanian Church Chronicle,* 6 Mar. 1852.
5. Ibid.
6. F. R. Nixon, *The Cruise of the Beacon* (Hobart, 1854), p. 42.
7. Report of Surveyor-General Power, Sept./Oct. 1854, TSA LSD 1/51/33.
8. John Thomas to the surveyor-general, Sept. 1861, TSA LSD 1/51/52.
9. T. Reibey, "Letter from the Venerable Archdeacon Reibey", *J&P LC Tas.,*

vol. 7 (1862), no. 17; Reibey, "Half-caste Islanders in Bass Straits", *J&P LC Tas.*, vol. 9 (1863), no. 48.

10. Surveyor-general to col. sec., 17 Feb. 1868, and George Everett to surveyor-general, 30 Nov. 1869, TSA LSD 1/51/32; J. E. C. Lord, "Report on the State of the Islands", *J&PP Tas.*, vol. 59 (1908), no. 57; *CN*, Apr. 1871.

11. Memo from Du Cane to ministers, 14 Aug. 1871, TSA CSD 7/45/833; *Tasmanian Government Gazette*, 30 Apr. 1872; A. W. Burbury, "Report on the Condition of Half Castes at Cape Barren Island Reservation", 25 Sept. 1929, TSA CSD 22/336/104/37.

12. M. B. Brownrigg, *The Cruise of the Freak* (Launceston, 1872), p. 79.

13. Stephen Murray-Smith, "Beyond the Pale", *P&P THRA* 20, no. 4 (Dec. 1973): 184.

14. Brownrigg, *Cruise of the Freak*, p. 6; Du Cane to ministers.

15. *Examiner*, 8 Mar. 1884.

16. Mrs. Claude Mansell, personal communication, 30 July 1973.

17. *Examiner*, 6 Feb. 1876; Murray-Smith, "Beyond the Pale", pp. 184–85; C. D. Rowley, *The Destruction of Aboriginal Society* (Canberra: ANU Press, 1970), p. 100.

18. *Tasmanian Government Gazette*, 15 Mar. 1881; Collis to chairman of Board of Education, 1 Aug. 1881, TSA CSD 13/6/168.

19. *Examiner*, 8 Mar. 1884.

20. P. R. Hart, "The Church of England in Tasmania under Bishop Montgomery" (M.A. thesis, U. Tas., 1963), p. 49.

21. *CN*, Dec. 1891, p. 563.

22. Register of Services, entry for 9 July 1899, TSA NS 373/11; *CN*, Aug. 1891, pp. 444–45.

23. *CN*, Dec. 1891, p. 563.

24. The inhabitants of CBI to Montgomery, 5 Feb. 1892, Montgomery Papers, Christ College, U. Tas.; E. W. Stephens diary, Nov. 1891, ML A1248/2.

25. Stephens diary, Sept. 1892.

26. *CN*, Aug. 1894, pp. 123–25; Report of J. Masters, Education Department, 7 Aug. 1893, TSA ED 3713/1077 110/732, and annual examination, Cape Barren School, 19 Nov. 1894, 110/733; E. W. Stephens to Montgomery, Nov. 1895, Montgomery Papers; anon. to minister for education, 12 Feb. 1896, TSA ED 3713/1077.

27. Montgomery to Rule, 9 Mar. and 7 Apr. 1896, and T. E. Mansell to Rule, 12 May 1896, TSA ED 3713/1077; Rowley, *Destruction of Aboriginal Society*, p. 96; Montgomery to minister for education, 4 Oct. 1896, TSA ED 3713/1077 110/335.

28. E. W. Stephens, "The Furneaux Islands", Stephens Papers, U. Tas. Lib.

29. C. E. Stephens to Montgomery, 28 Nov. 1899, Montgomery Papers; Register of Services, entry for 12 Aug. 1899; Hart, "Church of England in Tasmania", pp. 62–63.

30. Montgomery to police commissioner, 26 Aug. 1899, Montgomery Papers.

31. C. E. Stephens to Montgomery, 28 Nov. 1899, Montgomery Papers.

32. Ibid., 29 May 1900.

33. *Examiner*, 27 Aug. 1902.

16

The Tasmanian Aborigines in the Twentieth Century

By 1908 the people of Cape Barren Island bore characteristics common to Aboriginal populations in other parts of south-eastern Australia. They were predominantly of European descent; they generally inter-married; they were not homogeneous in physical appearance; they had no wish to look as white as possible; the older people liked to return to their place of birth to die; those of lighter colour liked to retain their identity as Aboriginal; they spoke English but retained remnant elements of former Aboriginal languages; and they had "covert" "idea-tional differences" that set them apart culturally from white society. Above all they knew they had origins different from whites, and although their culture was more like European culture than the former Aboriginal culture, much that was significant was based on Aboriginal tradition.[1]

In January 1908 Cape Barren Island and the two hundred Islanders were incorporated in the new Flinders municipality. The 250 white settlers considered the Islanders "spoon fed" because they had a reserve — a not uncommon attitude of local residents towards any Aboriginal group that had land. This jealousy became conflict when the Islanders refused to pay rates and taxes on the grounds they had not been con-sulted about the establishment of the council and were not represented on it. The attorney-general appointed the police commissioner, J. E. C. Lord, to investigate the conditions of the "half-castes and to make recommendations about the muttonbird industry". This was the first official expression of interest by the Tasmanian government in the affairs of the Islanders since the abortive attempt to bring Islander matters before parliament in 1902. The police commissioner's report became the basis of all succeeding reports until 1978.[2]

The report revealed three attitudes to "the problem of the reserve". The Flinders Council believed that the reserve should be thrown open to selection, with the Islanders having first option. Since most Islanders were financially unable to purchase land, the white residents would be able to take what land they liked. The police commissioner believed that the Islanders should "earn" legal security by taking out short-term homestead and agricultural leases, pursuing agriculture, and improving the land, and after a period of time they would become eligible for long-term leases. He also considered that a manager or overseer should be appointed to "strictly govern" the Islanders. Thus Lord's views were no different from Montgomery's. The Islanders believed the reserve should be granted to them outright with the muttonbird industry reserved for their exclusive use. But the government adopted Lord's suggestion and began to prepare legislation.[3]

In the process, the government decided to survey the boundary of the reserve and provide the Islanders with wire to fence it. Liquor laws were introduced, and new regulations for the muttonbird industry gazetted which set aside new islands as muttonbird reserves and prohibited grazing in the off-season. But the government failed to regulate the marketing of muttonbirds.

By June 1910 draft legislation was available, and in January 1911 an official party consisting of the governor, the premier, the minister for lands, and the chief health officer visited the reserve. They found 160 Islanders on the reserve, living in thirty-four houses. Seven of the houses were in good condition, eight were in fair condition, and nineteen in poor condition. The Islanders told the official party that if the reserve could not be granted to them, then they would prefer that each married man were leased forty hectares of reserve land and each single man ten hectares, in order to run cattle and sheep. They also wanted assistance to improve grasses and to develop suitable cattle. At the end of September copies of the bill were circulated to the Flinders council, the police commissioner, and the schoolmaster on Cape Barren Island, Captain J. W. Bladon.[4]

The bill made the minister for lands responsible for the welfare of the Islanders, while the secretary of the department of lands was to manage and regulate the use and enjoyment of the reserve and to supervise all matters affecting the interests and welfare of the residents. He had power to appoint anyone to carry out these duties at the reserve on his behalf. All land within the reserve area was to revert to the Crown for resurvey and subdivision into homestead blocks of a quarter-acre (1,012 square metres) and agricultural blocks of fifty acres (twenty hectares). Thus those Islanders who held freehold land on the reserve lost ownership. All Islanders over the age of eighteen, regardless of sex, were eligible for these blocks. After five years the blocks would become rent free if on the homestead block a house had been erected after two years and the lessee resided in it for at least six months of the year and

29. *Cape Barren Island Schoolchildren, with the Governor of Tasmania, Sir Harry Barron, January, 1911.* Tasmanian State Archives.

if the agricultural block had been "satisfactorily used". If the licensed occupier defaulted, the minister could cancel the licence and the block would be forfeited, leaving other people to apply for it. The Islanders were protected from seizure of land and goods, but if after three years anyone over twenty-one years of age was not a licensed occupier or lessee, he or she could be removed from the reserve. But they could select fifty-acre blocks (twenty hectares) elsewhere in Tasmania. No liquor was to be brought in or consumed on the reserve, and the act was to remain in force for twenty-five years.[5]

The Flinders council, the schoolmaster, and the police commissioner expressed satisfaction with the bill, but on the eve of its introduction to parliament on 21 November, a letter signed by H. G. Everett, on behalf of seventy other Islanders, appeared in the *Mercury* stating serious objections. They considered the quarter-acre homestead blocks too small, the restrictions and requirements on the agricultural blocks too severe, and the five-year period before the beginning of the rent-free lease too long. Instead they suggested that the homestead blocks should consist of five acres (two hectares) and that the rent-free lease should begin after one year. They also considered that unmarried eighteen-year-old women should not be eligible for blocks lest "outsiders" should be encouraged to marry into the community and thus threaten its identity. Above all they disliked the concept of a manager. They claimed they were capable of supervising their own affairs and recommended instead the appointment from among themselves of a committee of management empowered to make regulations for the welfare of the island.[6]

As a result of these objections, the bill was held over for another year. A compromise was reached on a number of the Islanders' objections, such as the rent-free period on the blocks beginning after three years instead of five and the homestead blocks increasing from a quarter-acre to three acres (1.2 hectares). But the concept of an Islander committee of management was rejected. The bill was finally introduced in parliament on 12 September 1912. In the second reading in the House of Assembly the premier said the Islanders were an indolent people by virtue of their Aboriginal ancestry, and although they had a "moral" right to the reserve, they could have no "legal" right until they had satisfied the conditions of the act. The assertion by an opposition member that the government should announce immediate recognition of the Islanders' legal rights was dismissed on the grounds that the Islanders were insufficiently grateful of the government's intentions. The *Cape Barren Island Reserve Act* 1912 became law on 6 December.[7]

The act was designed to encourage the Islanders to become "useful" citizens through government benevolence. Instead it ensured that the Islanders became institutionalized, with their movements and livelihood strictly controlled. Like the legislation establishing Aboriginal reserves in other states, the act reinforced the view that Aborigines were eligible for government regulation but ineligible for government assistance. But the main force of the act, the "overseer", was never appointed. The schoolmaster and the constable were considered sufficient evidence of law and order to intimidate the Islanders.

At first the government was pleased by the results. By 1914 the reserve had been resurveyed and the few freeholders compensated. Licences had been issued to twenty-seven families and new homes erected, and a thousand sheep, 104 cattle, and twenty horses had been purchased, pine trees had been planted, roads had been built, and gardens had been laid out. At the outbreak of the First World War twenty-one Islanders volunteered for service, six of whom gave their lives. The schoolmaster, J. W. Bladon, exhorted the Islanders to prove themselves equal to the white settlers by making great sacrifices of clothing and money. By the end of the war, their contributions were greater than those of the surrounding settlers.[8]

But by 1922 only a few Islanders had qualified for a ninety-nine-year lease, few had repaid housing loans, and most had failed to fence their agricultural blocks. Others had burnt down their homes when consumption killed members of their families. Some families had sub-let to relatives. The liquor laws had proved unenforceable. The mutton-bird industry had placed the Islanders deeper in debt, and no assistance had been provided with cattle or grasses — in contrast to the help received by new settlers on Flinders Island.[9]

In December 1922 the Islanders sent a petition to the minister for lands asking that the leasehold part of the act be amended to give them outright ownership of the reserve. "We are tired and disheartened," they wrote, "not through owing big debts, but for having nothing to show of what we are improving the land for. You will notice this ground is only held as a lease and may be cancelled at any time and by granting us a deed you will give us the encouragement to make our land self-supporting."[10]

In a briefing note to the minister, the secretary for lands, A. E. Counsel, explained that the two principal objects in passing the 1912 act had been to induce the people to take up and make homes on the reserve and to protect them from any dispossession from their allotments except by their own free will. Since the first part of the act had failed, because too few Islanders had taken out leases, he saw no reason to accede to the petitioners' request. "The present ninety-nine year lease or vesting land is practically a grant deed," he noted; "but I suppose the name 'lease' suggests an insecure title to those who don't understand its true value. . . . If it should be decided to grant the fee simple of the land, that is the allotments, stringent conditions must be imposed as to their giving up all rights to the balance of the Reserve or else the trouble will continue as bad as ever."[11]

The Islanders' view that the whole reserve should be granted to them, as individuals holding particular blocks, was beyond the understanding of the Tasmanian government at that time. The secretary for lands wanted to remove the children and appoint a manager to oversee the reserve. But he also realized that a manager would not necessarily produce guaranteed results, because the people did not want to work as agricultural labourers, and it was against the tenets of common law to remove children from their parents without their consent. At the same time Counsel admitted that the Islanders were exploited by white residents in the area, who charged high prices for food supplies and paid low prices for any stock or muttonbirds they purchased. Counsel perused other reserve legislation on the Australian mainland and came to the conclusion that all Aboriginal reserves suffered an absence of agricultural pursuits and lack of government expenditure. Cape Barren Island reserve, he concluded, needed expenditure far beyond the coffers of the Tasmanian government.[12]

In October 1924 a parliamentary inquiry also failed to reach a solution. It recommended the appointment of a new Crown lands bailiff to practise more fully the supervisory powers mentioned in the 1912 act; that pension payments should be made to the Islanders at the reserve, rather than at Whitemark on Flinders Island, so that the Islanders would not spend their cheques at the Whitemark Hotel; that the penalty provision of the act for such things as the absence of fencing should be enforced; that a short sealing season should be opened from December to February to allow the Islanders another supplementary industry; that no additional muttonbird licences should be granted to anyone but Islanders; that the school curriculum should be changed to ensure that practical subjects were taught; and that the residents should be allowed to elect annually a committee of five people to make suggestions for the administration of the reserve to the Crown land bailiff.[13]

The committee hoped a compromise would be reached in assisting with the muttonbird and sealing industries while keeping the regulations about leasehold. The Islanders saw the report as yet another attempt to restrict their movements, while the Flinders council saw it as a "sop" to the Islanders. In this impasse the government withdrew.

For the next five years the Islanders were at the mercy of the Flinders council. In 1924 the director of public health drew attention to the insanitary conditions on the reserve, but neither the council nor the department of public health would take action because the Islanders were in arrears with their local taxes, dog licences, and lease-hold payments. The council's medical officer was subsidized by the department of public health to treat those Islanders classified as "indigent" who had a leasehold on the reserve, but in 1930 he refused to attend the confinement of one of the Islanders, Mrs Clara Mansell, because of confusion over her indigent status. As a result her baby died. Yet without the subsidy it is doubtful whether the council would have been able to appoint a medical officer at all.[14]

Truant inspectors were often sent to the island to harass children who did not attend school, although the rate of attendance was usually higher than at most schools on Flinders Island. The Islander children at Flinders Island were also harassed. In February 1930 the head teacher at Lady Barron School denied that "he had taken no action to check the white scholars calling the half-caste scholars names", but later admitted that he caned the Islander scholars more often than white children.[15]

In June 1929 a lawyer from the attorney-general's department, A. W. Burbury, who had recently returned from observing the Pitcairn Islanders at Norfolk Island, was asked to investigate conditions on the reserve. He wrote the most perceptive report on the condition of the Islanders to date:

> How they live is a mystery. There is a store on the Reservation, but the half castes can get nothing except for cash. In the settlement there are about twenty-four dwellings, more than half mere shacks of two rooms: some few contain four rooms and about as many three rooms. Into these are crowded some 200 to 250 men, women and children. . . . Within the last two years at least ten marriages have taken place on the Reservation, but no further accommodation has been provided for the contracting parties. . . . they have an inferiority complex deeply ingrained, and they hate whites, regarding themselves as having been supplanted and exploited by white men. They say that the whites "took away their land and are now taking their kangaroos and mutton-birds . . ." the Act, too, has given them the belief that they have a claim on the State and that it was passed in recognition of their claim that their country had been taken from them by the whites. To an extent this view of theirs is justified, for, if the Act was not the result of a recognition that these people were entitled to something, why was it passed? . . . the Act was bound to fail because . . . success could only have been achieved under its provisions by a thrifty and hard-working tenantry who would develop and improve the land.[16]

He noted the Islanders' attachment to the reserve and their different view of life: "There is a warmth about them when speaking, the voices being soft and nicely lilted. They are fluent and convincing. In manner and courtesy they set an example which would put to shame many white folk."[17]

Burbury recommended that the government should acquire the whole of the island as a reserve, for the existing 2,428 hectares were inadequate for any economic pursuit, and that a missionary society should assume religious responsibility for the Islanders and the federal government assume financial responsibility, since it had more direct experience with Aboriginal problems in the Northern Territory. Failing that, the management of the reserve should be transferred to a "competent supervisor" whose duty would be to improve the land. He also recommended that an inquiry should be conducted into the mutton-bird industry and that the children should be encouraged to leave the reserve once they had finished school.[18]

The government again ignored the major recommendations relating to reserve land and approached both the Australian Board of Missions and the federal government to take over religious and financial responsibility for the Islanders. The chairman of the Australian Board of Missions, the Reverend J. S. Needham, visited the reserve in December 1930 to determine whether the Islanders were worthy of his association's missionary endeavours. He was horrified to find that "one man mentioned quite seriously, and he, to all appearances had no Tasmanian native blood in him — that if a case were brought in a Federal Court the Tasmanian Government would be forced to pay the half-castes rent for the island of Tasmania".[19] Needham dismissed the Islanders' desire for independence. Since they were not "fullbloods", the Australian Board of Missions could not assume any responsibility. Instead, he recommended that the Islanders should become part of the general community, for they had been too restive and ungrateful of previous attempts to help them.[20]

The federal government proved more sympathetic. At the end of 1931, as the full blast of the Depression was felt throughout Australia, a special unemployment grant was made available to the Islanders through the Flinders council. After initial problems with the council spending the money in other areas, the Islanders began to benefit. They were paid to mend roads, to repaint and renovate their homes, to buy seed, to lay out and plant their gardens, to dig wells, to put in water tanks, and to repair fences. By 1936 a hundred Islanders were paid from government funds. Social and sporting activities developed; frequent dances, horse races, and football matches were held. A series of good muttonbird seasons in the late 1930s further improved the situation. In this new prosperity the population increased to three hundred. The Islanders were to recall this period as the "good times". A new hall was built, and in 1939 a new church was constructed and a bush nurse appointed. The Islanders' diet improved because they were able to depend upon another income besides that obtained from muttonbirding.[21]

In this prosperity some Islanders gained the confidence to move to Launceston. This confidence was increased by the Second World War, which opened up new horizons. Many volunteered for service, while others were drafted under the Manpower Authority. The community was scattered. By 1944 only 106 remained from a pre-war level of 300.[22] At the war's end many Islanders remained on the Tasmanian mainland, in Melbourne, or on Flinders Island.

These changes led the government in 1944 to hold an inquiry to determine the future of the reserve. In 1937 the agreement by state and federal ministers to adopt an assimilation policy for Aborigines and the decision by the Commonwealth statistician after the 1944 Census of Aborigines not to include Aborigines who were less than "octoroon" had placed the status of the Islanders as an Aboriginal people in doubt. If they were not Aboriginal, then there was no need for a reserve. So in 1945 the Reserve Act was renewed for only five years. In this time the Islanders could decide whether to become agricultural farmers on the island or move to the Tasmanian mainland. After that, all reserve land not granted or selected by the Islanders would revert to the Crown and the reserve and laws relating to it would be abolished. The government hoped the Islanders would move to Launceston and become "abosrbed" into the white population. But the Islanders were angry. Once again they had been denied self-determination. Once again they had been defined, this time as white people, after having been defined as non-white for the previous seventy years.[23]

At the end of 1947, when complaints reached the press that the Islanders lived in squalor, another parliamentary select committee was sent to investigate conditions on the reserve. This committee discovered 130 Islanders in residence, none of whom had any desire to leave. The Islanders firmly believed the reserve had been bestowed by the government to their ancestors in 1881 as compensation for the loss of the island of Tasmania. But life had changed since the halcyon days of the 1930s. Apart from muttonbirding there was no regular work on the island, and no new houses had been built. But the committee could not recommend the development of projects on the reserve to assist the Islanders. Rather it recommended that the reserve should still be closed in 1951, that the Islanders should "be gradually absorbed into the rest of the Tasmanian population", and that their plea for recognition as a "special people" with Aboriginal ancestry should be dismissed.[24]

By denying the Islanders their Aboriginal ancestry, the select committee was considered "progressive". It was now widely believed that only the Islanders' poor living conditions had previously prevented them from becoming "useful" citizens. Whereas before the war they had been discouraged from leaving the reserve to reside in Launceston for fear they would "pollute" the white population, now they were urged to leave the reserve so they would become absorbed by the white population. For the Islanders, the report advocated cultural genocide.

The committee's arguments against continuation of the reserve were similar to those used in support of the closure of the American Indian reserves in the 1880s and of the Coranderrk and Lake Condah Aboriginal reserves in Victoria in 1939 and 1953 and the Cumeroogunga reserve in New South Wales in the same year — the inhabitants were no longer "real Aborigines", that is, "fullbloods". Although the terminology of the 1948 report had changed from that in the reports of Lord and Burbury, the basic attitude that the Islanders were a people incapable of determining their own future had not. In all three reports it was acknowledged that the Islanders regarded the reserve as their home, that it had been bequeathed to them by virtue of their Aboriginal ancestry in compensation for the loss of the island of Tasmania. Only in Burbury's report of 1929 — when he wrote, " . . . if the Act was not the result of a recognition that these people were entitled to something, why was it passed?" — were these claims examined. Burbury considered the act a dangerous recognition of Islander rights.

Before the act expired in 1951, the Islanders took out thirty-five leases on the reserve. Some bought cattle and sheep, and some homestead and agricultural blocks were fenced. But most "sat" on their land. They considered that they had already paid out for their land after the act had originally been passed in 1912. They were not going to pay for it again. Thus by the time the act expired only one lessee was eligible for a ninety-nine-year lease on his agricultural block. The government had a long-term objective of removal, but it was in no hurry to carry it out. With the legal termination of the reserve in 1951, the Islanders were expected to cease to exist.[25]

By 1958 only 120 remained. They preserved their existence by not co-operating with state health and welfare authorities, refusing to find employment off the island, and making strong expressions of attachment to the old reserve. Their bitterness and the prejudice of the surrounding white community were captured in a report on their condition to the bishop of Tasmania by the council clerk on Flinders Island, C. I. A. Booth, who was a former schoolteacher on Cape Barren. Booth considered the Islanders neither "white" nor "half-caste" but "coloured" and were a people of "unsettled temperament". They told him they belonged nowhere because the government did not recognize them as Aborigines and no one else recognized them as "white people". He thought they spent their money too fast, showed no ambition to improve themselves, disappeared when "welfare" visited the island, and had an innate inability to hold drink. Most serious of all, he thought they lacked moral principle, for their word was not their bond. They were unpunctual, inclined to "go slow" when left alone at their work, and seldom laboured beyond their usual time unless requested to do so. Yet they seldom argued over wage rates. Amongst older members of the community Booth noted an "undoubted dislike of whites". Yet like his predecessors, Booth found that the Islanders showed a "marked tendency towards courtesy when rightly approached, displayed a respect for elderly people and a great love for their children and expressed concern for the future of their own community".[26]

Outside interests gradually crept into the area. In 1960 a sixteen-thousand-hectare cattle run was established at Motter River on Cape Barren Island, some of which included land from the old reserve. The owner of the run offered attractive prices to Islanders for their leases, and some of them, unable to find regular work and concerned for the future of their children, sold up and went to Launceston.

By the mid-1960s half the remaining Islanders had taken up the offer of homes and jobs in Launceston from the social welfare department. A series of poor muttonbird seasons, unemployment, and the fact that no money had been spent on the island since 1944 induced them to leave. The fifty who remained refused to move or even to leave the reserve for short periods, because they were frightened the land might be taken from them in their absence. A similar situation had developed at the Framlingham Reserve in Victoria. The Islanders' resistance to assimilation at this time was part of a general resistance by Aboriginal communities in settled Australia threatened by removal or closure of reserves.

In Launceston the Islanders congregated in one of the poorer suburbs, Invermay, where they were often refused service in hotels and suffered discrimination in employment. But the older people missed "the quiet and peacefulness" of the island and looked forward to the muttonbird season when they could meet up with their own people again. Some were able to visit Cape Barren for some months, then Flinders, returning to Launceston at the end of the year. This migratory pattern had begun in the 1920s when the first families had gone to Launceston and was a variation of an earlier pattern established in the 1870s when the Islander families visited each other "until the neck of the flour bag became a little long".[27]

At the beginning of 1968, in an attempt to prod the government into final removal of the Islanders, the Flinders council suggested to parliament that another select committee be appointed to examine the future development of Cape Barren Island. The committee were impressed by the council's plea that there was much good land on Cape Barren, and estimated that 20,000 to 24,000 hectares were suitable for pasture and 240 hectares were ploughable. Some of this land was on the old reserve.[28]

The chief secretary, B. K. Miller, believing that if the remaining Islanders were presented with attractive alternative conditions they would leave, and realizing that the recent acquisition of powers from the referendum of May 1967 by the Commonwealth government to assist Aboriginal people would be a useful means of gaining funds for such a removal, decided to attend a meeting of Commonwealth and state ministers for Aboriginal affairs in July 1968. He hoped to gain assistance to house the Islanders in Hobart and Launceston.[29] While the chief secretary denied the Islanders their Aboriginal ancestry to lay claim to the old reserve, he used it to gain finance to house them on the Tasmanian mainland.

In support of Miller's policy, the *Mercury* in August ran a series of pro-assimilationist articles on the Islanders, but written in that patronizing manner to which Aborigines had become accustomed. The reporter found on Cape Barren a group of stubborn people living in squalor and refusing to move to Launceston to join their happy relatives, one of whose children had become a successful footballer. Those on Cape Barren were charming and eccentric people who refused to work and had a hatred of whites. If they were moved to Launceston they would not only lose these habits, they would find that they would be accepted by white society.[30]

The Islanders lost no time in pressing their case: "Instead of our having a hatred for white people, the boot is on the other foot. They have a set on us. Whose crime is it that we are of mixed blood? The government put us here. It is our home. We are happy, and all we ask is that work be made available for us. Then we shall have pleasure in inviting reporters to see for themselves whether we have to be stood over to be made to work."[31]

The Islanders were fighting "silent eviction", for it now seemed unlikely that they would "ever be masters of their own small domain". Those who stayed resented those who had departed, for in their view Launceston represented an invitation to "drunkenness, loose living, the hell of urban poverty". And although those who left denied these accusations, many wanted to return, "if some sort of future was allowed them at home".[32]

In August the chief secretary returned from Melbourne with twenty-five thousand dollars for Islander housing on the Tasmanian mainland. At this point the schoolmaster at Cape Barren, not known for his liberal views, spoke out: "I believe that any person who has made a place his home for many years should not be forced to leave it, by a person or by a government." A Launceston resident was even more to the point: "The Islanders have simply asked for an industry on their own land. Why can't we supply it?"[33]

In the Office of Aboriginal Affairs in Canberra there was similar concern over the allocation of funds. Charles Perkins, Aboriginal officer in the Office of Aboriginal Affairs, visited Tasmania late in 1968 and was not happy with the situation. Thus by the end of 1968 the lines of conflict had been drawn. On one side were the Islanders and their supporters in their clearly stated desire to remain on Cape Barren. On the other was the Tasmanian government and the Flinders council with their campaign to disperse the Islanders to Launceston. In the middle was an uncertain Commonwealth Office of Aboriginal Affairs.

By the middle of 1969 conflict had become confrontation. In May the Tasmanian Labor government, after twenty-five years in office, was defeated. In June two students representing Abschol, an organization providing scholarships for Aborigines to Australian universities, after a visit to Cape Barren persuaded the University of Tasmania Students Representative Council to pass a motion deploring the Tasmanian government's failure to support economic development on the island. In conjunction with the Islanders, the students decided to carry out their own feasibility study of the economic potential of the island and to try to raise finance for its economic resuscitation. By September, forty Islanders had signed an Abschol petition protesting against the removal policy.[34]

In April 1970 the Tasmanian Liberal government advertised for a "resettlement officer", to be located in Launceston, whose function would be "to advise and encourage families on Cape Barren Island to re-settle on the Tasmanian mainland in housing provided by Commonwealth funds and to assist such families generally with their social welfare".[35] For a year a battle raged between state and Commonwealth officials over the dispersal of the Islanders and the appointment of the resettlement officer, for the salary was to be paid from Commonwealth funds. By mid-1971 a compromise was reached. The resettlement officer's title was changed to "community development officer", who was to live on Cape Barren Island to assist in its redevelopment, using Commonwealth money.

The change in policy was accompanied by a growth in consciousness by the Islanders themselves. In August 1971 Abschol organized a conference of Islanders in Launceston, the first of its kind. The two

30. *The Corner, Cape Barren Island, 1974. Photo by Anne Bickford.*

hundred Islanders who attended from all over Tasmania and the Furneaux Islands found that nearly two thousand of their people were scattered across Tasmania and Australia. Much of the first day was spent in recrimination and bitterness, with many Cape Barren residents accusing their mainland Tasmanian relatives of betrayal. But by the second day they had begun to pick up the threads of their kinship patterns. The conference agreed to press for Islander title to the old reserve if not for the island as a whole. The conference acted as a catalyst for the Islanders in the way that the American Indian Chicago Conference of 1961 was a catalyst for American Indians.[36]

By the end of 1971 Cape Barren Island had seen an injection of Commonwealth money and for the first time since the Depression the Islanders had regular employment apart from muttonbirding. By the end of 1973, boxthorn had been cleared, roads repaired, concrete tanks installed, a retaining wall constructed and the cemetery and war memorial cleaned up. But no new homes had been built. An Islander council had been formed under the control of the community development officer, a dam had been started and school facilities improved, and the population had increased to ninety people, half of whom were children. But there had been almost no move towards self-determination because the Islanders had never been encouraged in the past to take themselves seriously. The community was split in their loyalty to the community development officer, because some feared that he was an authority figure they could not do without. Others were more optimistic.

As with all Aboriginal communities, the Islanders' problems are complex. There has been disquiet amongst the Islander community on the Tasmanian mainland that the Cape Barren people are now getting too much assistance at their expense. Nevertheless, various groups within the Islander people have emerged to fight for their own needs. This increasing sophistication, which was apparent at a conference of Islanders in Launceston in July 1973, contrasted with their uncertainty at the conference two years before.

Since then an Aboriginal Legal Service and the Tasmanian Aboriginal Centre have been established, with offices in Hobart and Launceston, and community councils set up on Flinders and Cape Barren Islands. The term *Islander* has been discarded for *Aboriginal Tasmanian,* and there has been an increase in the number of people who openly assert their Aboriginal identity from 671 in the 1971 census to 2,942 in the 1976 census. Inquiries have been conducted into Aboriginal Tasmanian education, employment opportunities, cases of discrimination, and the need for land rights, all of which have created an increased awareness

31. Poster advertising *The Last Tasmanian* with strip across the bottom accusing the film of racism. Photo by Eric Dury.

of Aboriginal Tasmanian identity, not only in the Aboriginal community but in some parts of the European community as well.[37]

This change in consciousness has not, however, extended to all parts of European Tasmania. A film released in 1978, *The Last Tasmanian*, refused to acknowledge that the present-day Aboriginal Tasmanian community had any continuity with the past Tasmanian Aborigines. Reaction to the film showed that many European Tasmanians had very little sympathy with or understanding of the significance of the identity issue to Aboriginal Tasmanians. An article in the *Mercury* expressed a common viewpoint when it said that "by trying to be different" Aborigines are likely to cause trouble, "and why stir up trouble when there is no need?"[38] It is still much easier for white Tasmanians to regard Tasmanian Aborigines as a dead people rather than confront the problems of an existing community of Aborigines who are victims of a conscious policy of genocide.[39]

NOTES

1. J. H. Bell, "Some Demographic and Cultural Characteristics of the La Perouse Aborigines", *Mankind* 5, no. 10 (1962): 431–37.
2. Flinders Council Minute Book, 26 Feb. 1908; Rowley, *Destruction of Aboriginal Society*, p. 182; J. E. C. Lord, "Report on the State of the Islands", *J&PP TAS.*, vol. 59, (1908), no. 57.
3. Flinders Council Minute Book, 2 June 1910; Lord, "State of the Islands".
4. Premier of Tasmania to warden of Flinders Council, 3 Mar. 1910, TSA PD 1/224/225; *Examiner*, 12 Jan. 1911; premier to Bladon, 20 Oct. 1911, Bladon Papers, U. Tas. Lib.
5. Premier to Bladon, 20 Oct. 1911.
6. *Mercury*, 21 Nov. 1911.
7. Bladon to premier, 20 Dec. 1911, Bladon Papers; *Mercury*, 13 Sept. 1912.
8. Cape Barren Island School and Punishment Book, 19 June 1916 and 3 Nov. 1918.
9. E. A. Counsel, secretary, Department of Lands, "Report on the Management of the Half Castes at Cape Barren Island", 4 Dec. 1922, TSA LSD 643/30/1646/22.
10. "Petition from Residents of Cape Barren Island Reserve to the Minister for Lands", 8 Dec. 1922, TSA LSD 643/30/1646/22.
11. Remarks by Counsel to minister for lands on back of petition, 12 Dec. 1922.
12. W. J. Mansfield, crown lands bailiff, Flinders Island, to secretary for lands, 18 Sept. 1922, and Rev. F. H. Gilles to premier, 14 Feb. 1923, TSA LSD 643/30/1646/22; Counsel, "Report".
13. "Report of the Select Committee Appointed 29 Oct. 1924 . . .", *J&PP Tas.*, vol. 91 (1924–25), no. 48.
14. A. W. Burbury, "Report on the Condition of Half Castes at Cape Barren Island Reservation", 16 Sept. 1929, TSA CSD 22/336/104/37; Flinders Council Minute Book, 5 July 1930.
15. Flinders Council Minute Book, 8 Feb. and 7 June 1930.
16. Burbury, "Report".

17. Ibid.
18. Ibid.
19. J. S. Needham, "Cape Barren Island", *ABM Review* 17 (1931): 171–72.
20. J. S. Needham, report to minister for lands, 24 Dec. 1930, TSA LSD 643/30.
21. Flinders Council Minute Book, 11 Oct. 1930 and 17 Jan. 1931; Brian King, "Barren Future" (typescript, *Four Corners*, ABC, Sydney, 18 May 1971); *Examiner*, 3 Oct. 1936; ministerial memo, minister for lands and works, 26 Feb. 1937, TSA CSD 22/416/104/10; "Report of the Secretary for Lands 1937–38", *J&PP Tas.*, vol. 119 (1938), no. 13.
22. "Report of the Secretary for Lands and Surveyor-General's Department 1944", *J&PP Tas.*, 131 (1944–45), no. 10.
23. Correspondence between Commonwealth statistician and chief secretary's department, 6 and 14 June and 18 and 23 Sept. 1946, TSA CSD 22/531/104/7; *Cape Barren Island Reserve Act* 1945.
24. *Examiner*, 17, 21, 25, 27, and 28 Nov. and 4 and 5 Dec. 1947; "Report of Joint Committee . . .", *J&PP Tas.*, vol. 139 (1948), no. 22.
25. *Expiration of Cape Barren Island Reserve Act 1945* 1951.
26. Victorian Aboriginal Group, *29th Annual Report* (1958); C. I. A. Booth, "The Half Castes of the Furneaux Islands", TSA CBI file.
27. P. Wagstaff, J. Gibson, and J. Manning, "Cape Barren Island" (typescript, SSRC Research File, Canberra, 1966); King, "Barren Future".
28. "Report of the Committee . . . to Examine . . . the Future Development of Flinders Island", *J&PP Tas.*, vol. 179 (1968), no. 15.
29. *Mercury*, 12 July 1968.
30. Ibid., 17, 19, 21, 22, 23, and 26 Aug. 1968.
31. Ibid., 29 Aug. 1968.
32. Connie Chobanian, "Cape Barren" (typescript, ABC, Sydney 1971), p. 20; King, "Barren Future".
33. *Examiner*, 23 Aug. and 3 and 11 Sept. 1968; *Mercury*, 30 Oct. 1968.
34. *Togatus* 41, no. 6 (May 1970); Ken Newcombe, "Their Barren Existence" (typescript, Hobart, 1970).
35. *Age*, 11 Apr. 1970.
36. Minutes of the Conference of Cape Barren Islanders, Launceston, 13–14 Aug. 1971 (Abschol Archives, U. Tas.); Nancy O. Lurie, "The Voice of the American Indian", *Current Anthropology* 2 (1961): 478–500.
37. Kerry Randriamahefa, *Aborigines in Tasmanian Schools,* Education Department of Tasmania Research Branch, Research Study no. 144 (April 1979); Lorna Lippmann, *A Somewhat Startled Realisation,* Office of Community Relations (Canberra: AGPS, 1978); "Report of the Aboriginal Affairs Study Group of Tasmania", *J&PP TAS.*, vol. 199 (1978), no. 94.
38. *Mercury*, 3 Apr. 1978.
39. Anne Bickford, "The Last Tasmanian: Superb Documentary or Racist Fantasy", *Filmnews,*.Jan. 1979.

17

Conclusion

The Tasmanian Aborigines have survived. But as this account has taken pains to emphasize, this has not been achieved without the enormous cost of near-extinction as a people and a continuing denial of their identity in the present.

Before European invasion and occupation, the Aboriginal inhabitants possessed a thriving culture which was clearly not in decline as some have claimed, and which was capable of adjusting to certain features of European society such as the sealing communities and agricultural settlement. The former provided the basis for the Islander communities which represent the major expression of Tasmanian Aboriginal society today. This is not to say that conflict and death were absent from race relations in these areas, but the piecemeal nature and extent of sealing and agriculture in Tasmania until 1820 did not have the disastrous consequences of the rapid and extensive pastoral occupation to follow.

The period of pastoral invasion (1820–30) caused the most serious dislocations to Aboriginal society and the greatest level of conflict. Here as elsewhere on the Australian mainland, Aborigines were compelled to defend their homeland with all the means at their disposal, for the massive alienation of land and resources without compensation under pastoralism made Aboriginal adjustment to this new situation impossible. At one point in 1828 there were more sheep in Tasmania than in New South Wales. In this situation, military and field police entered the picture, clearing Aborigines from "settled" areas in much the same way as was done in New South Wales at the beginning of pastoral settlement there. Martial law, that "higher" law invested with sanctity and savagery, was invoked to deal with the situation, as it was almost everywhere in the British Empire when a serious threat from below developed. Tasmania's governor, George Arthur, had already begun to think of banishing Aborigines to particular locations segregated from European settlements, while the settlers themselves formed "roving parties" to eliminate Aborigines altogether. The policy of segregation, with George Augustus Robinson as its instrument, was the precursor of segregated reserves for Aborigines which were instituted on the Australian mainland after 1880; the roving parties foreshadowed the private slaughter of Aborigines in Victoria, New South Wales, and Queensland after 1835.

If the hour finds the man, George Augustus Robinson was the man for that hour of history. But such concern which both he and Governor Arthur shared would always be tempered by the brutal facts of frontier war between Aboriginal and settler which ensured that the philanthropic motive was always subordinate and peripheral to the imperatives of pastoralism and economic development. In Tasmania as elsewhere, land rights for Europeans permeated all social relations; land rights for Aborigines did not exist. On Flinders Island it became obvious that neither Robinson nor anyone else could arrest Aboriginal mortality. A fatalistic ideology surfaced as the Aborigines died one by one; it became allied with an excessive, grim monitoring of the fate of the two remaining "traditional" Aborigines, William Lanney and Truganini. Science, which showed scant concern for the Tasmanians while alive, showed great interest now that it appeared inevitable that they would die. When William Lanney died in 1869, two scientists severed his head from his body in order to examine it for "scientific" purposes and replaced it with the head of a European. This act, in a rather grisly, bizarre fashion, symbolized what Robinson had been doing with his charges at Flinders Island. Truganini, who died in 1876 as the celebrated "last Tasmanian", escaped such mutilation but reappeared as a display in the Royal Society of Tasmania Museum in 1904 where she remained until 1947.

These dramatic developments had obscured the reality of the Cape Barren Island community, which had endured the vicissitudes of invasion, dislocation, culture shock, and constant harassment from missionaries, government officials, and teachers. At the same time such isolation had enabled them to converge as an accultured Aboriginal–European community, based on muttonbirding and other traditional activities, determined to manage their own affairs as best they could.

In the twentieth century, their demand for recognition as an Aboriginal community resulted in the *Cape Barren Island Reserve Act* of 1912, which acknowledged their Aboriginal identity but not their culture or society. While the community had a certain security on the reserve, they were expected in return to undertake agriculture, a mode of production they had already rejected. Despite their service in two world wars, the reserve was withdrawn in 1951, as part of the assimilation policy which declared that the Islanders had to live "like white people" and leave the island so that their land could be used by cattle farmers. But the Islanders' stubborn refusal to disperse enabled a more sympathetic federal government in 1971 to bring some life back into the community. Despite this, European Tasmanians have managed to convince themselves and the world that they had carried out the swiftest and most efficient act of genocide ever.

The history and present circumstances of the Aboriginal Tasmanians reviewed here exemplify in a particularly stark form many features of the uneasy, unequal relationship between Aboriginal and other Australians. Some were and are more apparent than real, as this account has shown, but in various ways Tasmania represented a kind of "ideal type" of colonial society which the colonists on the mainland compared with their own, usually to the detriment of Tasmania. Tasmania had more convicts than any other colony and had them for a longer period; consequently Tasmania was less able to shake off the "convict taint" which was such a source of division in the early colonial Australian society. Tasmania's environment was more "English" than the rest of Australia and hence was a constant source of emulation for those transplanted British who wished to refashion their colony of adoption or sojourn into another England. Tasmania to all appearances had wiped out its Aboriginal population more thoroughly than anywhere else in Australia. Tasmania adopted the punitive raid against the Aboriginal depredations, although not to the zealous extent of colonists on the mainland. Tasmania underwent pastoral development more rapidly than almost anywhere in the colonies, although it did not maintain its dominant position as a supplier of raw wool. Tasmania adopted segregated reserve policies earlier than any other colony. And Tasmania denied identity to the Aboriginal descendants for longer than any other colony or state, partly because there were not supposed to be any Tasmanian Aborigines left alive after 1876.

Yet this portrayal of Tasmania as an "ideal type", like all ideal types, is meant to highlight and accentuate reality, not substitute for it. The intention is not to single out Tasmanian society, past or present, as an aberrant case in the Australian context but rather as a mirror that reveals the real nature of those "other" Australians across Bass Strait whose brutal march to "progress" at the expense of the Aborigines was in many cases far more destructive than the Tasmanian precedent. The indigenous population on the mainland was far greater than in Tasmania, and the loss of life was correspondingly greater — on both sides. Whole tribes were wiped out in New South Wales, Victoria, and Queensland. Tasmania was the proving ground of European technology, warfare, culture, and political economy which, emerging victorious in Tasmania, swept across the mainland as an expression of manifest destiny. The defeated Aborigines of Victoria, New South Wales, and Queensland were herded into reserves or placed in missions, or they clung to the fringes of settlement. The most notorious segregated reserve system for Aborigines — that of Queensland in 1897 — was expressly modelled on Robinson's spectacular, blind failures. Agrarianism was the most universal ideology foisted on Aborigines.

Europeans have never adjusted or adapted to the Aboriginal presence in Australia. This is a problem not confined to Tasmania, although there are certain features such as the denial of identity to the descendants which exacerbate the problem there. As one Aboriginal Tasmanian has put it: "It doesn't matter how many bloodlines there are in you, subconsciously you will identify with one or the other. And I can't help but identify with Aborigines because society picks me out as an Aborigine."[1] Another Aboriginal Tasmanian, Michael Mansell, has said, "We are the only race of people that I know of on earth, the Tasmanian Aborigines, who have to daily justify our existence."[2]

To most whites, Aborigines still have to prove themselves respectable and acceptable. It is one of the tragic ironies of Western society that the violence used by whites to dispossess minority groups was either never publicized or was justified by a specifically constructed ideology. Now that these dispossessed minority groups have had to resort to similar tactics to restore prestige, they are vilified. This is as true of the assassination of Earl Mountbatten in Ireland in 1979 as with the siege by the Sioux at Wounded Knee in South Dakota in 1973.

In the Australian context, the anthropologist/historian Charles Rowley has pointed out: "We have inherited quite a grim history as so many other nations have; and for many reasons we must learn to apply to the facts of our own past and to current attitudes the same sociological principles which it is much easier to apply to situations elsewhere."[3] Historians have the task of assisting in this reinterpretation of our past and towards a basic readjustment of our world outlook. Henry Reynolds has already pointed out that "of all aspects of the past the fate of the Aborigines demands the greatest expansion of our historical imagination". In this process we may learn a little of the "dark underside" of the Australian mind: "the violence, the arrogant assertion of superiority, the ruthless single-minded and often amoral pursuit of material progress and the need to develop mature self-awareness."[4]

Some attempts have already been made in a more popularized form to understand the racist fears and prejudices that Europeans have manifested without change since first invasion. Others have tried to give a more compassionate account of the Aborigines' personal experiences. A sustained attack has also been launched on school textbooks.[5] Aboriginal Australians are also contributing to this expanded view of Australian history. Kevin Gilbert in 1973 gave his analysis of the oppression that has continued unchanged since first invasion and celebrated the Aboriginal patriots: "those who have refused to sell out, have refused to pay that ultimate 'price of survival' demanded by the white boss . . . and to the mass of blacks, 'poor buggers all', who are still waiting".[6]

The present policy of the Australian government on Aboriginal self-determination, like most policies involving social change, needs committed public servants, preferably Aboriginal, an assured budget, and time to develop concepts of self-determination and to decide what assistance they want. The difficulties remain of making generalizations and prognostications about the future of Aboriginal Australians of which the Aboriginal Tasmanians are a part. Economic factors and policy and administrative changes will still determine the outcome of Aboriginal/European relations. Like most oppressed minorities, Aboriginal Australians are particularly sensitive to paternalism and arrogance.

The problem of Europeans and their inability to understand themselves has always amazed Aborigines. From first settlement, Aborigines exclaimed at the senseless brutality of European society, the excesses of authoritarian control, and the drive for conformity. Indeed, Aboriginal society presented a challenge to long-held beliefs of concepts of the human soul and its relationship to the land. While Aborigines thought that their society was superior to the invader's, they also understood that there would never be an opportunity to become part of European society while Europeans held "strange" ideas about them. In Aboriginal eyes the Europeans may have had a superior technology, but they used this technology in a senseless obliteration of a landscape they did not understand. To Aborigines, therefore, Europeans are a shallow people who are in constant fear not only of the people whose land they have appropriated but of the land itself. They are also afraid of external forces who will in turn expropriate their ill-gotten gains. Until Europeans have learned to cope with these problems and have resolved them, they will remain a problem for Aborigines.

NOTES

1. Interview with "P. B." from *Genocide without Blood and Guts*, mimeograph (Hobart: Tasmanian Aboriginal Information Centre, n.d. [1978]), p. 10.

2. Comment by Michael Mansell from "The Last Tasmanian", *Monday Conference,* 4 September 1978, transcript, Sydney, ABC, p. 8.
3. C. D. Rowley, *The Destruction of Aboriginal Society* (Canberra: ANU Press, 1970), pp. 8–9.
4. Henry Reynolds, ed., *Aborigines and Settlers* (Melbourne: Cassell Australia, 1972), pp. xi–xii.
5. Lorna Lippmann, *Words or Blows* (Ringwood, Vic.: Penguin, 1973); Humphrey McQueen, *Aborigines, Race and Racism* (Ringwood, Vic.: Penguin, 1974); Jack Horner, *Vote Ferguson for Aboriginal Freedom* (Sydney: ANZ Book Co., 1974).
6. Kevin Gilbert, *Because a White Man'll Never Do It* (Sydney: Angus and Robertson, 1973), frontispiece.

Appendix 1. Aborigines Accounted for in the Literature, 1800-35

Tribe	Captured	Shot	With Sealers	With Settlers	Total
SOUTH EAST	14	1	3	26	44
OYSTER BAY	27	67	8	14	116
BIG RIVER	31	43	0	4	78
NORTH MIDLANDS	23	38	3	4	68
BEN LOMOND	35	31	3	3	72
NORTH EAST	12	43	28	2	85
NORTH	28	80	8	0	116
NORTH WEST	96	59	21	5	181
SOUTH WEST	47	0	0	0	47
	313	362	74	58	807

Appendix 2. Number of Europeans Killed by Individual Tribes, 1800-35

NORTH MIDLANDS	26
BIG RIVER	60
OYSTER BAY	50
NORTH	15
NORTH EAST	7
BEN LOMOND	20
SOUTH EAST	2
NORTH WEST	3
SOUTH WEST	0
	183

Note: Numbers include Europeans from outside the settled districts such as sealers, whalers, timber-getters, stockmen, and explorers.

Appendix 3. Aborigines at Flinders Island and Oyster Cove, October 1835 to May 1876

Name	Sex	Age in 1835	Other Names	Relations, Territory	Date of Death
1. Achilles	M	30	Rowlebanna	Wife: Maria Ben Lomond	Between 1845 and March 1847
2. Adam	M	born 7 June 1838		Mother: Sarah Father: Eugene	1857
3. Adelaide (Queen)	F	26	Drometeemetyer	Husband: King William Oyster Bay	4 March 1839
4. Adolphus (Prince)	M	7	Timemeniddic	Mother: Larratong Father: Wymurric West Coast	Between 1845 and March 1847
5. Agnes	F	38	Meelathinna Blind Poll	Husband: George Robinson Ben Lomond	1847
6. Ajax (Count)	M	47	Moultelargine (= Kalebunna?) Jacky	Son: Jack Allen Brother: Umarrah Stoney Creek	Between February 1844 and March 1846
7. Albert	M	22	Warwee (Wowwee)	Wife: Emma Port Sorell	8 April 1838
8. Alexander	M	23	Druemerterpunner Long Billy	Wife: Caroline Big River	Between April 1851 and 1854
9. Alfred (King)	M	29	Purngerpar Big Billy	Wife: Pauline Big River	Between February 1844 and March 1846
10. Algernon	M	28	Memerlannelargenne Charley	Father: Umarrah Stoney Creek	20 February 1837
11. Alpha[1, 2] (Count)	M	43	Wooraddy Doctor	Wife: (ii) Truganini Sons: (i) Peter Bruny (ii) Davy Bruny (by first wife)	July 1842

Appendix 3. (cont.)

Name	Sex	Age in 1835	Other Names	Relations, Territory	Date of Death
12. Alphonso	M	28	Neernerpaterlargenne Big Jemmy	Wives: (i) (ii) Truganini Big River	1847
13. Amelia	F	18	Kittewer	Mother: Racerdunnupe Husband: Neptune Daughter: Emily Son: Moriarty Sandy Cape	Between April 1851 and 1854
14. Andrew	M	18	(? = Dewooradedy) Dray's Jerry	Wife: Sophia West Coast	Before December 1843
15. Andromache (Queen)	F	43	Larratong	Husband: Wymurric Son: Adolphus West Coast	16 August 1837
16. Anne[3]	F	36	Pierrapplener Dinah, Diana	Formerly with sealer Robert Rew	Before December 1843
17. Arthur	M	23	Wetaleer Jemmy	Big River	Between February and June 1839
18. Augustus	M	14	Thermanope Ben	Wife: Bessy Clark West Coast	29 August 1860
19. Barnaby Rudge[4]	M	6–10 in 1844		Mother: Narbrunga Father: John Lanna Brothers: William Lanney, Charles, Pleti, Francis North West	Between 1847 and 1851
20. Benjamin	M	18	Pendewurrewic	Macquarie Harbour	29 August 1837
21. Bessy	F	10	Pangernowidedic Bessy Clark	Mother: Tingernoop Husbands: (i) Augustus (ii) European Port Davey	12 February 1867

	Sex	Age	Little Jacky	Big River	
24. Caroline	F	35	Gunneyanner	Husband: Alexander Big River	10 July 1860
25. Catherine[3]	F	38	Narrucer	Husband: Noemy Daughters: Catherine Martha	29 November 1850
26. Catherine	F	born 26/1/1839	Morenang	Mother: Catherine Father: Noemy Sister: Martha	1848
27. Charley	M	10	Drunteherniter Rawee Charley Clark	Mother: Toindeburer Sandy Cape	Between April 1851 and 1854
28. Charles[4]	M	5–8 in 1844		Mother: Nabrunga Father: John Lanna Brothers: William Lanney, Barnaby Rudge, Pleti, Francis North West	Between April 1851 and 1854
29. Charlotte (Queen)	F	35	Luggenemenener	Husband: King George Daughter: Eliza Sandy Cape	21 March 1837
30. Charlotte	F	child		Mother: Harriet North East	20 June 1838
31. Charlotte[2, 3]	F		Carereen Kalloondo Sarah	Son: Johnny Franklin	
32. Christopher	M	33	Meterluererparrityer Dick, Richard	Ben Lomond	26 February 1838
33. Clara	F	16	Tedeheburer	Father: Wyne Sister: Mahanna Husband: Edward West Coast	c. August 1843
34. Cleopatra	F	17	Ryinrope	Daughter: Helen Pieman River	31 July 1837

Appendix 3. (cont.)

Name	Sex	Age in 1835	Other Names	Relations, Territory	Date of Death
35. Columbus	M	32	Lenergwin	Son: Pyboke Point Hibbs	28 January 1837
36. Constantine	M	33	Makeaduru Big Jacky	Central VDL	29 December 1837
37. Cuish[3, 5]	F		Parthemeenna		May 1851
38. Daniel	M	46	Lenudel Gohanne, "Dick"	Sandy Cape	8 June 1837
39. Daphne[3]	F	32	Dromethehenner Cranky Bet	Brother: Buonaparte Swanport	Between April 1851 and 1854
40. David Bruny[6]	M	11	Myyungge Davy Bruny	Father: Woorraddy Brother: Peter Bruny Wife: Matilda Bruny Island	Between 1847 and 1851
41. Deborah	F	23	Larmoderick	Husband: Rodney Daughter: born April 1837 West Coast	3 March 1838
42. Dick[1]	M	28	Druerertattenanne Cranky Dick	Wife: Louisa Ben Lomond	November 1850
43. Doctor	M		Topderarerener	Oyster Bay	December 1836/ January 1837
44. Edmund	M	23	Toeernac	West Coast	26 March 1851
45. Edward[1]	M	18	Little Billy	Wife: Clara West Coast	February 1839
46. Eliza	F		Eliza Robinson	Mother: Charlotte Father: George	27 June 1838
47. Elizabeth (Queen)	F	38	Big Bet, Waterloo Bet	Husbands: (i) Montepellerate (ii) William Robinson	17 November 1837

No. & Name	Sex	Age	Aboriginal name	Relations	Date
48. Emmy		Born 3/3/1838		Mother: ?ana Father: Neptune Brother: Moriarty	
49. Emma[3]	F	28	Little Tuery Meethecaratheeanna	Husband: Albert St Patrick's Head	8 May 1863
50. Eugene	M	26	Nicermenic	Wife: Sarah Son: Adam Robbins Island	November 1850
51. Eveline	F	28	Wongerneep	Husband: Romeo Daughter: Mathinna Port Davey	30 September 1837
52. Evannah	F		Tanleboneyer	Husband: Mannalargenna Ben Lomond	11 October 1836
53. Fanny[1,6]	F		Planobeena Jock (= Fanny Hardwicke?)	Husband: Napoleon Brother: Ajax	Between April 1851 and 1854
54. Fanny[7]	F	born 1835	Fanny Cochrane	Mother: Sarah Father: Cochrane (sealer) Sister: Mary Ann Husband: Smith (European)	After October 1903
55. Flora[3]	F	26	Pelloneneminner Bangum	Husband: Punroonner Ben Lomond	27 May 1860
56. Francis[4]	M			Mother: Nabrunga Father: John Lanna Brothers: William Lanney, Barnaby Rudge, Charles, Pleti North West	Before 1844
57. Francis	M	43	Big Mary's Jemmy	Oyster Bay	10 May 1838
58. Frederick	M	25	Pallooruc Tommy	Wife: Ryinrope West Coast	Between April 1851 and 1854
59. George (King)	M	46	Rolepa Old Tom	Wife: Charlotte Daughter: Eliza Sons: Walter George Arthur, Timmy, Ben Lomond	February 1839

Appendix 3. (cont.)

	Name	Sex	Age in 1835	Other Names	Relations, Territory	Date of Death
60.	George	M	14	George Clark		24 October 1836
61.	George	M	28	George Robinson	Wife: Agnes Ben Lomond	Between April 1851 and 1854
62.	Hannah[7]	F			Mother: Maria	1848 (?)
63.	Hannibal	M	29	Parley, Palle Parlin	Wife: Tinedeburrie Macquarie Harbour	Between February 1844 and March 1846
64.	Harriet[2,3]	F	34	Wottecowwidyer Watty Thompson's Sall	Daughters: Charlotte, Mary Ann Thompson Son: Tommy Thompson Cape Portland	Between 1851 and 1854
65.	Hector	M	30	Kartitteyer East Coast	Father: Mannalargenna	15 October 1837
66.	Helen	F	25	Corrobbery Twopence	Big River	13 June 1838
67.	Helen	F	infant		Mother: Cleopatra	18 December 1837
68.	Henrietta[3]	F	32	Thielewanna Big Mary	Daughters: Nancy, Hannah McSweeney Birches Rocks	Between April 1851 and 1854
69.	Henry	M	38	Parpomelenyer	Wife: Lucy Big River	c. December 1843
70.	Isaac[1,2]	M	18	Lacklay Jemmy	Wife: Matilda Surrey Hills	1839
71.	Jack Allen[8]	M		Batman's Jack Tillarbunner	Father: Ajax Ben Lomond	10 February 1864
72.	James	M	27	Little Jacky	Wife: Susan Daughter: Jessy	Before June 1839

No.	Name	Sex	Age	Looerrymner	Oyster Bay	
73.	Jane	F	43			February 1839
74.	Jemima	F	26	Cranky Poll	Port Sorell	18 November 1837
75.	Jenny[1]	F	16	Semiramis	Husband: Robert Ben Lomond	28 February 1839
76.	Jessy	F	3		Father: James Stoney Creek	Before February 1844
77.	John	M				Before June 1839
78.	John[4]	M		John Lanna	Wife: Nabrunga Sons: William Lanney, Pleti, Barnaby Rudge, Charles, Francis	Before 1844
79.	Johnny[2]	M		Johnny Franklin	Mother: Charlotte	
80.	Joseph	M	28	Rose's Jemmy	Wife: Rose	Before August 1841
81.	Juliet[3]	F	26		Cape Portland	May 1851
82.	Kit	F	38	Kitty, Old Kit	Husband: Samuel Tomahawk River	15 October 1837
83.	Lalla Rookh[1,6]	F	23	Truganini	Father: Mangerner Husbands: (i) Woorraddy (1829–42) (ii) Alphonso (1842–47) Recherche Bay	8 May 1876
84.	Leonidas	M	24	Doluwungege Dawunga David	Wife: Patty Surrey Hills	9 August 1844
85.	Louisa[3]	F	25	Drummernerloonner Jumbo	Mother: Poolrener Husbands: (i) Dick (ii) Tippo Saib Cape Portland	Between 1847 and 1851
86.	Lucy	F		Mytermoon	Husband: Henry Big River	Between March and October 1847
87.	Mahanna	F	9	Moyhenung Pillah	Sister: Clara Father: Wyne Pieman River	13 October 1837

Appendix 3. (cont.)

Name	Sex	Age in 1835	Other Names	Relations, Territory	Date of Death
88. Mannalargenna	M	Very old		Wife: Evannah Son: Hector Daughters: Wapperty, Nimerana George Bay	4 December 1835
89. Margaret[3, 9]	F	38	Woretermoeteyenner Bung (Pung)	Husband: Phillip Mussel Roe River	After 1841
90. Maria[3]	F	48	Old Maria	Husband: Achilles	Between August 1848 and January 1849
91. Maria	F		Charlotte, Maria II	Stoney Creek	30 March 1837
92. Martha	F	born 1835		Mother: Catherine Father: Noemy Sister: Catherine	2 February 1851
93. Mary	F	26	"Wild Mary" Wilhelmina	Big River	15 February 1851
94. Mary Ann Cochrane[6, 7]	F	16		Mother: Sarah Father: Cochrane (sealer) Sister: Fanny Husbands: (i) Walter George Arthur (ii) Adam Booker (European)	August 1871
95. Mary Ann Thompson[7, 10]	F	6		Mother: Harriet Brother: Tommy Thompson	1841
96. Mathinna[11]	F	1		Mother: Eveline Father: Romeo	1 September 1856
97. Matilda[6]	F	16	Pyterrunner	Mother: Tingernook Husbands: (i) Isaac (ii) Davy Bruny Port Davey	Between April 1851 and 1854

	Sex	Age		East Coast	Between March and October 1847
98. Matilda[5, 12]	F	30	Maria Mathabelianna (? = Maytepueminner)		
99. Matthew	M	35	Jacky McCracky	Arthur River	3 February 1837
100. Milton	M		Panenemeroick	Sandy Cape	3 September 1837
101. Moierune	F			Husband: Loathdiddebope	30 March 1837
102. Moriarty	M	born 1840		Mother: Amelia Father: Neptune Sister: Emily	Between April 1851 and 1855
103. Nabrunga[4]	F			Husband: John Lanna Sons: William Lanney, Barnaby Rudge, Charles, Pleti, Francis	1843
104. Nancy[7]	F	1-5	Younah	Mother: Henrietta Father: sealer Robbins Island	Between March 1847 and April 1851
105. Napoleon[1, 2]	M	23	Pevay Tunnerminnerwait Cape Grim Jack	Wife: Fanny Brother: Rodney Robbins Island	Executed 1842
106. Neptune	M	21	Reinderberg Drinene	Wife: Amelia Son: Moriarty Daughter: Emily North Coast	21 March 1851
107. Nimrod	M	28	Kangaroo Billy	Big River (?)	30 December 1836
108. Noemy	M	32	Marwerreek	Wife: Catherine Daughters: Catherine, Martha West Coast	Between April 1851 and 1855
109. Nomercuer	F			Sandy Cape	8 October 1837
110. Nooerner	F	21		Big River	
111. Noweberric	F	35		Husband: Omega Cape Grim	13 December 1835

Appendix 3. (cont.)

	Name	Sex	Age in 1835	Other Names	Relations, Territory	Date of Death
112.	Omega	M	23		Wife: Noweberric Cape Grim	22 February 1837
113.	Patty[3]	F	28	Goneannah Cuneenner Coonia	Husband: Leonidas	29 July 1867
114.	Pauline	F	28	Little Sally	Husband: Alfred Big River	Between August 1838 and January 1839
115.	Peter[2]	M	10	Droyyerloinne Peter Bruny	Father: Woorraddy Brother: Davy Bruny Bruny Island	Between August 1838 and January 1839
116.	Peter	M	23	Marnetti Peter Pindar	West Coast	Between February 1844 and March 1846
117.	Petuck	F			Husband: Heedeek West Coast (?)	Between February and June 1839
118.	Phillip	M	31	Bung's Jacky	Wife: Margaret Campbell Town	1 March 1839
119.	Ponedimeunep	F			Western	25 October 1837
120.	Pleti[4]	M	adol.		Mother: Nabrunga Father: John Lanna Brothers: William Lanney, Barnaby Rudge, Charles, Francis North West	1847 (?)
121.	Rebecca[3, 13]	F	32		Husband: Rodney Son: Robert Great Forester River	29 April 1841
122.	Robert[1, 2]	M	21	Timmy	Wife: Jenny Ben Lomond	Executed 1842
123.	Robert	M	born 1838		Mother: Rebecca Father: Rodney	Between 13 August 1838 and 10 January 1839

#	Name	Sex	Age	Other name	Relations / Location	Date
124.	Rodney	M	28	Pendowtewer	Wife: Rebecca / Brother: Napoleon / Son: Robert / West Coast	4 August 1838
125.	Romeo	M	35	Towterrer	Wife: Eveline / Daughter: Mathinna / Port Davey	30 September 1837
126.	Sabina[3]	F	37	Tylo, Crook	Cape Grim	3 March 1839
127.	Samuel	M	25	Karly / Kit's Jacky	Wife: Old Kit / Tomahawk River	3 February 1837
128.	Sarah[3]	F	33	Tarenootairrer / Tib	Husband: Eugene / Daughters: Mary Ann Cochrane / Fanny Cochrane / Son: Adam / Ben Lomond	3 October 1858
129.	Sophia	F	35	Dray	Husband: Andrew / South West Coast	29 August 1861
130.	Susan	F	34	Maniyercoyertutcher / Lockjaw Poll	Husband: James	Between August 1838 and January 1839
131.	Thomas	M	26–27 (38?)	Heedeek	Wife: Petuck / Sandy Cape	20 April 1841
132.	Thomas[14]	M	12	Thomas Bruny	Bruny Island	
133.	Thomas[2]	M	9	Tommy Thompson	Mother: Harriet / Sister: Mary Ann Thompson	
134.	Tidderup	F				1 June 1838
135.	Timmy	M	18	Maulboyheenner	Father: George / Brother: Walter George Arthur / Ben Lomond	Between June 1839 and August 1841
136.	Tinedeburric	F	35		Husband: Hannibal / Little Swanport	9 February 1837
137.	Tingernoop	F			Daughters: Bessy Clark, Matilda / Port Davey	May 1851

Appendix 3. (cont.)

Name	Sex	Age in 1835	Other Names	Relations, Territory	Date of Death
138. Tippo Saib	M	23	Calerwarrermeer Jacky	Big River	2 September 1860
139. Walter George Arthur[6]	M	15		Father: George Brother: Timmy Wife: Mary Ann Cochrane Ben Lomond	May 1861
140. Wapperty,[3] 15	F		Wobberrertee	Father: Mannalargenna St Patrick's Head	12 August 1867
141. Washington	M	28	Maccamee	Big River	Between April 1851 and 1860
142. William (King)	M		Tongerlongter	Wife: Adelaide Oyster Bay	20 June 1837
143. William Lanney[4]	M	1842 aged 7		Mother: Nabrunga Father: John Lanna Brothers: Barnaby Rudge, Charles, Pleti, Francis North West	3 March 1869
144. William Robinson	M	26	Pannerbuke	Wife: Elizabeth West Coast	12 January 1838
145. Wyree	F			Cox Bight	16 March 1837

NOTES

1. Absent from Wybalenna from March 1836 to July 1837 with George Robinson, jun., in search of Aborigines on the Van Diemen's Land mainland.
2. Went to Port Phillip with G. A. Robinson in February 1839 and did not return.
3. From sealers.
4. Arrived at Wybalenna in December 1842 from the north-west, where captured by sealers.
5. Joined the settlement in 1847.
6. Absent from Wybalenna from February 1839 to July 1842, at Port Phillip with G. A. Robinson.
7. Part-Aboriginal.
8. Came from Port Phillip in 1842; previously with John Batman.
9. Went to join part-Aboriginal daughter at Perth, Tasmania, in 1841.
10. Arrived at Wybalenna in June 1836, left Flinders Island in August 1841 with M. L. Smith, and possibly returned to Flinders Island in 1849 with Smith.
11. Lived with Sir John and Lady Franklin from 1839 to 1843.
12. Joined the establishment in May 1836.
13. Arrived at Wybalenna on 21 May 1837.
14. Arrived at Wybalenna in June 1836.
15. Arrived at Wybalenna in 1847.

Bibliography

MANUSCRIPT COLLECTIONS

Mitchell Library, Sydney (ML)

Official Sources

A339	Government and General Orders, New South Wales, 1816–1819.
A341	General and Garrison Orders by Governor Collins, 1803–8.
A1205	Dispatches to the governor of New South Wales, vol. 16, 1829.
A1219	Dispatches to the governor of New South Wales, vol. 30, 1838.
A1227	Dispatches to the governor of New South Wales, vol. 38, 1842.
A1352	Orders and proclamations of Lt.-Gov. Sorell, 1817–22.
A3490	Colonial secretary, out letters, 1810.
A4042	Governor King's letterbooks, 1797–1806.
C186	Correspondence of P. G. King with Lord Hobart and Governor Collins, 30 August 1802–15 March 1806.
C190	Van Diemen's Land. Register of Deaths, 1803–20.

Other Sources

A76	Bedford Papers.
A78–3	Banks Papers, Brabourne Collection, vol. 4. Bonwick Transcripts: vol. 3, box 51, pp. 892–97; vol. 4, box 52, pp. 1205–07 and 1268–74; vol. 5, box 53, pp. 1508–10; vol. 7, box 56, pp. 1919–21.
A106	Riley Papers, vol. 1.

A133–2   Diary of Rev. John McGarvie, 1826–28.
A316   Gunn papers.
A573   Flinders Island Papers.
A575   Calder Papers, miscellaneous.
A586   Sorell Papers.
A612   Tasmanian Aborigines.
A614   MS Account of the Aborigines of Van Diemen's Land by Rev. John Braim.
A860   Rowland Hassall Papers, 1818, vol. 2, pt. 1.
A1063–65   Thomas Scott Papers, 3 vols.
A1248/2   Writing notes and correspondence of E. W. Stephens.
A1604   Letters of Sir John Franklin to Strzelecki.
A1744   Allen Cunningham. Journal of a Visit to Macquarie Harbour, 1819.
A1992   Marsden Papers, vol. 2.
C228   George Bass. Journal Describing . . . the Coasts and Harbours of Van Diemen's Land, from Notes made on Board . . . *Norfolk* in 1798 and 1799.
A2161–
220   Arthur Papers: vol. 11, Sealers (A2172); vol. 15, Correspondence 1830 (A2176); vol. 23, Backhouse (A2183); vol. 28, Aborigines (A2188); vol. 39, Bedford (A2199); vol. 40, Bedford (A2200); vol. 49, Jorgensen (A2209); vol. 50, Gilbert Robertson (A2210).
A7022–92   Robinson Papers: vols. 11–13, Journals, Flinders Island, 1835–1839 (A7032–34); vol. 18, Journal, Port Phillip, 1841–42 (A7039); vols. 21–24, Letterbooks, 1829–39 (A7042–45); vols. 41–53, Correspondence and other papers, Flinders Island Settlement, 1832–39 (A7062–74); vols. 54–56, Correspondence and other papers, 1841–44 (A7075–77); vol. 67, Various journals and papers, 1850–52 (A7088).
            Uncat. MSS, set 214, item 1. Papers of William Thomas.

Archives Office of New South Wales, Sydney (AO)

1161   Examination of William Whitcomb, Port Dalrymple, 2 Feb. 1806. Miscellaneous correspondence relative to Aborigines.
2/8130   Colonial secretary. Appendix A: special bundles 1794–1825, Van Diemen's Land 1807–16. Remarks on the Country and Settlements formed in Van Diemen's Land, 1809.

Tasmanian State Archives, Hobart (TSA)

Official Sources

Colonial Secretary's Office (CSO)

1/37/658	Aboriginal children sent to England 1821 and 1823.
1/40/734	Aboriginal children sent to England.
1/240/4072	Correspondence relating to the Aborigines on Bruny Island, 1828.
1/240/5803	Welsh to col. sec., 6 June 1827.
1/316/7578/1	Miscellaneous correspondence and reports, 1824–31, relating to atrocities committed by the Aborigines.
1/317/7578/2	Reports by G. A. Robinson.
1/318/7578/3	Reports by G. A. Robinson.
1/319/7578/4	Papers relating to the Aborigines Committee.
1/320/7578/5	Reports by police magistrates *re* roving parties.
1/321/7578/6	Applications for position of storekeeper at Bruny Island 1829; applications to join parties in pursuit of Aborigines; applications for indulgences and rewards; letters from James Parish.
1/322/7578/7	Applications to go out after Aborigines; applications for rewards; requisitions for supplies.
1/323/7578/8	Jackson's reports on the islands in the straits; suggestions *re* capture of Aborigines; answers to questions circulated by Aborigines Committee.
1/324/7578/9	Papers relative to the Line (1830).
1/325/7578/10	Flinders Island papers.
1/326/7578/11	Miscellaneous material, chiefly relating to the roving parties; and some papers dealing with the Line.
1/327/7578/12	Papers relating to Sydney Aborigines; to the eligibility of Bruny Island for an Aboriginal Establishment; to the two Aboriginal boys held by Batman.
1/328/7578/13	Proclamations relating to the Aborigines; issue of firearms to the parties and other matters relating to the Line; material relating to Gilbert Robertson; papers relating to the Port Davey expedition.
1/329/7578/14	Papers relating to the roving parties and to the Line.
1/330/7578/15	Correspondence with Major Abbott, Edward Curr (*re* Goldie Affair), Gilbert Robertson, and others; reports on the killing of Aborigines and captures; some Flinders Island papers.
1/331/7578/16	Papers *re* Gilbert Robertson, 1828–31.
1/332/7578/17	Minutes of the Aborigines Committee.

1/807/17237   Correspondence between Robinson and colonial secretary, 1835.
5/182/4317   Case of Malcolm Laing Smith, 1839.
8/42/952   Case of Malcolm Laing Smith, 1842.
8/53/1191   Case of Harriet Thompson, 1842.
8/136/2731   Case of Malcolm Laing Smith, 1844.
8/157/1166   Papers relating to Flinders Island, 1842–43.
11/26/216   All subjects in connection with Flinders Island, 1846–47.
11/27/658   Report of Lt. Matthew Friend on the Flinders Island Aboriginal Establishment, 31 Oct. 1846.
24/24/582   Malcolm Laing Smith, 1847.
24/66   Report of the Surveyor-General on the Islands of Bass Strait, 1849.
24/93/3033   Correspondence by colonial secretary to Denison, Jan. 1850.
24/105/3351   Memorial of Malcolm Laing Smith, 25 Aug. 1846.
24/271/5453   Milligan and Oyster Cove, 1847.
24/284/6314   Milligan and Oyster Cove, 1854.

Chief Secretary's Department (CSD)
1/76/2029   M. L. Smith to colonial secretary 5 Dec. 1855–Mar. 1856 *re* Aborigines at Oyster Cove.
4/77/231   Correspondence with Royal Society of Tasmania, 1864.
7/26/215   Correspondence relating to Truganini.
7/33/450   Burial of Truganini, 1876.
7/45/833   Memo. Du Cane to Ministers, 14 Aug. 1871.
10/31/488   Burial of Truganini, 1876.
13/6/168   Correspondence with Malcolm Collis to Chairman of Board of Education, 1 Aug. 1881.
22/336/104/37   A. W. Burbury, Report on the Condition of the Half Castes at Cape Barren Island Reservation, 25 Sept. 1929.
22/343/104   Cape Barren Island, 1930.
22/416/104/10   Ministerial memo, minister for lands and works, 26 Feb. 1937.
22/531/104   Correspondence between the Commonwealth statistician, Roland Wilson, and the Chief Secretary's Department, 6 and 14 June and 18 and 23 Sept. 1946.

Education Department (ED)
3713/1077   Correspondence relating to the education of the children at Cape Barren Island, 1890–1901 (110/335–110/733).

Governor's Office (GO)
52/2   Governor's Office, in letters 1823–26.
1/65   Inwards dispatches, Apr.–June 1847, vol. 78.
Lands and Survey Department (LSD)
1/51/32   Surveyor-general to colonial secretary, 17 Feb. 1868, and other papers.
1/51/33   Report of Surveyor-General Power, Sept./Oct. 1854.
1/51/52   Remarks on Bass Strait Islands by John Thomas, to the surveyor-general, Sept. 1861.
643/30   Correspondence file 1913–30, including folios 1646/22, 554/23, and 1231/29.
Premier's Department (PD)
1/224/108–225 Cape Barren Island, 1910.
Premier's Office (PO)
108/2/10   C. E. Stephens to premier of Tasmania, 27 Oct. 1910.

Other Sources

LSD no. 11   Journal of Charles Grimes [James Meehan].
NP61   Diary of James Sutherland.
Pol 38/6   Depositions and associated papers, Launceston Police Office.
4/1692   Oyster Cove Visitors' Book, 1858–66.
CBI file   C. I. A. Booth, "The Half Castes of the Furneaux Islands", February 1959 (typescript report to the bishop of Tasmania).
M/M no. 79   Anon. Material on Cape Barren Island.
NS 373/11   Register of Services, Church of the Epiphany, Cape Barren Island, 1889–1906.

Public Record Office, London (PRO)

Dispatches from Van Diemen's Land to the Colonial Office, London
CO 280/16   Dispatches, Jan.–June 1828.
CO 280/21   Dispatches, July–Dec. 1829.
CO 280/35   Dispatches, July–Dec. 1832.
CO 280/45   VDL. Blue Book, 1823.
CO 280/93   Dispatches, Jan.–Mar. 1838.
CO 280/108   Dispatches, Mar.–June 1839.
CO 280/121   Dispatches, Oct.–Dec. 1840.
CO 280/133   Dispatches, July–Aug. 1841.
CO 280/169   Dispatches, Apr.–June 1844.

CO 280/179   Dispatches, Jan.–June 1845.
CO 280/180   Case of Dr Jeanneret, 1844–46.
CO 280/195   Dispatches, July–Oct. 1846.
CO 280/209   Dispatches, Jan.–June 1847.
CO 280/215   Dispatches, 5–7 Dec. 1847.
CO 284/80   Report of Oyster Cove Aboriginal Station, Jan. 1858–
               May 1859.

Royal Society of Tasmania (University of Tasmania Library)

8/RS/190/D34 John Hudspeth, Diary.
              Bladon Papers.
              Stephens Papers.

State Libary of South Australia

A1819   Marjory Rose Casson, "The Tasmanian Aborigines"
              (typescript, 1958).

Christ College, University of Tasmania

BC 46 CBI   Montgomery Papers, papers relating to Cape Barren
              Island.

Flinders Council, Whitemark, Flinders Island

Flinders Council Minute Book, July 1903–Dec. 1912, June 1913–June
              1917, July 1917–Aug. 1919, Oct. 1927–Jan. 1931.

Cape Barren School, Cape Barren Island, Tasmania

Cape Barren Island School and Punishment Book, 1898–1938.

University of Tasmania Archives

Parker Papers.

Macquarie University Library

Victorian Aboriginal Group: Annual Reports, 1929–64.

National Library of Australia (ANL)

MS 3251   Launceston Police Office, depositions (Aborigines and
             bushrangers).
MS 3311   H. J. Emmett, "The Black War in Tasmania".

Australian Institute of Aboriginal Studies (AIAS)

Microfilm MF 30/3255.
Ernest Westlake, Tasmanian notes [1908–10], from Pitt Rivers
             Museum, vols. 1, 2, 3, and 4.

PARLIAMENTARY PAPERS : GREAT BRITAIN (BPP)

Year Vol. No.
1812   11   341   *Report from the Select Committee on Transportation.*
1816   450   *Papers relating to His Majesty's Settlements at New
                   South Wales, 1811–1814.*
1823   10   136   *Report of Commissioner Bigge on the State of Agri-
                   culture and Trade in New South Wales.*
1831   19   259   *Copies of all correspondence between Lieutenant-
                   Governor Arthur and His Majesty's Secretary of State
                   for the Colonies, on the Subject of the Military
                   Operations lately carried out against the Aboriginal
                   Inhabitants of Van Diemen's Land.*
1834   44   617   *Aboriginal Tribes, 1834.*
1836   7   538   *Report from the Select Committee on Aborigines
                   (British Settlements) together with the minutes of
                   evidence, appendix and index (5 Aug. 1836).*
1837   7   425   *Report from the Select Committee on Aborigines
                   (British Settlements) with the minutes of evidence,
                   appendix and index (26 June 1837).*
1837   19   518   *Report from the Select Committee on Transporta-
                   tion; together with the minutes of evidence, appendix
                   and index (14 July 1837).*
1837/ 22   669   *Report from the Select Committee on Transporta-
38   tion; together with the minutes of evidence, appendix
                   and index (3 Aug. 1838).*
1839   34   526   *Australian Aborigines. Copies of extracts of des-
                   patches relative to the massacre of various aborigines
                   in Australia, in the year 1838, and respecting the trial
                   of their murderers (12 Aug. 1839).*

1844   34   637   *Aborigines (Australian colonies). Copies of extracts from the despatches of the Governors of the Australian colonies, with the reports of the protectors of aborigines and any other correspondence to illustrate the condition of the aboriginal population of the said colonies, from the date of the last papers laid before Parliament on the subject (papers ordered by the House of Commons to be printed, 12 August 1839, no. 526)* (9 Aug. 1844).

PARLIAMENTARY PAPERS : TASMANIA

J. Milligan, "Vocabulary and Dialects of Aboriginal Tribes in Tasmania". *J&P LC Tas.* (1856), paper 7.

T. Reibey, "Letter from the Venerable Archdeacon Reibey, on the Subject of the Half-caste Islanders in the Straits". *J&P LC Tas.*, vol. 7 (1862), no. 17.

T. Reibey, "Half-caste Islanders in Bass Straits". *J&P LC Tas.*, vol. 9 (1863), no. 48.

Statistics of Tasmania 1844–1864. *J&P LC Tas.* (1864).

Board of Education Report for 1878. *J&P LC Tas.*, vol. 28 (1879).

Report of Dr Vine upon the fevers in the Islands. *Journals of the House of Assembly,* vol. 37 (1879), no. 56.

Board of Education Report for 1882. *J&P LC Tas.*, vol. 35 (1883), no. 88.

Flinders Island: Report by Mr John Brown. *J&PP Tas.*, vol. 12, (1887), no. 62.

J. E. C. Lord, "Report upon the State of the Islands, the Condition and Mode of Living of the Half-Castes, the existing Methods of regulating the Reserves, and Suggesting Lines for Future Administration". *J&PP Tas.*, vol. 59 (1908), no. 57.

"Report of the Select Committee appointed 29 October 1924, to inquire into and report upon the best means of dealing with the half-caste problem on the Furneaux Group of Islands". *J&PP Tas.,* vol. 91 (1924–25), no. 48.

"Report of the Secretary for Lands 1937–38". *J&PP Tas.,* vol. 119 (1938), no. 13.

Ministerial statement, minister for lands and works, 1939. *J&PP Tas.*, vol. 121 (1939), no. 7.

"Report of the Secretary for Lands and Surveyor-General's Department 1944". *J&PP Tas.*, vol. 131 (1944–45), no. 10.

"Report of the Joint Committee of the House of Assembly and Legislative Council Appointed to Enquire into Matters Connected with the

Flinders Island Municipality". *J&PP Tas.*, vol. 139 (1948), no. 22.
"Report of the Committee Appointed by the State Government to
Examine Several Matters concerned with the Future Development of
Flinders Island". *J&PP Tas.*, vol. 179 (1968), no. 15.
"Report of the Aboriginal Affairs Study Group". *J&PP Tas.*, vol. 199
(1978), no. 94.

ACTS : TASMANIA

An Act to require sealers and others to depart the Straits 6 Will. IV, no.
15, 1836.
Cape Barren Island Reserve Act 1912, 3 Geo. V, no. 16.
Cape Barren Island Reserve Act 1945, 9 Geo. VI, no. 14.
Expiration of Cape Barren Reserve Act 1945 1951, 9 Geo. VI, no. 14.

NEWSPAPERS AND PERIODICALS

Advocate (Burnie), 18 July 1929.
Advocate (Launceston), 1829–35.
Argus (Melbourne), Jan. 1909–Jan. 1910.
Asiastic Journal, Sept. 1820.
Black Action, Journal of the Aboriginal Information Service, Tasmania.
1976–1980.
Church News (Hobart), May 1866, 1871–99.
Colonial Advocate (Hobart), 1828.
Colonial Intelligencer, or the Aborigines Friend (London), 1847–48.
Colonial Literary Journal; and Weekly Miscellany of Useful Information
(Sydney), vol. 1, June-Dec. 1844.
Colonial Times (Hobart), 1826–31.
Colonist (Hobart), 1838.
Cornwall Chronicle (Launceston), 1839–47.
Derwent Star and Van Diemen's Land Intelligencer (Hobart), 29 Jan.
1810.
Examiner (Launceston), 1842–1975 (discontinuous).
Gentlemen's Magazine (Hobart), 15 Feb. 1881.
*Ross's Hobart Town Almanack and Van Diemen's Land Annual for
1834 and 1836* (Hobart).
Hobart Town Courier, 1827–35, 1840–47.
Hobart Town Gazette, 1816–27.
Illustrated London News, vol. 46, 7 Jan. 1865.
Launceston Independent, 1831.
Mercury (Hobart), 1860–1979 (discontinuous).
New South Wales Magazine (Sydney), Feb. 1842.

South Asian Register (London), Jan. 1820.
Sunday Examiner Express (Launceston), Apr. 1970 and Aug. 1971.
Sydney Gazette, 1803–24.
Tasmanian (Hobart), 1831, 1837.
Tasmanian and Port Dalrymple Advertiser (Launceston), 1825, 1827, 1829.
Tasmanian Church Chronicle (Hobart), 6 Mar. 1852.
Tasmanian Democrat (Hobart), 16 June 1894.
Tasmanian Government Gazette (Hobart), 1871–1951 (discontinuous).
Tasmanian Illustrated Supplement (Hobart), vol. 1, no. 10 (20 Oct. 1866).
Van Diemen's Land Almanack (Hobart), 1831–34.
Van Diemen's Land Annual (Hobart), 1831–35.

REFERENCE WORKS

Australian Dictionary of Biography. Edited by Douglas Pike. Vols. 1–7. Melbourne: Melbourne University Press, 1966–79.
Eldershaw, P. R. *Guide to the Public Records of Tasmania.* 3 vols. Hobart: Archives Office of Tasmania, 1951–65.
Ferguson, J. A. *Bibliography of Australia.* Vols. 1–4. Sydney: Angus and Robertson, 1941–55.
Guide to Collections of Manuscripts Relating to Australia. Canberra: National Library of Australia, 1965.
Historical Manuscripts of Tasmania – Reports 1–5. Hobart: University of Tasmania, 1964.
Historical Records of Australia. Series 1, vols. 1–26 (1914–25). Series 3, vols. 1–6 (1921–23).
Historical Records of New South Wales. Vol. 1, part 2 (1899). Vol. 5, (1900).
Hope, J. H., S. Murray-Smith, and F. I. Norman, "Bibliography of Bass Straits 1797–1971". *Proceedings of the Royal Society of Victoria* 85 (25 May 1973): 79–116.
Index to Bibliographies. Series 4, no. 126, 1964–69. Compiled by I. Boleszny. Adelaide: State Library Research Service, South Australia, 1969.
Plomley, N. J. B. *An Annotated Bibliography of the Tasmanian Aborigines.* Occasional Paper of the Royal Anthropological Institute, no. 28. London, 1969.

UNPUBLISHED TYPESCRIPT MATERIAL

Albrecht, Paul G. E. "Social Change and the Aboriginal Australians of Central Australia". Bombay, 1970.

Barwick, Diane E. "Coranderrk and Cumeroogunga: Pioneers and Policy". Canberra, 1972.

Canteri, Carl. "The Origins of Australian Social Banditry: Bushranging in Van Diemen's Land 1805–1818". London, 1973.

Chobanian, Connie. "Cape Barren". ABC, Sydney, 1971.

Jones, Rhys. "Tasmanian Tribes". Seminar paper, Department of Prehistory, RSPS, ANU, Mar. 1971.

————. "A Hunting Landscape". Seminar paper, ANU, 1972.

King, Brian. "Barren Future". *Four Corners,* ABC, Sydney, 18 May 1971.

Macknight, C. C. "Macassans and Aborigines in the Northern Territory". Department of Prehistory, RSPS, ANU, 1968.

Moore, Bob. "The Last Tasmanian". *Monday Conference,* ABC, Sydney, 4 Sept. 1978.

Newcombe, Ken. "Their Barren Existence: The Story of Abschol's Involvement with the Cape Barren Islanders Since the Beginning of June 1969 up to May 1970". Hobart, 1970.

Reynolds, Henry. "The Unrecorded Battlefields of Queensland". Townsville, Feb. 1974.

Ryan, Lyndall. "Report to the Australian Institute of Aboriginal Studies on Truganini". Canberra, AIAS, Oct. 1974.

Summers, John. "Everard Park and the Administration of Aboriginal Welfare in the North West of South Australia". Seminar paper, Politics Department, Flinders University, 1972.

Wagstaff, P., J. Gibson, and J. Manning. "Cape Barren Island". SSRC Research File. Canberra, Feb. 1966.

Wales, Eleanor. "Flinders Island". Prehistory Department, UNE, Armidale, 1978.

THESES

Barwick, Diane E. "A Little More than Kin: Regional Affiliation and Group Identity Among Aboriginal Migrants in Melbourne". PhD, ANU, 1963.

Beckett, Jeremy. "A Study of a Mixed-Blood Aboriginal Minority in the Pastoral West of New South Wales". MA, ANU, 1958.

Bladel, Frances M. "British Tasmanian Relations, 1803–1828". BA, University of Tasmania, 1969.

Bowdler, Sandra. "Hunter Hill, Hunter Island". PhD, ANU, 1979.
Bridges, Barry. "Aboriginal and White Relations in New South Wales, 1788–1855". MA, University of Sydney, 1966.
Calley, Malcolm J. C. "Social Organisation of Mixed-Blood Communities in North-Eastern New South Wales". PhD, University of Sydney, 1959.
Campbell, Ian. "The Relations between Settlers and Aborigines in the Pastoral District of New England, 1832–1860". BA, University of New England, 1969.
Curthoys, Ann. "Race and Ethnicity: A Study of the Response of British Colonists to Aborigines, Chinese and non-British Europeans in New South Wales, 1856–1881". PhD, Macquarie University, 1973.
Fink, Ruth. "Social Stratification: A Sequel to the Assimilation Process in a Part-Aboriginal Community". MA, University of Sydney, 1955.
Franks, S. M. "Land Exploration in Tasmania 1824–42". MA, University of Tasmania, 1959.
Gale, Fay. "A Study of Assimilation: Part-Aborigines in South Australia". PhD, University of Adelaide, 1960.
Harrison, B. W. "The Myall Creek Massacre and Its Significance in the Controversy over the Aborigines during Australia's Early Squatting Period". BA, University of New England, 1966.
Hart, P. R. "The Church of England in Tasmania under Bishop Montgomery, 1889–1901". MA, University of Tasmania, 1963.
Hart, Philip R. "J. A. Lyons: A Political Biography". PhD, ANU, 1967.
Hartwig, M. C. "The Process of White Settlement in the Alice Springs District and Its Effects upon the Aboriginal Inhabitants 1860–1894". PhD, University of Adelaide, 1965.
Hausfeld, R. G. "Aspects of Aboriginal Station Management". MA, University of Sydney, 1960.
Hormann, B. L. "Extinction and Survival: A Study of the Reaction of Aboriginal Populations to European Expansion". PhD, University of Chicago, 1949.
Iredale, Robyn R. "The Enigma of Assimilation: The position of the Part-Aboriginal in New South Wales". BA, University of Sydney, 1965.
Johnston, Sue. "The New South Wales Government Policy towards Aborigines 1880–1909". MA, University of Sydney, 1970.
Jones, Rhys. "Rocky Cape and the Problem of the Tasmanians". PhD, University of Sydney, 1971.
Lourandos, H. J. "Coast and Hinterland: The Archaeological Sites of Eastern Tasmania". MA, ANU, 1970.

Oldmeadow, K. S. "The Science of Man: Scientific Opinion on the Australian Aborigines in the Late 19th Century; the Impact of Evolutionary Theory and Racial Myth". MA, ANU, 1968.

Prentis, M. D. "Aborigines and Europeans in the Northern Rivers Region of New South Wales, 1823–1881". MA, Macquarie University, 1972.

Reece, R. H. W. "The Aborigines and Colonial Society in New South Wales before 1850, with Special Reference to the Period of the Gipps Administration 1838–1846". MA, University of Queensland, 1969.

Reynolds, Henry. "The Island Colony". MA, University of Tasmania, 1963.

Rhee, Hendrik S. "The Black Line and Governor Arthur's Aboriginal Policy". BA, University of Tasmania, 1972.

Stokes, H. J. W. "The Settlement and Development of the Van Diemen's Land Company Grant in North-Western Van Diemen's Land 1824–1860". BA, University of Tasmania, 1963.

Taylor, John C. "Race Relations in South East Queensland, 1840–1860". BA, University of Queensland, 1967.

ARTICLES TO 1900

Barnard, James. "Observations on the Statistics of Van Diemen's Land for 1848 . . . ", *P&P RST* 1, no. 1 (1849–51): 102–34.

Broadfoot, John "J. B.". "An Unexpected Visit to Flinders Island in Bass Straits". *Chambers' Edinburgh Journal,* 20 Sept. 1845, pp. 187–89.

Calder, J. E. "Some Account of the Country Lying between Lake St Clair and Macquarie Harbour". *Tas. Jour. Nat. Sci.* 3 (1849): 415–29.

Davies, R. H. "Some Account of the Habits and Natural History of the Sooty Petrel (Mutton Bird)". *Tas. Jour. Nat. Sci.* 2 (1843): 13–16.

———. "On the Aborigines of Van Diemen's Land". *Tas. Jour. Nat. Sci.* 2 (1846): 409–20.

Dove, T. "Moral and Social Characteristics of the Aborigines of Tasmania, as Gathered from Intercourse with the Surviving Remnant of Them Now Located on Flinders' Island". *Tas. Jour. Nat. Sci.* 1 (1842): 247–54.

Friend, M. C. "On the Decrease of the Aborigines of Tasmania". *Tas. Jour. Nat. Sci.* 3 (1847): 242–43.

Horton, W. "Letter from Van Diemen's Land". *Weslayan Methodist Magazine* 46 (1823): 832–34.

Montgomery, H. H. "A Mutton Bird Island". *New Review* 7 (1892): 233.

PRINTED WORKS TO 1900

Atkins, Rev. T. *Reminiscences of Twelve Years' Residence (1836–1847) in Tasmania and Australia.* Malvern, 1869.

Backhouse, James. *A Narrative of a Visit to the Australian Colonies.* London, 1843.

Backhouse, James, and C. Tylor, *The Life and Labours of G. W. Walker.* London, 1862.

Beattie, J. W. *Photographs of Aborigines at Oyster Cove.* Hobart, 1860.

Betts, T. *An Account of the Colony of Van Diemen's Land.* Calcutta, 1830.

Bischoff, James. *Sketch of the History of Van Diemen's Land.* London, 1832.

Bonwick, James. *The Last of the Tasmanians.* London, 1870.

Breton, W. H. *Excursions in New South Wales, Western Australia, and Van Diemen's Land, During the Years 1830, 1831, 1832 and 1833.* London, 1833.

Bride, T. F., ed. *Letters from Victorian Pioneers: Being a Series of Papers on the Early Occupation of the Colony, the Aborigines etc.* Melbourne, 1898.

Broughton, Archdeacon W. G. *Charge Delivered to the Clergy of New South Wales, 15 November 1829.* Sydney, 1829.

Brownrigg, M. B. *The Cruise of the Freak.* Launceston, 1872.

Calder, J. E. *Some Account of the Wars, Extirpation, Habits, etc. of the Native Tribes of Tasmania.* Hobart, 1875.

Collins, David. *An Account of the English Colony in New South Wales.* London, 1804.

Cunningham, Peter. *Two Years in New South Wales.* London, 1827.

Curr, E. M. *An Account of the Colony of Van Diemen's Land.* London, 1824.

Delano, Amasa. *A Narrative of Voyages and Travels.* Boston, 1817.

Denison, Sir William. *Varieties of Vice-Regal Life.* 2 vols. London, 1870.

Dixon, James. *Narrative of a Voyage to New South Wales, and Van Diemen's Land, in the ship Skelton.* Edinburgh, 1822.

Evans, G. W. *A Geographical, Historical and Topographical Description of Van Diemen's Land.* London, 1822.

Fenton, James. *A History of Tasmania.* Hobart, 1884.

Flinders, Matthew. *A Voyage to Terra Australis.* London, 1814.

Godwin, Rev. B. *Emigrant's Guide to Van Diemen's Land.* London, 1823.

Haydon, G. H. *Five Years' Experience in Australia Felix.* London, 1846.

Heeres, J. E., ed. *Abel Tasman's Journal of his Discovery of Van Diemen's Land and New Zealand in 1642 with Documents Relating to His Exploration in Australia in 1644.* London, 1898.

Henderson, Capt. John. *Observations on the Colonies of New South Wales and Van Diemen's Land.* Calcutta, 1832.

Howitt, William. *Colonization and Christianity: A Popular History of the Treatment of the Natives by the Europeans in 'All Their Colonies.* London, 1838.

Hull, H. M. *Royal Kalendar, and Guide to Tasmania for 1859.* Hobart, 1859.

Jeanneret, Henry. *Vindication of a Colonial Magistrate.* London, 1854.

Jeffreys, Charles. *Van Diemen's Land: Geographical and Descriptive Delineations of the Island of Van Diemen's Land.* London, 1822.

Labillardière, J. J. H. de. *An Account of a Voyage in Search of La Perouse . . .* 2 vols. London: Debrett, 1800.

————. *An Account of a Voyage in Search of La Perouse . . .* London: Stockdale, 1800.

Ling Roth, Henry, trans. *Crozet's Voyage to Tasmania, New Zealand and the Ladrone Islands, and the Philippines in the years 1771–1772.* London, 1891.

Lloyd, G. T. *Thirty-three Years in Tasmania and Victoria.* London, 1862.

Martin, R. M. *The British Colonies.* 3 vols. London, 1851.

Merivale, H. *Lectures on Colonization and Colonies.* 2nd ed. London, 1861.

Meston, Archibald. *Queensland Aborigines: Proposed System for Their Improvement and Preservation.* Brisbane, 1895.

Nixon, F. R. *The Cruise of the Beacon.* Hobart, 1854.

Pasco, Crawford. *A Roving Commission: Naval Reminiscences.* Melbourne, 1897.

Péron, François. *A Voyage of Discovery to the Southern Hemisphere Performed by Order of the Emperor Napoleon, During the Years 1801, 1802, 1803 and 1804.* Translated from the French. London, 1809.

Prinsep, Mrs A. *The Journal of a Voyage from Calcutta to Van Diemen's Land.* London, 1833.

Prout, J. S. *Tasmania Illustrated.* Hobart Town, 1844.

Robinson, G. A. *Address to the Aborigines' Protection Society of New South Wales, 19 October 1838.* Sydney, 1838.

Stokes, John Lort. *Discoveries in Australia.* 2 vols. London, 1846.

Strzelecki, P. E. de. *Physical Description of New South Wales and Van Diemen's Land.* London, 1845.

Sturt, Charles. *Two Expeditions into the Interior of Southern Australia.* 2 vols. London, 1833.

Wentworth, W. C. *A Statistical, Historical and Political Description of the Colony of New South Wales, and Its Dependent Settlements in Van Diemen's Land.* London, 1819.

West, John. *The History of Tasmania.* 2 vols. Launceston, 1852.

Westgarth, William. *A Report on the Condition, Capabilities and Prospects of the Australian Aborigines.* Melbourne, 1846.

Woolley, C. A. *Tasmanian Aborigines at Oyster Cove.* Hobart, 1866.

ARTICLES FROM 1900

Barwick, Diane E. "And the Lubras are Ladies Now". In *Woman's Role in Aboriginal Society,* ed. Fay Gale. Canberra: AIAS, 1970.

———. "Changes in the Aboriginal Population of Victoria 1863–1966". In *Aboriginal Man and Environment in Australia.* ed. D. J. Mulvaney and J. Golson. Canberra: ANU Press, 1971.

———. "Coranderrk and Cumeroogunga: Pioneers and Policy". In *Opportunity and Responses: Case Studies in Economic Development.* ed. T. Scarlett Epstein and D. H. Penney. London: 1972.

Basedow, Herbert. "Relic of the Lost Tasmanian Race: Obituary Notice of Mary Seymour". *Man* 14 (1914): 161–62.

———. "Diseases of the Australian Aborigines". *Journal of Tropical Medicine and Hygiene* 35 (1932): 177–85.

Bell, J. H. "Some Demographic and Cultural Characteristics of the La Perouse Aborigines". *Mankind* 5, no. 10 (1962): 425–538.

———. "Assimilation in New South Wales". In *Aborigines Now: New Perspectives in the Study of Aboriginal Communities.* ed. Marie Reay. Sydney: Angus and Robertson, 1968.

Berndt, R. M. "External Influence". *Hemisphere* 9, no. 3 (March 1965): 2–9.

Berry, R. J. A. "A Living Descendant of an Extinct (Tasmanian) Race". *PRSV* 20 (1907): 1–20.

Bickford, Anne. "The Last Tasmanian: Superb Documentary or Racist Fantasy". *Filmnews,* Jan. 1979.

Bridges, Barry. "The Aborigines and the Law: New South Wales 1788–1855". *Teaching History* 4, pt 3 (Dec. 1970): 40–70.

Bryden, William. "Tasmanian Museum and Art Gallery Historical Note". *P&P RST* 100 (1966): 25.

Buchner, L. W. G. "Notes on Certain of the Cape Barren Islanders". *Report of the Australasian Association for the Advancement of Science,* 1913, pp. 446–47.

Capell, Arthur. "What Do We Know of the Tasmanian Language?", *RQVM* n.s. 30 (1968): 1–12.

Cleland, J. B. "Diseases Amongst the Australian Aborigines". *Journal of Tropical Medicine and Hygiene* 31 (1928): 234.

Crowther, W. E. L. H. "The Passing of the Tasmanian Race". The Halford Oration. *Medical Journal of Australia,* 3 Feb. 1934, pp. 147–60.

———. "The Final Phase of the Extinct Tasmanian Race 1847–1876". *RQVM,* n.s. 49 (1974): 1–30.

Curthoys, Ann. "Destruction of Aboriginal Society". *Arena,* no. 27 (1971): 37–48.

De Vore, Irven. "A Hunter-Gatherer Society". In *Man the Hunter,* ed. Richard B. Lee and Irven de Vore. Chicago: Aldine Press, 1968.

Dunbabin, Thomas. "Men Who Vanished: Sidelights on the Lost Tasmanian Race". *Mankind* 1 (1935): 258–60.

Dunstan, D. A. "Aboriginal Land Title and Employment in South Australia". In *Aborigines in the Economy,* ed. Ian G. Sharp and Colin M. Tatz. Brisbane: Jacaranda Press, 1966.

Elkin, A. P. "Aborigines and Whites". *Meanjin* 9 (1949): 279–85.

———. "Reaction and Interaction: A Food Gathering People and European Settlement in Australia". *American Anthropologist* 53 (1951): 164–86.

Fink, Ruth. "The Caste Barrier – An Obstacle to the Assimilation of Part-Aborigines in the North West of New South Wales". *Oceania* 28, no. 2 (Dec. 1957): 130–56.

Giblin, R. W. "Robert Brown at Port Dalrymple". *P&P RST* (1929): 25–32.

Hainsworth, D. R. "Iron Men in Wooden Ships: The Sydney Sealers 1800–1820". *Labour History,* no. 13 (Nov. 1967): 19–26.

Hamilton, Annette. "Blacks and Whites: Cultural Change in Australia". *Arena,* no. 20 (1972): 34–38.

———. "Aboriginal Man's Best Friend?". *Mankind* 8, no. 4 (Dec. 1972): 287–95.

———. "Aboriginal Cultures: Management or Autonomy". *Arena*, no. 34 (1974): 16–23.

Harper, N. D. "Historical Aspects of Race and Culture Contact". *Mankind* 1 (Feb. 1935): 270–71.

Hartwig, M. C. "Aborigines and Racism: An Historical Perspective". In *Racism: The Australian Experience*, ed. Frank Stevens. Vol. 2, *Black versus White*. Sydney: ANZ Book Co., 1972.

Hausfeld, R. G. "Dissembled Culture: An Essay on Method". *Mankind* 6, no. 2 (Nov. 1963): 49–51.

Hiatt, Betty. "The Food Quest and the Economy of the Tasmanian Aborigines". *Oceania* 38, no. 2 (1967): 99–133; no. 3 (1968): 190–219.

———. "Woman the Gatherer". In *Woman's Role in Aboriginal Society*, ed. Fay Gale. Canberra: AIAS, 1970.

Hicks, George L., and David I. Kertzer. "Making a Middle Way: Problems of Monhegan Identity". *Southwestern Journal of Anthropology* 28, no. 1 (spring 1972): 1–24.

Hudspeth, W. H. "Experiences of a Settler in the Early Days of Van Diemen's Land". *P&P RST* (1935): 139–54.

———. "Leaves from the Diary of a Van Diemen's Land Official". *P&P RST* (1946): 37–39.

Inglis, Judy. "One Hundred Years at Point McLeay, South Australia". *Mankind* 5, no. 12 (Nov. 1962): 503–7.

Jennings, J. N. "The Submarine Topography of Bass Strait". *PRSV* 7 (1959): 49–72.

Jones, Rhys. "A Speculative Archaeological Sequence for North Western Tasmania". *RQVM*, n.s. 25 (Dec. 1966): 1–12.

———. "Fire-Stick Farming". *Australian Natural History* 16 (1969): 224–28.

———. "Tasmanian Aborigines and Dogs". *Mankind* 7, no. 4 (Dec. 1970): 256–71.

———. "The Demography of Hunters and Farmers in Tasmania". In *Aboriginal Man and Environment in Australia*, ed. D. J. Mulvaney and J. Golson. Canberra: ANU Press, 1971.

———. "The Tasmanian Paradox", in *Stone Tools as Cultural Markers: Change, Evolution and Complexity*, ed. R. V. S. Wright. Canberra: AIAS, 1977.

———. "A Note on the Discovery of Stone Tools and a Stratified Prehistoric Site on King Island, Bass Strait". *Australian Archaeology* 9 (1979): 87–94.

Kalokerinos, Archie. "Some Aspects of Aboriginal Infant Mortality". *Medical Journal of Australia* 1 (1965): 185–87.

Lurie, Nancy O. "The Voice of the American Indian: Report on the

American Indian Chicago Conference". *Current Anthropology* 2 (1961): 478–500.

Macknight, C. C., and A. G. Thorne. "Two Macassan Burials in Arnhem Land". *Archaeology and Physical Anthropology in Oceania* 3, no. 3 (Oct. 1968): 216–22.

McRae, M. D. "Port Davey and the South West". *P&P THRA* 8 (1960): 46–50.

Maddock, Ken. "Give Us Land, Not Philanthropy". *Tharunka* [A Black and White Issue], July 1970.

Malcolm, N. W. G. "Short Notes on the Inhabitants of Cape Barren Island, Bass Strait, Tasmania". *Man* 20 (1920): 145–49.

Mansell, Michael, "Land Rights for Tasmania's Aborigines". *Arena,* no. 50 (1978): 92–97.

Meston, A. L. "The Problem of the Tasmanian Aboriginal". *P&P RST (1936): 85–92.*

——— . "The Half Castes of the Furneaux Group". *RQVM,* no. 2 (1947): 1–52.

——— . "The Van Diemen's Land Company 1825–1842". *RQVM,* n.s. 9 (1958): 1–40.

Mulvaney, D. J. "Beche-de-mer, Aborigines and Australian History". *PRSV,* n.s. 79, pt 12 (Sept. 1966): 449–57.

Murray-Smith, Stephen. "Beyond the Pale: The Islander Community of Bass Strait in the 19th Century". *P&P THRA* 20, no. 4 (1973): 167–200.

[Needham, J. S.] "Cape Barren Island". *ABM Review* 17 (1931): 171–72.

Neville, A. O. "The Half-Caste in Australia". *Mankind* 4, no. 7 (Sept. 1951): 274–90.

Plomley, N. J. B. *"Friendly Mission: The Tasmanian Journals and Papers of G. A. Robinson 1829–1834.* A Supplement". *P&P THRA* 18, no. 1 (1971): 1–32.

Plomley, N. J. B., and W. J. C. Wilkinson. "Introduced Disease as a Cause of Death among the Tasmanian Aborigines". *Journal of Anatomy* 98 (1964): 489.

Reay, Marie. "A Half-Caste Aboriginal Community in North Western New South Wales". *Oceania* 15 (1945): 296–323.

——— . "Native Thought in Rural New South Wales". *Oceania* 20, no. 2 (1949): 89–118.

——— . "The Background of Alien Impact". In *Aboriginal Man in Australia: Essays in Honour of Emeritus Professor A. P. Elkin,* ed. R. M. and C. H. Berndt. Sydney: Angus and Robertson, 1965.

Reber, Grote. "Aboriginal Carbon Dates from Tasmania". *Mankind* 6 (1965): 264–68.

Reece, R. H. W. "Feasts and Blankets: The History of Some Early Attempts to Establish Relations with the Aborigines of New South Wales, 1814–1846". *Archaeology and Physical Anthropology in Oceania* 2, no. 3 (1967): 190–206.

Reynolds, Henry. " 'That Hated Stain': The Aftermath of Transportation in Tasmania". *Historical Studies* 14, no. 53 (1969): 19–31. 31.

Ryan, Lyndall. "Outcasts in White Tasmania". *Mankind* 8, no. 4 (1972): 249–54.

———. "The Extinction of the Tasmanian Aborigines: Myth and Reality". *P&P THRA* 19 no. 2 (1972): 61–77.

———. "The Struggle for Recognition: Part-Aborigines in Bass Strait in the Nineteenth Century". *Aboriginal History* 1, pt 1 (1977): 27–51.

Scott, Peter. "Land Settlement". In *Atlas of Tasmania*, ed. J. L. Davies. Hobart: Dept. of Lands and Surveys, 1965.

Serventy, D. L. "Mutton-birding". In *Bass Strait: Australia's Last Frontier*, Sydney: ABC, 1969.

Sharp, Nonie. "White is Right". *Arena*, no. 35 (1974): 8–14.

Shaw, A. G. L. "A Colonial Ruler in Two Hemispheres: Sir George Arthur in Van Diemen's Land and Canada". *P&P THRA* 17, no. 3 (1970): 80–102.

Stanner, W. E. H. "The Aborigines". In *Some Australians Take Stock*, ed. J. C. G. Kevin. London: Longmans, Green, 1939.

———. "Durmugan, A Nangiomeri". In *In the Company of Men*, ed. J. B. Casagrande. New York: Harper, 1960.

———. "Aboriginal Territorial Organisation, Estate, Range, Domain and Regime". *Oceania* 36 (1965): 1–26.

———. "The History of Indifference thus Begins". *Aboriginal History* 1, pt 1 (1977): 3–26.

Thorne, A. G. "The Racial Affinities and Origins of the Australian Aborigines". In *Aboriginal Man and Environment in Australia*, ed. D. J. Mulvaney and J. Golson. Canberra: ANU Press, 1971.

Tindale, N. B. "Tasmanian Aborigines on Kangaroo Island, South Australia". *Records of the South Australian Museum* 6 (1937): 29–37.

———. "Summary of the Half-Caste Problem in South Australia". *Proceedings of the Royal Geographical Society of Australia, South Australian Branch* 42 (Nov. 1941): 66–159.

———. "Results of the Harvard-Adelaide Universities Anthropological Expedition, 1938–1939. Growth of a people: formation and development of a hybrid aboriginal and white stock on the islands of Bass Strait, Tasmania, 1815–1949". *RQVM*, n.s. 2 (1953): 1–64.

Tomlinson, John. "Land Rights or Death". *Australian Journal of Social Issues* 9, pt 1 (1974): 45–55.

Warner, W. Lloyd. "Malay Influences on the Aboriginal Cultures of North-Eastern Arnhem Land". *Oceania* 1, no. 5 (1932): 476–95.

White, Doug. "Aboriginal Resistance". *Arena*, no. 35 (1974): 4–8.

PRINTED WORKS FROM 1900

Anderson, Hugh. *Out of the Shadow: The Career of John Pascoe Fawkner.* Melbourne: Cheshire, 1962.

Bass Strait, Australia's First Frontier. Sydney: Australian Broadcasting Commission, 1969.

Baudin, Nicholas. *The Journal of Post Captain Nicholas Baudin.* Adelaide: Libraries Board of South Australia, 1974.

Beattie, J. W. *Our Straits Islands.* Hobart: *Mercury,* 1911.

Beaglehole, J. C., ed. *The Journals of Captain James Cook on his Voyages of Discovery.* Vols. 1 and 3. London: Hakluyt Society, 1955 and 1967.

Bethell, L. S. *The Story of Port Dalrymple.* Hobart: Government Printer, n.d.

Bowden, K. M. *The Life of George Bass.* Carlton, Vic.: Melbourne University Press, 1952.

———. *Captain James Kelly of Hobart Town.* Carlton, Vic.: Melbourne University Press, 1964.

Brown, Dee. *Bury My Heart at Wounded Knee.* London: Eyre and Spottiswoode, 1970.

Brown, P. L., ed. *The Narrative of George Russell of Golf Hill.* London: Oxford University Press, 1955.

———. *Clyde Company Papers.* Vol. 1: *Prologue.* London: Oxford University Press, 1941.

Campbell Town, Tasmania. Campbell Town Municipal Council, 1966.

Chilcote, Ronald D., ed. *Protest and Resistance in Angola and Brazil.* Berkeley: University of California Press, 1972.

Clark, C. M. H. *A History of Australia.* Vols. 1–4. Carlton, Vic: Melbourne University Press, 1962–78.

Corris, Peter. *Aborigines and Europeans in Western Victoria.* Canberra: AIAS, 1968.

Crawford, The Hon. Mr Justice, W. F. Ellis, and G. H. Stancombe, eds. *Diaries of John Helder Wedge 1824–1835.* Hobart: RST, 1962.

Cumpston, J. S. *Kangaroo Island 1800–1836.* Canberra: Roebuck Books, 1970.

———. *The Furneaux Group, Bass Strait: First Visitors 1797–1800.* Canberra: Roebuck Books, 1972.

Davies, David. *The Last of the Tasmanians.* Sydney: Shakespeare Head Press, 1973.

Davies, J. L., ed. *Atlas of Tasmania.* Hobart: Dept. of Lands and Surveys, 1965.

Dunmore, John. *French Explorers in the Pacific.* 2 vols. London: Oxford University Press, 1965 and 1969.

Eiseley, Loren C. *Darwin's Century.* London: Gollancz, 1959.

Ellis, Vivienne Rae. *Trucanini: Queen or Traitor?* Canberra: AIAS, 1981.

Fairchild, H. N. *The Noble Savage: A Study in Romantic Naturalism.* New York: Columbia University Press, 1928.

Frame, Donald M., ed. *The Complete Works of Montaigne.* London: Hamish Hamilton, 1958.

Fraser, J. F. *Australia: The Making of a Nation.* London: Cassell, 1910.

Gale, Fay. *A Study of Assimilation: Part-Aborigines in South Australia.* Adelaide: Libraries Board of South Australia, 1964.

————. ed. *Woman's Role in Aboriginal Society.* Canberra: AIAS, 1970.

————. *Urban Aborigines.* Canberra: ANU Press, 1972.

Genocide without Blood and Guts. Mimeograph. Hobart: Tasmanian Aboriginal Information Centre, n.d. [1978].

Giblin, R. W. *The Early History of Tasmania.* Vol. 1, 1603–1804, London: Methuen, 1929. Vol. 2, 1804–1828, Carlton, Vic.: Melbourne University Press, 1939.

Gilbert, Kevin. *Because a White Man'll Never Do It.* Sydney: Angus and Robertson, 1973.

Glover, Margaret. *History of the Site of Bowen's Settlement, Risdon Cove.* Hobart: National Parks and Wildlife Service, 1978.

Goffman, Erving. *Asylums.* Harmondsworth Mddx.: Penguin, 1968.

Green, F. C., ed. *A Century of Responsible Government in Tasmania.* Hobart: Government Printer, 1956.

Gunson, Niel, ed. *Australian Reminiscences of L. E. Threlkeld, Missionary to the Aborigines, 1824–1859.* 2 vols. Canberra: AIAS, 1974.

Hainsworth, D. R., ed. *Builders and Adventurers.* Melbourne: Cassell, 1970.

Hare, Rosalie, and Ida Lee, eds. *The Voyage of the Caroline from England to Van Diemen's Land and Batavia in 1827–1828.* London: Longmans, Green, 1927.

Harris, Stewart. *This Our Land.* Canberra: ANU Press, 1972.

Hartwell, R. M. *The Economic Development of Van Diemen's Land 1820–1850.* Carlton, Vic.: Melbourne University Press, 1954.

Hartz, Louis. *The Founding of New Societies.* New York: Harcourt, Brace, 1964.

Hasluck, Paul. *Black Australians: A Survey of Native Policy in Western Australia 1829–1897.* 2nd ed. Carlton, Vic.: Melbourne University Press, 1970.

Heizer, Robert F., and Alan J. Almquist. *The Other Californians: Prejudice and Discrimination under Spain, Mexico and the United States to 1920.* Berkeley: University of California Press, 1971.

Horner, Jack. *Vote Ferguson for Aboriginal Freedom.* Sydney: ANZ Book Co., 1974.

Jordan, Winthrop D. *White Over Black: American Attitudes Towards the Negro 1550–1812.* Chapel Hill, NC: North Carolina University Press, 1968.

Kermode, Frank. *Caliban and the Noble Savage.* London: 1957.

Kiernan, V. G. *The Lords of Human Kind.* London: Weidenfeld and Nicolson, 1969.

Lee, Richard B., and Irven de Vore, eds. *Man the Hunter.* Chicago: Aldine Press, 1968.

Lippmann, Lorna. *Words or Blows: Racial Attitudes in Australia.* Ringwood, Vic.: Penguin, 1973.

———. *A Somewhat Startled Realisation.* Office of Community Relations, Canberra: AGPS, 1978.

Long, J. P. M. *Aboriginal Settlements.* Canberra: ANU Press, 1970.

Loone, A. W. *Tasmania's North East.* Launceston: *Examiner*, 1928.

Lovejoy, Arthur O. *The Great Chain of Being: A Study in the History of an Idea.* Cambridge, Mass.: Harvard University Press, 1957.

Lovejoy, Arthur O., and George Boas, *Primitivism and Related Ideas in Antiquity.* Baltimore: Johns Hopkins Press, 1955.

McCarthy, F. D., ed. *Aboriginal Antiquities in Australia.* Canberra: AIAS, 1970.

McKay, Anne, ed. *Journals of the Land Commissioners of Van Diemen's Land 1826–1828.* Hobart: University of Tasmania in conjunction with the Tas. Hist. Res. Assn., 1962.

McNally, Ward. *Goodbye Dreamtime.* Melbourne: Nelson, 1973.

McQueen, Humphrey. *Aborigines, Race and Racism.* Ringwood, Vic.: Penguin, 1974.

Mannoni, Octave. *Prospero and Caliban: The Psychology of Colonisation.* 2nd ed. New York: Praeger, 1964.

Melville, Henry. *The History of Van Diemen's Land from the Year 1824–1835 Inclusive.* Sydney: Horwitz-Grahame, 1965.

Micco, Helen Mary. *King Island and the Sealing Trade 1802.* Canberra: Roebuck Society, 1971.

Mollison, B. C. *A Chronology of Events Affecting Tasmanian Aboriginal Ancestors and their Descendants.* Hobart: Psychology Dept., U. Tas., 1974.

————. *Briggs Family Genealogy to August 1974.* Hobart: Psychology Dept., U. Tas., 1974.

————. *The Genealogies of the Eastern Straitsmen.* Hobart: Psychology Dept., U. Tas., 1974.

————. *The Tasmanian Aborigines: Tasmanian Aboriginal Genealogies with an Appendix on Kangaroo Island (to October 1976).* Vol. 3, pt 1. Hobart: Psychology Dept., U. Tas., 1977.

————. *Tasmanian Aboriginal Genealogies.* Vol. 3, pt 2: *The Briggs Family Genealogy (to September 1976).* Hobart: Psychology Dept., U. Tas., 1977.

Mollison, B. C., and C. Everitt. *A Chronology of Events Affecting Tasmanian Aboriginal People Since Contact with Whites (1772– 1976).* Hobart: Psychology Dept., U. Tas., 1976.

Moore, F. C. T., trans. *The Observation of Savage Peoples, by Joseph-Marie Degerando.* London: Routledge and Kegan Paul, 1969.

Moore-Robinson, J. *Tasmanian Nomenclature.* Hobart: *Mercury*, 1911.

Mulvaney, D. J., and J. Golson, eds. *Aboriginal Man and Environment in Australia.* Canberra: ANU Press, 1971.

Murray-Smith, Stephen, ed. *Mission to the Islands: The Missionary Voyages in Bass Strait of Canon Marcus Brownrigg 1872–1885.* Hobart: Cat and Fiddle Press, 1979.

Nicholls, Mary, ed. *The Diary of the Rev. Robert Knopwood 1803– 1838.* Launceston: Tasmanian Historical Research Association, 1977.

Perkins, Charles. *A Bastard Like Me.* Sydney: Ure Smith, 1975.

Perry, T. M. *Australia's First Frontier.* Carlton, Vic.: Melbourne University Press/ANU Press, 1963.

Plomley, N. J. B., ed. *Friendly Mission: The Tasmanian Journals and Papers of George Augustus Robinson 1829–1834.* Hobart: Tasmanian Historical Research Association, 1966.

————. *A Word-list of the Tasmanian Aboriginal Languages.* Launceston: author, 1976.

————. *The Tasmanian Aborigines.* Launceston: author, in association with the Adult Education Division, Tas., 1977.

Randriamahefa, Kerry. *Aborigines in Tasmanian Schools.* Education Department of Tasmania Research Branch, Research Study no. 144, April 1979.

Reay, Marie, ed. *Aborigines Now: New Perspectives in the Study of Aboriginal Communities.* Sydney: Angus and Robertson, 1964.

Reece, R. H. W. *Aborigines and Colonists: Aborigines and Colonial Society in New South Wales in the 1830s and 1840s.* Sydney: Sydney University Press, 1974.

Reynolds, Henry, ed. *Aborigines and Settlers.* Melbourne: Cassell Australia, 1972.

Reynolds, John. *Launceston, History of an Australian City.* Melbourne: Macmillan, 1968.

Rimmer, W. Gordon. *Two Early Views of Van Diemen's Land.* Hobart: Dept. of History, U. Tas., 1965.

Roe, Michael. *Quest for Authority in Eastern Australia 1835–1851.* Carlton, Vic.: Melbourne University Press, 1965.

Rowley, C. D. *Aboriginal Policy and Practice.* 3 vols. Canberra: ANU Press. Vol. 1, *The Destruction of Aboriginal Society* (1970). Vol. 2, *Outcasts in White Australia* (1971). Vol. 3, *The Remote Aborigines* (1971).

Salisbury, Richard F. *Vunamami.* Carlton, Vic.: Melbourne University Press, 1970.

Scott, Ernest. *The Life of Captain Matthew Flinders, R.N.* Sydney: Angus and Robertson, 1914.

Sharland, Michael. *Stones of a Century.* Hobart: Oldham, Beddone & Meredith, 1957.

Smith, Bernard. *European Vision and the South Pacific 1768–1850.* London: Oxford University Press, 1960.

Smith, Patsy Adam. *Moonbird People.* Adelaide: Rigby, 1965.

Solomon, R. J. *Tasmania.* Sydney: Angus and Robertson, 1972.

Stevens, Frank, ed. *Racism: The Australian Experience.* 3 vols. Sydney: ANZ Book Co., 1971–73.

Stieglitz, K. R. von. *History of Bothwell and Its Early Settlers at the Clyde in Van Diemen's Land.* Launceston: Telegraph Printery, 1958.

Triebel, L. A., and J. C. Batt. *The French Exploration of Australia, with Special Reference to Tasmania.* Hobart: Government Printer, 1957.

Turnbull, Clive. *Black War: The Extermination of the Tasmanian Aborigines.* 2nd ed. Melbourne: Cheshire-Lansdowne, 1965.

Van den Berghe, Pierre L. *Race and Racism: A Comparative Perspective.* New York: Wiley, 1967.

Walker, James B. *Early Tasmania.* Hobart: Government Printer, 1902.

Warrington, John, ed. *Aristotle's Politics and the Athenian Constitution.* London: Dent, 1959.

West, John. *The History of Tasmania.* Edited by A. G. L. Shaw. Sydney: Angus and Robertson in association with the Royal Australian Historical Society, 1971.

Wurm, S. A. *Languages of Australia and Tasmania.* The Hague: Mouton, 1972.

Index